Royal Flourish

by

Christopher Rubinstein

Edited by Daniel Rubinstein

**Grosvenor House
Publishing Limited**

Christopher Rubinstein is hereby identified as author of this
work in accordance with Section 77 of the Copyright, Designs
and Patents Act 1988

The book cover picture is copyright to Gunner Byskov

This book is published by
Grosvenor House Publishing Ltd
28-30 High Street, Guildford, Surrey, GU1 3HY.
www.grosvenorhousepublishing.co.uk

A CIP record for this book
is available from the British Library

ISBN 978-1-907652-31-8

Contents

Introduction

At the core of this book are the events of some sixteen weeks of WW2 running from March to mid-July 1941. Why the selection of this period?

The principal thread running through this book, is that of the intended grand deception of Hitler by Churchill. In Churchill's own words 'the theme' of the third volume of his history of World War Two, *The Grand Alliance,* reads in capital letters: 'HOW THE BRITISH FOUGHT ON WITH HARDSHIP THEIR GARMENT UNTIL SOVIET RUSSIA AND THE UNITED STATES WERE DRAWN INTO THE GREAT CONFLICT'.

How was Churchill to alleviate and escape the "hardship" Britain faced as the sole resistor of Nazi domination?

Germany invaded Russia on 22 June 1941 and by that date although the USA remained nominally at peace with Germany - and Japan - her vital role in support of Britain had taken on the dimension of near belligerency. It is correctly taken for granted that Churchill wanted the USA as a full ally of Britain in WW2 as soon as possible. However, it is also contended, (and the evidence appears in this book), that Churchill was keen for the USSR to become an ally of Britain as soon as possible.

In June 1992 the then Home Secretary Douglas Hurd told the House of Commons in a formal statement that royal documentation relating to Rudolf Hess was kept at Windsor

Castle and that nothing could be said about when it would be disclosed to the public. Present indications (including a climate where the Freedom of Information Act has since been enacted) are that further information will be released by 2020.

The printed and spoken word, music and visual image may seem to have little connection with the strategic decisions referred to in this book, but they are significant factors informing the prosecution of the war. Press, radio and cinema, pageantry for the multitude, the place and function of official and unofficial humour, wit and sarcasm impacted on the lives of ordinary people. Their reactions to events remain in the background of this book.

Editor's Introduction

This book is effectively a re-working of an extensive (and in his view complete) manuscript finalised by my father in early 2005, Sadly his sudden death on 3rd August 2005 put an abrupt end to any possible release of the book in its then form. Upon a reading of the manuscript, I took the decision (aided greatly by my very capable wife) to revise its structure, eliminate some of the more abstruse material, and to offer some further clarification to readers new to this historical period. I should immediately volunteer my own lack of advanced historical knowledge of this specific period beyond a 1970's "A" Level standard although my general reading (mostly of my father's book collection!) of this period has been far from negligible.

The episode of Hess's flight to Britain has proved a fertile breeding-ground for every species of historian(self-styled or otherwise) to offer their up their opinion. These include the scholarly and responsibly journalistic (such as Louis C. Kilzer's perceptive book "Churchill's Deception", which my father did not discover, and Martin Allen's work "The Hitler/Hess Deception", which he was well aware of. It will be noted that the conceptual "starting point" of this book is an implicit agreement with the theory that Churchill set out to dupe Hitler into thinking that there were those in Britain with sufficient influence to topple Churchill and make peace with the Third Reich so as to give Hitler a false sense of security and prompt his invasion of the USSR. The content of more recent books such as "Behind Closed Doors" by Laurence Rees (published in 2005 and drawing heavily on newly-opened Soviet archives), do not impinge on or detract from the essential thesis put forward in this book.

However, this historic incident has invited more than its fair share of perfunctory paranoia (usually involving supposed evidence of an "impostor" replacing Hess as prisoner), proceeding to theories betraying vile racism and neo-nazism. It is almost as though to explore the motivation for Hess's flight is automatically to expose oneself as a member of the irrational majority who have broached the subject (a state of affairs not unsatisfactory to those who actually refuse to release the secret documents).

My father's book is part of that large minority of studies in this areas that places Hess's action in an unsensationalist, dispassionate light; however, the context of Churchill's undoubted ruthlessness in prosecuting the war and the sheer grandiose oddness of Hess's journey must entail bold interpretation of available facts, and my father's interpretation effectively paraphrases Sir Arthur Conan Doyle's famous creation ; "Once one has eliminated the impossible, then that which remains must be the truth, however implausible".It is worth mentioning in this context that my father's uncle was Ewen Montagu, instigator of the famous "The Man Who Never Was" deception of the Nazis. Whilst it would not be appropriate to cite her as a formal source, some conversations did take place with his widow, Mrs. Iris Montagu, as to the plausibility of the theories advanced in this book . My father was also the grandson of Solomon J. Solomon, the artist and pioneer of military camouflage during World War 1. The idea of deception for an honourable purpose appears to have attracted our forebears!

It would also be a profound misconception of this book were it to be seen merely to narrowly expound yet another theory seeking to explain Hess's flight. It will be readily discerned that the book gives a detailed analysis of the dire domestic and diplomatic position of Britain during the period, and an overview of the contemporaneous situation in Germany and the USSR. It is somewhat unusual that my father's political outlook was progressive and socialist, and it is therefore no liberal hagiography of Churchill nor is it a kneejerk "one minute's hate" towards any of the main protagonists involved. For example, Churchill's absolute commitment to the victory of civilised values is recognised, but it is emphasised that he was simultaneously waging a ruthless and inherently unscrupulous method of struggle, above and beyond the use of armed might. More recent studies have strongly suggested that he became a sincere and wholehearted admirer of Stalin, at least during the war years; not something that would be later publicly emphasised in any way.

Of course studies of this period will continue to be published and debated. This book is intended to be an accessible contribution to that debate.

CHAPTER 1

Caught in the Net

The day Rudolf Hess, Deputy Fuhrer of the Third Reich, left Germany, he appeared to act naturally. He horseplayed with his three – year - old son. Entertained at lunch was his friend the Nazi ideologist, Rosenberg. After lunch, Hess left home to travel to the airfield near Augsberg where his new plane - unarmed - was ready. The first part of his flight ended at an airfield in northern Germany where his plane was refuelled.

The flight of Hess northward over the North Sea was guided by German radio beams transmitted from a German station in Denmark. In his later grandiloquent (and inaccurate) description of his flight, he kept this fact under wraps. He flew in daylight turning to moonlight, westward towards Dungavel House. He apparently made a brief detour to fly near Alnwick Castle, the seat of the pro-fascist Duke of Northumberland. His plane was detected, but RAF fighters then about to intercept the Messerschmitt were called off, much to the frustration of their pilots - including two eager Czechs - who wanted to make a "kill".[i]

Hess neared the airstrip at Dungavel where the landing lights came on and were then switched off. The reason for that incident remains unknown. Hess must have been looking for the airstrip lights but now he was becoming desperate as he was low on fuel. Therefore he had to bail out and let his plane crash, which it did in open country. He 'landed' unarmed, and with a broken ankle sustained upon his parachute landing. He was in a minute or two accosted by a Scottish ploughman and also by two sergeants from a local 'secret' signals unit. The world was led to believe the ploughman found him on his own. Hess, who was openly and fully co-operative, was helped to hobble to the farm cottage nearby. He politely declined the offer of a cup of tea from his 'captor's' mother, drinking a glass of water instead. Hess showed to his hosts photos of his wife and son and said he was "Alfred Horn". He gave his Iron Cross to one of the sergeants. The time was almost midnight on Saturday 10 May.

A Home Guard detachment, various soldiers and a special constable came to the cottage. Hess said that he had intended to land at Dungavel and he wished to be taken to meet the Duke of Hamilton. He was taken by car to a local Home Guard HQ in a Scout hut, and then to a Scout Hall nearer to central Glasgow again escorted by Home Guards. A Polish Consular official, who had been in Intelligence in pre-war Poland, was present as an interpreter. He and Hess conversed in German for about two hours. Apparently no note was taken! No one else present understood much German. Hess was still considered to be "Alfred Horn", though his resemblance to Hess was noticed and laughed away by the captive who however insisted that he had an urgent message for the Duke of Hamilton, and that they had a mutual friend. A major from the Royal Observer Corps who was present, recognised Hess. Any fuller explanation for his expectation that he would be greeted by the Duke of Hamilton, has yet to be forthcoming.

The Duke of Hamilton as the senior RAF Intelligence officer on duty should have interrogated Hess without delay to comply with standard RAF practice. He stayed away. He had been told that there was a captured German airman to be interrogated. One has to conclude that he contacted British Intelligence and was ordered to take no action until after dawn. The suggestion that he met Hess anyway that night more or less "in the street" would appear to lack any substantial foundation.

Of course no one in Britain then knew for certain who the airman was. Whatever might have been the messages exchanged between Intelligence services, it would have seemed improbable that the Deputy-Fuhrer of Germany had actually arrived in Britain and in so dramatic a fashion.

Hess himself must have wondered whether he was among friends or enemies. At premises in the grounds of Dungavel House,(itself a wartime hospital), there were apparently waiting various VIPs, among them the Duke of Kent. The Duke of Hamilton himself was at Turnhouse but one of his brothers was present. If Hess had been taken to Dungavel House instead of to Glasgow, there was the risk of his being out of the control of the authorities completely loyal to Churchill.

One has to appreciate that the would-be appeasers waiting to meet Hess, and those very many more they purported to represent, were by no means united. It was one thing to learn what Hess had to say and to learn what the present condition of the enemy might be, and quite another to look forward to a peace on Nazi terms. As far as Churchill was concerned, there was danger in letting Hess say anything to anyone. The Home Guard was ordered to take Hess to Glasgow, whereas the eligible local army unit might have received orders from its immediate commander to take him to Dungavel House. Churchill must have been informed that night by telephone of the arrival of someone who might be Hess, and among those at Dungavel must have been an informer for the Prime Minister. Hess himself was convinced that many top people in Britain were keen for peace between Britain and Germany so as to facilitate a German invasion of the USSR.

The unexpected presence of the Polish Consular Official may be explained by the Polish government in exile in Britain being told in advance of the likely arrival of Hess, perhaps by or through the Duke of Kent. While it is hard to imagine these

Poles warming to the German in any way , their aim must nonetheless have been to learn what Hess had to say.

The disappointed men awaiting Hess at Dungavel would hardly have been comforted by reading the *Sunday Dispatch* of 11 May. Its regular columnist, the Marquess of Donegall (sic) positively advised all would-be appeasers to read *If Hitler Comes* : '*It is all horribly plausible were we ever to weaken in spirit.*' His comments may have been prompted to mark Churchill's total rejection of Hess's intentions, but it is surely the case that the Marquess would not have been told much of the truth.

The interview with the Pole ended, Hess was taken in a Home Guard car driven by their Major Barie to Maryhill Barracks, Glasgow. It was about 2am on the Sunday . The Guardroom was quiet. The Major had to sound the horn repeatedly to attract attention. The Major, sitting upright in bed with his pyjamas on, was saluted by the Second Lieutenant. Hess, (still identified as "Horn"), was placed in a cell with blankets. Before long, he was taken to a nearby military hospital for treatment for his ankle injury.

That Sunday morning, the Duke of Hamilton and an aide inspected Hess's crashed plane. It remains unknown what documents they found, if any. By about l0am, the Duke and Hess entered into a discussion at the military Hospital, the Duke's aide excluded at the request of Hess. No full transcript of this discussion exists. The previous night, there had been prepared an inventory of what the prisoner had brought with him in the ample pockets of his top-quality flying suit. This inventory (still a secret), is mentioned in the letter the Major wrote to the C-in-C of the local army unit, in which he complains of the indiscipline and slackness in the guardroom.[ii] .

The inventory would certainly have listed a number of medicaments, many homeopathic, which Hess had with him.

These were later listed separately. One may reasonably infer that Hess brought with him something in writing about his mission, which the authorities in Britain wished to conceal, and it seems to have been the case he had a list with him of notable men in Britain whom he believed were willing to negotiate peace.

The handwritten note prepared by the Duke officially presents his summary of that first interview with Hess. It remains unclear when this note, which may now be read at the PRO, was prepared. A typewritten copy, which would appear to have been from a typewriter at 10 Downing Street, is also available.[iii] The contents are far from convincing, and it looks as if the Duke's own handwritten statement of the conversation between him and Hess *post-dates* the meeting between the Duke and Churchill which took place in the early hours of Monday morning.

According to the handwritten note, Hess opens by claiming their personal acquaintance dating from the time of the Berlin Olympic games. He writes of his and Hitler's desire for a generous peace with Britain, including however the German hegemony of Europe. Otherwise, there will be a complete German victory. He discloses his expectation that the King would facilitate his return to Germany shortly. What Hess omits, according to this questionable document, is any suggestion that Hitler approved his coming to Britain or of a German invasion of the USSR. Probably Hess said much more to the Duke than is contained in the published version of their talk. However, the obvious fact that Hess did not know whether he was among friends or enemies would probably have set constraints to what he was prepared to disclose at this early stage. Out of loyalty to Hitler and the Nazi cause, could he risk fully mentioning Operation Barbarossa? Did he have to improvise? If so, this would help to explain all his threats and boasts. It is commonsense to presume that the Duke would have been non-committal in his response to whatever Hess had to offer, however outwardly sympathetic. It is true that during the summer Hess indicated that he continued to trust the Duke.[iv] Hess also asked for his 'aunt' in Switzerland to be notified by telegram of his arrival in Britain. This was not done, whatever he may have been told. The Duke telephoned Churchill himself soon after this private discussion with Hess. Churchill's hostess at Ditchley Park, (where Churchill was spending the week-end), was told Sunday morning by Churchill, that the Duke would be spending Sunday night as another guest. The Duke did telephone the Foreign Office on the Sunday.[v] The news of Hess as conveyed by the Duke was later described by the officials concerned as if some kind of fantasy of the Duke's ; these descriptions are internally inconsistent and Churchill must have realised he had better display an attitude of seeming disbelief. That the Duke himself apparently told Churchill that he wished to see the King straightaway, met with Churchill's order that the Duke should meet him *first*, later that day.

The Duke duly flew south but his journey was prolonged by his mistakenly thinking he had to go to Chequers. So it was late at night that the Duke arrived at Ditchley Park. Churchill made his famous remark that he would first watch a Marx Brothers film, irrespective of this ostensibly sensational news received. The Duke and Churchill met in private at around midnight, but for part of the time Sir Archibald Sinclair, Secretary of State for Air and confidant of Churchill, was also present. The Duke was sworn to secrecy. Five days later he was a guest at lunch at Buckingham Palace, and described the King as *'very curious'* about Hess, and he tactfully told the King *'it is indeed extraordinary how little the Nazis understand us'*. On 19 May, the Duke sent to the King's principal private secretary a letter and sealed box of documents. Nearly four years later, Hamilton was forbidden by Churchill to travel to the USA, where he would have been grilled by journalists asking awkward questions.

The four hours of the Churchill-Hamilton discussion, Sunday night and Monday morning, would have addressed how the Duke was to narrate his meeting on Sunday morning with Hess to satisfy the War Cabinet. One must recall that the Duke had refused on 25 April to volunteer to go to neutral Portugal to meet his old friend Haushofer,and had on 10 May actually changed his mind and had duly written to British Intelligence. Whatever the Duke thought of how the war might develop, his private talk with Churchill on the night of 11/12 May must have persuaded him, (if it were necessary), to be fully loyal to Churchill's cause to fight and defeat Germany in WW2.

It is hard to believe that the Duke was not sure Hess himself had arrived, but the War Cabinet on the Monday 12th May, as usual under Churchill's total influence, decided that the best course was to send the Duke and Ivone Kirkpatrick, (who had met Hess in Berlin pre-war), to Scotland straight away more certainly to identify Hess and personally to ascertain his mission, and duly to report to London.

Meanwhile the British public was kept totally uninformed and the *Daily Record* was censored. The first news was to come from Germany at 8pm on Monday, when the Duke and Kirkpatrick were on their way to the castle by Loch Lomond where Hess was now under guard. Their journey by air was maddeningly slow due to headwinds. They arrived after midnight, while Hess was continuing to write copious notes. It seems the papers which he had brought with him and on which he was relying had already been confiscated.

Kirkpatrick listened to a long monologue from Hess but the Duke, who had last had any proper sleep the previous Friday night, was nodding off! Hess after his initial disappointment, had recovered his composure. He analysed in detail Anglo-German relations since 1904. He gave his proposals for ending WW2 , but without disclosing Barbarossa. He did however say that German demands on Russia might lead to war. Hess asserted that he was acting without Hitler's knowledge but that he knew Hitler's mind intimately so he had the implied authority of the Fuhrer. He was on typical Nazi ground when he insisted that if Britain were not now to negotiate a peace with Germany, then Luftwaffe and U-boat attacks would bring Britain to its knees. Hess knew how to intimidate Germans but not Kirkpatrick, and after some four or five hours of growing tedium and irritation, Kirkpatrick had heard enough! An early cooked breakfast was provided for him and the Duke, and they could at last relax. Hess was left as once more a solitary prisoner.

The Foreign Office had phoned Kirkpatrick in the early hours expecting firm information and he had told them their call was premature - except he was able to confirm that the prisoner was Hess. He phoned by 11am to give a full report but added that he found the problem of extracting any worthwhile information from Hess too difficult for him to handle. Hess for his part would have realised that he could not trust Kirkpatrick. Kirkpatrick then advised that Hess should be housed under the auspices of the Duke, and that the Duke's brother should act as an interpreter and that Hess should be interviewed by a senior Conservative whom Hess might trust. Kirkpatrick could not raise the issue of the royal letter, but was ordered to interview Hess again. He was told to encourage Hess to believe that his proposals were being considered in London. The next interview was in the afternoon. Possibly Hess was transferred to a nearby mansion where a guard of honour stood.

Hess now told Kirkpatrick and the Duke of Hamilton that Germany harboured no aggressive designs against either Ireland or the USA, and that there should be no negotiations with Churchill. A third interview from which the Duke was absent, took place on Thursday morning. Hess mentioned further issues of a possible peace settlement in relation to Italy and Iraq, and indemnities. Hess also said that at any further discussions a German representative of his own choice should be present. In fact two such possible candidates had already been brought in their internment to a camp not far away! A frustrated Kirkpatrick returned to London later on Thursday 15 May, by when much had transpired since the Monday afternoon. It is known that Kirkpatrick enjoyed a close relationship with 'C' (Sir Stewart Menzies) who headed MI6. Possibly the Duke of Kent met Hess at this stage.

A news announcement on Berlin radio at 8 pm on Monday evening reported that Hess had flown from Germany solo despite a personal ban by Hitler in the interests of his health, and that Hess suffered from hallucinations. As he had disappeared, it had to be presumed he was dead. The Fuhrer had already ordered certain arrests.

This was the cue for a hastily summoned press conference at 10 Downing Street at 11.20pm, when the Minister of Information, Duff-Cooper, announced that Hess was in Britain. The morning papers on Tuesday 13 May led an unprecedented euphoria. Readers could believe that Hess was a political fugitive and that there was a total split in the leadership of Nazi Germany. The Foreign Office, which had the benefit of Kirkpatrick's phoned reports, was beginning to feel only disappointment and anger-Hess was no "fugitive." Cadogan found his time preoccupied and wasted. Eden by the Wednesday found nothing of use in the Hess incident. Meanwhile on the Tuesday (13 May) Churchill ordered that Hess should be treated as a PoW with the deemed rank of a Major-General, and kept in seclusion.

Whereas most Nazis, post-war, expressed the opinion that Hitler knew in advance and approved the plan of Hess to fly to Britain, Hitler acted melodramatically when he learned at about lunchtime on 11th May of the disappearance of Hess, as if the news came as a complete surprise. Hess had ordered his adjutant Hauptmann Karlheinz Pintsch to travel to Berchtesgaden with a letter to give to Hitler, unless news came of his safe arrival and welcome in Britain. What should be done had in fact been prearranged by Hess with Hitler. As no news came of Hess, the adjutant duly obeyed. Hitler displayed feigned amazement and anger which became real when he read the letter to him from Hess. It had become clear that Hess-with his foreknowledge of Barbarossa-was in unfriendly British hands and this was a situation with potentially terrifying consequences, as Goebbels noted in his diary of 15th May. Most of the company tried to reassure Hitler that Hess must have perished on his journey, but he remained unconvinced - though he said he wished Hess were dead. The best step seemed to be for German radio to make its announcement at 8pm Monday evening. No news at all had come from Britain.

Once the news was released more than three hours later that Hess was in Britain, Hitler reacted promptly. He summoned a meeting of about seventy top Nazis including his Gauleiters, for Tuesday afternoon 13 May. His aim was damage limitation. The fact that Hess, the Deputy-Fuhrer, the second most important Nazi, had voluntarily become a captive of the enemy, struck at the core of Nazi ideology. As Goebbels bitterly recorded, the demoralisation of millions of Germans was an inevitable consequence .The 1ine taken by Hitler was perhaps the optimum available. Hess was an idealist who was afflicted by 'hallucinations' and had 'messianic delusions'. He imagined he could negotiate with the Duke of Hamilton. He had been influenced by astrologers, clairvoyants, fortune tellers and others... 'If the man were not mad he would deserve to be shot'.

Many would-be prophets were now arrested, and their activities made illegal. It was useful to treat them as scapegoats. It was also a safeguard in case any of them with insights and misgivings let alone Communist sympathies, might imperil Barbarossa, now less than six weeks away. As for astrology, Hess may be compared with Julius Caesar of Shakespeare's drama, who recognised superstition as a political weapon. The night of 10/11 May was generally forecast as of astrological significance – a most unusual alignment of planets. Hess had probably been misled, partly by British Intelligence, into a belief that the alleged British peace movement had some faith in astrological prediction, and perhaps black magic.

Among those arrested in Germany, was Albrecht Haushofer. In custody he wrote a statement for Hitler. For his own protection this was bland but he said about Hess privately on 11 May: '*This motorised Parsifal wants to bring peace to Hitler, and he imagines that he could get round the Churchill government and could sit down at the negotiating table with the King*'. Haushofer was released early in July by when Hitler believed the USSR was being conquered. He lost his job at the German Foreign Office but continued to lecture in politics at a Berlin institute of higher education. More than three years later he was arrested as one of the conspirators against Hitler's rule and was imprisoned without trial until the SS murdered him shortly before VE day. He must have known more about the mission of Hess than he admitted to Hitler, but how much more is unclear.

The intense German disillusionment was dispelled to Goebbels' relief by the end of the week. The German invasion of Crete on 20 May opened a new chapter for sensational news. By the end of May Hess's wife was receiving a state pension.

The German media on Tuesday 13 May improved on its radio announcement of Monday evening with an elaboration of Hess as a victim of malign occult influences. On the Wednesday it claimed that Hess had flown to meet the Duke of Hamilton with a wild scheme of negotiating peace. Inevitably, the publicising of this story in the British media on Thursday 15

May gave a new twist to the Hess episode. The MoI, (obviously directed by Churchill with the aim of convincing Hitler that Hess was being taken seriously), released the news that the Duke and Hess were friends. The fury of the Duke at this slur on his character led to a formal retraction of this assertion a week later by Sinclair on behalf of the government in the House of Commons. The Duke privately asked Churchill *'what do you tell your wife if a prostitute flings her arms around your neck'?* Churchill found this rhetorical question most amusing! The Duke was promoted to Group-Captain at the end of May.

The British Communists, meanwhile, published a pamphlet which contained the allegation of friendship between the Duke and Hess. The Duke commenced a libel action. The Attorney-General became worried that the defendants might subpoena Hess to give evidence at the trial, no date for which was yet fixed. If a subpoena were issued, the legal question would arise as to whether the government would have to facilitate service of the subpoena on Hess personally and in due course, his presence in Court as a witness. The Attorney-general mistakenly believed that the banned *Daily Worker* was still appearing as a daily newspaper.[vi] In the event the libel case was settled, and there was a fairly short court hearing on a date in February 1942. By then, the Red Army and the USSR were immensely popular in Britain, and there was every incentive to avoid an ugly dispute in public.

In Court, the Defendants through their counsel apologised for the libel on the Duke, but the Defendant Harry Pollitt, (once again the General Secretary of the CPGB), was exonerated. He had taken no part in the slur. There was no award of damages, and each side was left to bear its own legal costs apart from a contribution, not announced in Court, to the Duke's costs.[vii]

The weakness of the Duke's case was his friendship with Haushofer and the latter's close friendship with Hess, about which the Defendants probably knew enough to make the Duke hesitate to go to trial. Counsel for the Duke was probably unwittingly misleading the Court when he said the Duke had, without delay, interrogated Hess after his capture.

Why had no less a personage than the Deputy Fuhrer of the Third Reich, suddenly parachuted into Scotland? And why was this stunningly bizarre episode quickly left behind during the war itself, later to be buried in secret archives to this very day, the bones of the facts picked clean over the years by legions of conspiracy-theorists (varying in their degrees of sanity), let alone those with more sinister political beliefs? This book seeks to explain why Hess's motivation for risking imprisonment for life (let alone the noose), was far stronger than has hitherto been suggested.

CHAPTER 2

Holding the Fort

The background to Hess's strange "visit" lies in the deeply uncertain progress of the war for Britain in the sixteen weeks after March 1941 – until Germany's invasion of the Soviet Union. Britain had won the Battle of Britain. Would it now lose the war? Although the majority of the population was aware of the war, according to the official estimate, about forty per cent of adults generally declined to take any notice of war news. Naturally the official wish to influence morale for the war effort concentrated on that sixty per cent of adults who were likely to take some interest.[viii] They were seen to respond to what was guardedly publicised in broadcasts, newspapers, journals and magazines, books and pamphlets, photographs, cartoons, cinema newsreels, and especially feature films. Attention was given to German broadcasts intended to demoralise British listeners, minimal though this influence was by the Spring of 1941. The charming and brilliant con-man, William Joyce (Lord Haw-Haw), broadcasting for the Nazi regime, had ceased to make more than a marginal impact. Even his slight appeal was far ahead of those of the cynical German *New British Broadcasting Station* and the coarse *Workers' Challenge*, both pretending to come from Britain.[ix] It was the job of Ministry of Information (MoI) to learn about public morale from diverse sources including surreptitious reading of personal correspondence. Its weekly reports, marked 'secret', show how important the Government deemed civilian enthusiasm for the war effort to be and how it might be maintained and boosted.[x]

Incalculable numbers of personal experiences and contacts also contributed to thoughts and feelings about the war. The boundary line between truth and fiction was often indistinct, because all but a tiny number of people lacked any significant knowledge or strategic understanding of the conflict. The vast majority relied on what they inwardly felt and were persuaded to accept as truth. So most people still reacted to war news according to their cherished beliefs. These constituted a spiritual capital including, for most people, a confidence that the war was one of good against evil and could and would be won by Britain, whatever the disappointments. Given the political democracy widely believed to exemplify British values in contrast to the obvious barbarism of Nazism and Hitler's absolute rule, there was a general reliability of loyalty. In this context, Churchill's impressive public speeches sustained morale. At the root of his rhetoric was his deep passion for the survival of the British Empire and Commonwealth, the Monarchy and Parliament. He confirmed the entrenched political beliefs of a majority of adults, and despite his personal agnosticism or perhaps atheism, he had the nous to appear supportive of a liberal-minded Christianity. His calculated emphasis on freedom and democracy appealed across the political spectrum, only excluding the extreme wings of opinion. His genius in the political field and his practical application of it, more than compensated for a frequent lack of substance. His style of defiance of Hitler and Nazi Germany, especially given the many privations and sacrifices of wartime, made a unique contribution to the British war effort. It was the British equivalent to that of Hitler for the German war effort.

Vital for morale was the official spreading of various fallacies and rumours about the progress and conduct of the war. Concerns centred on the possibility of a German invasion of Britain. ENIGMA information available to Churchill in 1941, together with intelligence gathered from aerial reconnaissance, showed the risk as minimal. Provided British defences were strong enough Hitler would be deterred from even attempting an invasion. If invaders landed, they could be repulsed. So, both the army and the Home Guard could feel deeply motivated to continue training.[xi] An extreme tale to boost morale was that of 26 sharks being held to release into the Channel if there were an invasion.[xii] Everyone was officially advised to always carry a gas mask, for fear of German use of poison gas. This advice was widely disregarded as were orders to this effect to servicemen on leave.[xiii]

In an attempt to raise morale depressed by the Blitz on British cities, where high civilian casualties and much damage to civilian buildings were at least local general knowledge, the myth was cultivated that the RAF was badly damaging the German war effort with its night raids on targets in Germany. In fact, the attempt of the previous winter to hamper synthetic oil production in Germany was a total failure. By the beginning of March 1941, it must have become clear to Churchill, as a result of aerial photographs, that RAF bombing was causing at most minor damage to German industry and cities. RAF bombers mostly failed to find their targets.[xiv] Losses of planes and aircrews were growing, and only a handful of four-engined bombers were as yet in service. One of these was shot down by mistake by RAF fighters over Surrey, an event naturally remaining unpublicised.

The media gave the public a grossly distorted and exaggerated impression of RAF raids on Germany. Soon the Ministry of Information wanted publication in Britain of the RAF leaflets dropped on Germany, threatening Germans with mass destruction. The Ministry of Economic Warfare refused to co-operate. It was feared that publication would give the impression that the RAF would be as evil as the Luftwaffe in the indiscriminate bombing of cities. The interested public was more or less equally divided about the morality of bombing enemy civilians. Those who wanted this new RAF policy did not know it had already been inaugurated, as many military targets were elusive. American opinion could be dangerously influenced against Britain, if this were made public. The MEW was scared that should there be unauthorised publication, the Official Secrets laws could not be invoked, because the enemy was already in possession of the leaflets! The dispute between the two Ministries was settled by Beaverbrook as an arbitrator finding for MEW.[xv] However, an unofficial campaign gathered momentum for the mass destruction of German cities and civilians. It was claimed this would bring victory, as the German people would not have the moral fibre to withstand such an onslaught. Equally erroneously, it was implied that the RAF would soon be in a position to make devastating raids.

William Hickey, alias the leftwinger Tom Driberg, the gossip columnist of the Beaverbrook owned *Daily Express*, was himself perturbed at the callous response of many correspondents to the paper on the issue of bombing German children. He raised the matter by mentioning in his column a 'sweet little' six year old German girl by name. The hostile letters he received provided evidence of ongoing brutalisation in Britain. Yet the clamour for revenge met with more support from people in safe areas than from survivors of the Blitz, who knew first-hand of the deaths and maiming of children from German bombs.[xvi]

Fallacies were also entertained about the effectiveness of the blockade of Germany and occupied Europe. MEW held conflicting views. *The Times*, triumphalist, reported with scorn ersatz methods of packaging goods advertised at the Leipzig Trade Fair in February.[xvii] In the long-term, the blockade did tell against it, but the German economy could stand the strain for the immediate future.

One real landmark for the development of the war in Britain's favour was the passing into law in the USA of Lend-Lease on 11 March, its reference number for the record intentionally

H.R.1776. Lend Lease involved the supply by the US of massive quantities of war materials to Britain in exchange for the use of naval bases in Newfoundland, Bermuda and the British West Indies. Now the growing involvement of the USA could be reckoned a certainty. However, huge and vital imports to Britain previously ordered from the land of the dollar still had to be paid for with practically exhausted financial reserves. Much never arrived as it was sunk in transit, The much publicised first Lend-Lease shipment, which included carefully chosen nourishing foods, was to arrive by June.[xviii] The hope of increasing American aid to the UK was in itself a great boost for British morale.

Lend-Lease excepted, March was at first a ferocious month for Britain, particularly because of the night time Blitz on British cities and losses in the "Battle of the Atlantic", as it was named by Churchill. However, the war in North and East Africa, in the Mediterranean and in Albania over the frontier from Greece, had seen, since November, victories over the Italians. It was uncomfortable to realise that the Germans had not been involved in this fighting. When the Luftwaffe had intervened against Malta and attacked the Royal Navy in the Mediterranean as from January 1941, the results were gloomy. An unwise spirit of complacency reigned during the second half of March. Hopes soared in the last five days of the month, only for morale soon badly to decline.

A deceptively bright interpretation of the considerations prevailing in most of March is exemplified by BBC talks given by the Czech Foreign Minister in exile in London, Jan Masaryk, to an audience in his homeland, which had been under German occupation for some two years. His aim was to inspire mostly middle-class Czechs to remember their patriotism and not to fall for the Nazi line that Bohemia and Moravia were inherently part of Greater Germany. His argument was upbeat in defence of democracy and political freedom whilst deriding '*the scum*' who had voluntarily accepted German citizenship. It pointedly relied on alleged Anglo-American military strength and co-operation.[xix] Reaction to his talks was mixed. Dr Goebbels, the German Minister of Propaganda, records in his diary satisfaction with industrial output for the German war machine in occupied Bohemia and Moravia.[xx] In contrast, German cultural penetration was limited. Nazi dismay at absence of success here is evident.

In Britain, contemporary diaries show impressively how personal and war experiences mingled for their authors. A twenty year old lance-bombardier in a Searchlight unit near London, public school educated, enters for 23 March: '*As it was a national day of prayer, & Jean wanted to go to their church, Union Church at Mill Hill Broadway, which is Congregational, I went with Jean and was very pleased I went, though Mr Reid, the minister, was not a very impressive speaker. One of the ladies in the choir sang solos from Mendelssohn's* (sic) *Elijah excellently ("Hear, O Israel" & "Be not afraid")*'. His entry for 26 March however contains depressing war news: '*It was announced that the Yugoslavian government had signed an agreement with the Axis powers against the wishes of the population - particularly the Serbs*'.

A professional diarist, forty year old Charles Graves, younger brother of the distinguished literary figure Robert, had his diary published volume by volume during the war. His home was in the West End of London and much of his spare time he spent undergoing training in his local Home Guard unit in St. Marylebone. As well as describing conversations with well-known people, usually in the best restaurants and bars or on a golf course, he had the useful habit of detailing the expensive and luxurious meals he enjoyed when was he ate out. 26 March: ...*We (CG and Alan Herbert MP) lunched at Carr's in Aldwych. He had a very small piece of salmon (3s 6d) and I had sausages and bacon and mushrooms (3s 10d), with turnips, parsnips and potatoes, coffee, a glass of port or two, and admittedly a couple of two-bob cigars...'.*

Most of the population, however, had insufficient food. Meat, bacon, fats, eggs, sugar and tea were strictly and sparsely rationed. Cheese rationing at the rate of one ounce a week was soon to be introduced with more for agricultural workers and vegetarians. The Ministry of Food at first overlooked Forestry workers. The meat ration which was reduced by twopence to one shilling a week in retail value at the end of March, included corned beef when and where fresh meat was unavailable. Unrationed foods, beer and cigarettes were often in short supply or priced beyond the means of many. There was a virtual nationwide shortage of onions, as Brittany was part of occupied France, and the Mediterranean was closed to trade with Egypt. When a consignment of oranges arrived from Spain under a recently negotiated commercial agreement, their distribution was bungled. Milk rationing was introduced but the arrangements for this were not properly planned out. The press told the story with a photograph of the coalminer who only had a beetroot sandwich to eat. The Black Market flourished.[xxi] Profiteering in the sale of unrationed goods was rampant. Only some foods were price controlled. The wealthy could dine out lavishly, and unrationed food, such as poultry and game and fresh fish, could be bought retail at a high price not least in comfortable and safe areas. Prosecutions of Black Marketeers and illegal profiteers were infrequent and hardly all that punitive, in that a retailer could be fined or occasionally imprisoned, but their customers, among them 'pillars of the community', escaped prosecution.

The statistics and official information about food supplies were accordingly kept a close secret. The German sinkings of merchantmen carrying precious cargoes to Britain were bad enough, and it was prudent not to count on the Battle of the Atlantic being won easily, if at all. Churchill reflected on the possibility of a 'basal' diet comprising mainly bread, milk, sugar, home produced vegetables, legumes and oatmeal. A *National Wheatmeal Loaf* was introduced with much publicity but oatmeal was notoriously often in short supply. When the meat ration was reducing as from the beginning of the year, the consumption of bread, unrationed, was substantially increasing. Stocks of grain fell from a minimum safe level of 13mil. tons, representing three months' estimated consumption, to a risky $11^1/_2$ mil. tons. Lend-Lease food supplies - at first a trickle and then a growing flow from June onwards - eventually prevented disaster. A few people benefited from private American and other foreign food parcels. It was unlawful to solicit these from abroad. A titled lady had her begging letter to a friend in Eire read by a censor. She was prosecuted and fined.

The Ministry of Food made many gaffes, and the reputation of the Minister, Lord Woolton, a big businessman, marginally suffered. Among the official achievements was the intelligent study of diet by scientists. On balance the health of the nation did not worsen, although an average adult loss of weight from pre-war to the summer of 1941 was estimated at 10 lbs. Despite some setbacks, including a greater incidence of tuberculosis and rickets, the physical health of the nation as a whole actually improved. Near full employment, higher wages compared with pre-war, rationing and some price controls were among the causes. The incidence of mental ill-health formally diminished, but many problems e.g. for children who were evacuees, went largely ignored. There was a marked increase in juvenile delinquency and theft offences including looting facilitated by bomb damage.[xxii]

Agriculture in Britain became another weapon of war. Far less food and fodder were being imported. Some food stores were destroyed in the Blitz. Before the war, farming in Britain had been a depressed industry despite state intervention for products such as milk, potatoes and sugar beet. Closer trade relations within the Commonwealth and Empire had also struck at British farming. The recovery in wartime was slower than it should have been. There was a partial but inadequate spurt in production from the summer of 1940, but this marked the beginning of the implementation of better drainage and of supplies of artificial fertilisers and tractors.

A foremost critic of government sloth was Lloyd George,[xxiii] himself a farmer, who recollected the threat of starvation in WW1 when he had been Prime Minister. He drew attention to the urgency of ploughing up the maximum of derelict land for essential crops. Farm workers enjoyed exemption from call-up but there was a drift to better paid war factory jobs and the forces. Their smaller numbers were offset by the Woman's Land army, aliens and conscientious objectors, and a temporary lending of army Pioneers - which was not demobilisation. Their low wages were belatedly increased by government order. Housing and hostel conditions were eventually improved, but the government was dilatory in its approach.

Increased production of grain, mostly for bread, and milk, potatoes, vegetables and sugar beet was state policy dictated, financially aided and enforced. Inefficient farms were taken over to be managed by local agricultural committees. Meat and eggs were treated as less vital. Animal feedstuffs were in short supply but non-farmers, whether in town or country, were encouraged to keep pigs and poultry on a small scale, mostly to be fed with domestic left-overs. Wasting food was made a crime. A woman was fined for feeding stale bread to birds and her case was widely publicised.

Horse racing, and the diversion of hay and oats for the animals, became a public issue, with press correspondence and questions asked in Parliament. A compromise was found so that the bloodstock industry could survive the war, and horse racing on a reduced scale continued as a major sport. There were grumbles because of the conspicuous attendance at race-courses of hundreds of privately owned vehicles belonging to the wealthy, with coaches for the less affluent. Precious imported petrol was considered to be wasted as a result of this 'pleasure driving'.[xxiv]

The public Dig for Victory propaganda campaign could theoretically mean no shortage of vegetables for many families and institutions. Another pronounced step forward was an increasingly systematic provision of cheap canteen meals throughout industry. Long distance lorry drivers tired however of meals at pull-ups too often consisting of the joked-about wartime sausage. Locally run *'British Restaurants'* first appeared in March, serving affordable and generally nutritious meals. The chosen title followed Churchill's rejection of *'Communal'* as smacking of Communism.

Industry presented a plethora of problems for the developing war economy. Coal mining,[xxv] a basic, saw a steep decline in production. As the foreign markets for British coal had disappeared, the reduced production did not as yet matter much. But, on scrutiny, the future looked grim. The high incidence of ill-health among miners, the depreciation of pits, lack of investment during the inter-war years and low wages were to have serious consequences for productivity. Added to these disadvantages was the drift away from mining jobs to better paid employment in munitions factories and to the services. The old 'stick' of unemployment had disappeared and this led to much absenteeism and demoralisation. Mandatory direction and retention of employment under the 'essential works' order, was only a partial solution.

The Battle of the Atlantic could be won or lost as a result of production and efficiency in shipbuilding, ship repair and the speedy throughput of cargoes in ports. Speed of work was of the essence. The Labour MP, Manny Shinwell, outside the

Government of his own volition, was an outspoken and well-informed critic.[xxvi] Though his call for former shipyard workers to be released from the forces went unheeded, they did enjoy exemption from call-up. The blitz on ports caused especial hardships for dockworkers, only partly compensated for by an end to the much hated system of casual employment. Grievances arising over work during unsocial hours, and related difficulties of meals and transport were remedied, most often only after threats - and occasionally the reality - of unofficial strikes.

Ernest Bevin, Minister of Labour and National Service, was much respected but his active presence certainly did not resolve all conflicts and problems. Bottlenecks in the supply of materials and inadequate numbers of skilled workers significantly inhibited the war effort. The Minister of Aircraft Production (who was Lord Beaverbrook until 1st May) was ruthless in his supervision, but there was barely adequate production of modern warplanes. The production of the first four-engined bomber, the Short Stirling, was badly delayed due to German bombing in 1940. The boasting about new warplanes disguised much grim technological inadequacy.[xxvii] However, hundreds of planes were now being purchased from the USA, ultimately to become thousands supplied under Lend-Lease. As for tanks, they could be seen in the countryside, allegedly ready to meet an invasion. They were produced in fair quantity but effective, up to date designs were non-existent. There was a cover-up over their poor quality, but early in July a new Conservative MP, Lieutenant-Colonel R.A Brabner,[xxviii] formerly an officer in the Middle East, angrily told the House of Commons of the high incidence of mechanical breakdown. His allegations were unconvincingly denied. The Germans already had by now first-hand knowledge of the battlefields where British tanks had failed.

The expansion of the war economy with an almost complete absence of male unemployment led to the registration of young women, excluding many mothers, for war work either in industry or the services. The secondary problems raised by this unprecedented extension of conscription caused much disruption and discussion, but the principle was accepted as unavoidable. Industry was hit by the war much more than could be publicly admitted. Management had to cope with many new obstacles due to shortages of materials, delays in transport and absence of skilled labour. Despite government attempts at co-ordination and allocation of materials and skilled labour, much war production was inefficient and enforced idleness in factories was not uncommon. Workforces would often suffer from sleeplessness, due to the Blitz or threat of Blitz, homelessness if there was bomb destruction or damage, difficulties with travel, ill-health, malnourishment, absence of works canteens and family problems. Small wonder productivity was often low. Allegations of blame came from each side of industry. Attempts made both at the top and locally, by trade unions and employers' organisations, to remedy all such problems were only partly successful.

Churchill himself left it to his colleagues to deal with the war economy and social issues. It was the Labour Party, part of the coalition government, which claimed credit for achievements of the war effort in industry and home affairs, as outlined in its manifesto for its 1941 Whitsun annual Conference: '*The area of the social services has been increased. Largely through the care and determination of the Trade Unions, the standard of life has been well safeguarded. The health of the workers has been protected by the maintenance of the factory codes, and by the institution of factory doctors, canteens and nurseries. Labour, national and local, has taken its share in civil defence; and in every sphere its activities have done much to improve the provision for the safety and comfort of citizens. The social protection of our people has been facilitated by the alert and continuous watch which has been kept over financial policy. Interest rates have been kept down. The Treasury has assumed powers over the Banks which assure their full co-operation in the policy upon which Parliament decides, The dangers of inflation, ever present in war-time, have been kept to a minimum'.*[xxix] The Labour historian G.D.H.Cole held these claims to be justified. He added that in most respects the record compared very favourably with that of WW1. An extensive, if incomplete, abolition of the hated means test was another advance, though by the Spring of 1941 there was near full employment in any event.

An attempt to steamroller through Parliament far-reaching proposals to diminish the number of small businesses, and thus release manpower for war production, failed. This approach, which the House of Commons disapproved, centred on a wartime trusteeship by surviving businesses, of the goodwill of those businesses forced to close. The implications for small businesses, even though small shopkeepers were not included, were forbidding. The scheme was abandoned.[xxx]

Wartime politics was unusual as conflict between the major parties was suspended, as were local government elections. This was the Party truce which lasted despite grumbles. The War Cabinet, over which Churchill presided as Prime Minister and Minister of Defence, had eight members. Lord Beaverbrook as Minister of Aircraft

Production was the closest confidant of Churchill. Clement Attlee, as leader of the Labour Party and Lord Privy Seal, was businesslike and trustworthy, and chaired key committees when Churchill was absent, and in practice supervised Parliamentary business. The effective boss of the war economy was Sir John Anderson as Lord President of the Council. His brusque efficiency, and sometime colonial role as Governor of Bengal, contributed to his reputation as authoritarian and pompous. Anthony Eden, the Foreign Secretary, had a great flair for diplomacy, but his poor sense of judgement was already known to insiders. Because of his popularity with the public, he appeared an obvious heir to Churchill. Ernest Bevin, whose ministry has already been mentioned, was recognised as a massive political presence formerly dominating the trade union movement. Outside his own immediate sphere, his contribution could be defined as that of 'gut reaction'. The two other members of the War Cabinet had lesser status. However, they connected with the backbenchers. The Chancellor of the Exchequer, Sir Kingsley Wood, once close to the late and by now largely despised Neville Chamberlain, was politically indispensable. Moreover, the tax system in the budget of early April was to be innovative including much steeper rates of taxation with income tax up to 10/- in the £. and, for the first time, post-war credits. The third man from the Labour Party, Arthur Greenwood, a popular and experienced figure, had responsibility for post-war reconstruction but as a Minister without Portfolio. Of the eight active members of the War Cabinet, five were Conservative or on the Conservative side. Four of the eight had no departmental responsibilities. The leader of the Liberal Party of some twenty MPs, Sir Archibald Sinclair was Secretary of State for Air. He was close to Churchill but not a member of the War Cabinet, although often in attendance at its meetings. Viscount Halifax, the British ambassador in Washington, retained nominal membership of the War Cabinet.

In March 1941, the firmest supporters of the government on the back benches came from the more than one hundred and forty Labour MPs, who generally felt a stronger ideological antagonism to fascism than the Conservative majority of more than twice as many. Most of the latter, despite their patriotism did not have that edge for all their distrust and dislike of Hitler. They felt a positive detestation of Communism in contrast to Labour's categorical distancing. Many ordinary Labour Party members had reservations about Communism which fell short of hatred. Irrespective of such likes or dislikes, the USSR was occasionally thought of as a potential ally by some in the centre and on the Left. This view was shared by few Conservatives, but among this minority was Churchill. For strategic and political reasons, he kept this view to himself.

On the extreme right of British politics were the fascists, of whom over nine hundred were interned as potential traitors, mostly on the Isle of Man. The selection of internees was somewhat arbitrary and occasionally unjust, but a prime aim was to intimidate the very many more people, many of whom would not have defined themselves as fascists, who might want to negotiate a peace with Germany on Nazi terms. Also interned either on the Isle of Man - or by now in Canada or Australia - were those enemy aliens who continued to be distrusted. The scandal of the mass internment of *'enemy'* aliens (mainly anti – Nazi Germans and refugees from occupied nations) the previous summer, undertaken hurriedly in panic and causing some tragic suicides in the process, had by now largely been superseded. Those aliens, once classified as enemy, who were keen to support the war effort were mostly free by March 1941. Some of their services became exceptionally valuable.[xxxi]

A fear of Churchill's must have been that defeatism could prevail in Parliament if there were severe reverses during the summer of 1941. For the time being, what could be more attractive for the potentially treasonable than to keep their heads below the parapet, and await events? An occasional expression of belief that the real enemy was Communism and the USSR was a sign of this game of patience. Early in March, a Communist candidate in a by-election in the industrial Lowlands of Scotland, secured 15% of the vote. A secret MoI report warned *'that a situation of some danger is revealed and a close watch ought to be kept on developments in this area'*. Many at the top of society privately entertained misgivings about the future of Britain, and most of them feared Communism. At a meeting of MPs on 2 April to which 63 MPs had been invited and 23 attended, the question of a need for a negotiated peace was implied, though no action as such followed the discussion.[xxxii]

Churchill had to take account of this potential of defeatism yet could not risk offending most of its adherents. Many in the Conservative Party nursed doubts about his hope of ultimate victory. The Conservatives who had faith in his total defiance of Nazism were a bare majority in their party. Because those who were responsible for disseminating propaganda of hope for victory had to believe in its truth if they were going to give value, Churchill tolerated discussion of war aims which assumed a complete defeat of fascism and the victory of democracy from a left-wing standpoint. In this approach might be found one of the seeds of the future, ostensibly surprising, Labour victory of 1945.

The celebrated novelist and dramatist J.B. Priestley, was the greatest protagonist of the broad ideology of the non-Communist Left. His immensely popular morale boosting radio broadcasts gave him a reputation for challenging Conservative political values, while adroitly recognising their contribution to national unity. His astute broadcasts perceptibly shifted the centre of gravity of political belief to the Left. He was eventually banned from further broadcasting. Charles Graves recalls in his diary for 26 March 1941 asking Beverley Baxter (a well-known Conservative MP and influential journalist doubtful about Churchill's leadership) whether he had been singing in his bath *'Who killed Cock Robin'*? The best record of optimism about a victorious post-war Britain as superior to the Britain of the 1930s may be found in the New Year number of the mass circulation weekly, *Picture Post*. Experts, mostly left-wing, gave their opinions about what could and should be done for a planned economy and a welfare state. There were fetching photographs to drive their points home. However, according to a poll a few weeks after this *Picture Post* appeared, only a small minority of readers had a specific memory of it.

The Labour Party as a party of government had to show great restraint because of the wartime party truce. So the small but active Communist Party represented a definite challenge. To many on the left, its self-imposed handicap was that it stood by the entitlement of the USSR to remain neutral, and following Moscow's interpretation of events, saw the war as '*an imperialist war*', therefore discounting any call to patriotism. This stance had led to the official banning of its newspaper the *Daily Worker* on 21 January. Officially it was accused of impairing the war effort by discouraging production and damaging morale. But there was notably no prosecution. The paper had exposed instances of industrial mismanagement, deficiencies in Air Raid Protection (ARP), and unnecessary privations, and had led vehement campaigns against these. Minutes of high level discussions by ministers show embarrassment and muddle about this attack on '*free speech*'. The opposition was morally powerful although ineffective. There were probably several reasons for the ban . The Home Secretary, Herbert Morrison, the Labour Party's chief disciplinarian, disliked the Communist Party, as did the officials of the Trades Union Congress. The paper severely criticised their frequent deviation from socialist principles. Earlier in January the paper had mocked the leading Labour Party theorist, Harold Laski. Late in 1940 the paper had praised Lord Beaverbrook for his realism about the USSR, but a few days before the ban it reminded its readers that as late as 1939 he had sent Hitler birthday greetings. Perhaps most significantly, Churchill and Beaverbrook must have been afraid that the paper might spoil any plan to bring the USSR into the war as an ally of Britain. Such a fear could not wisely be recorded.[xxxiii]

Morrison, Beaverbrook and others, had been alarmed by the success of 'The People's Convention' of 12 January which was a triumph for many on the Left, including Communists. Many active trade unionists and others had attended or supported the weekend mass meeting at a London hotel. The weakness of the eight point programme for a people's government and a people's peace, which won some sympathy on the left, was the assumption that German workers could and would destroy the Nazi regime if there were a people's government in Britain. The view was that such a rebellion would facilitate genuine anti-fascist peace negotiations.

Yet this mistaken belief stemmed partly from the official propaganda of the phoney war of a year or so previously that the German economy was likely to collapse under the strain of war. The chief personality of the People's Convention was the Labour Independent MP and prominent lawyer D.N.Pritt. Certainly pro-Soviet, Pritt declined to become a Communist. In the parliamentary debate of 29 January forced upon the government in protest against its ban on the *Daily Worker*, he interestingly complimented Churchill as a major safeguard against the influence of those members of the 'upper class' who might seek peace with an undefeated Nazi Germany. The huge majority of MPs who supported the ban on the *Daily Worker* held their ground, winning the vote 323 -6.

The Labour Party and the TUC officially maintained their total opposition to the Communist Party. Anti-Communist views in the mass media peaked from mid-January onwards. Yet primarily because of the presence in industry of Communist shop stewards and other left-wingers in the Unions, the mass media soon dropped its overt anti-Communist campaign. The mass circulation *Daily Express,* owned by Beaverbrook, had divided Communists into two categories: patriots and '*dullards who* (thought) *they could outwit Hitler'.*[xxxiv] The latter were considered dangerous. It was claimed that much popular support for the "People's Convention" had been fabricated (e.g. there had been forging of signatures in workplaces). Then these allegations were abruptly discontinued. Peter Howard, a superstar of the Beaverbrook press, was soon complimenting the sole Communist MP Willie Gallacher. In the Communist poll in the Dumbarton by-election at the end of February, a clandestine observer for MoI alluded to the high incidence of goodwill towards the Communist candidate that resulted from his airing the real grievances of local people.

In this by-election Gallacher campaigned for a more efficient and democratic war effort and significantly made no claim that the war was *'imperialist'*. A Scottish nationalist intended to stand, but he was a serving soldier and the War Office did not oblige quickly enough with permission. He happened to be the elder brother of the Communist candidate. Conservatives and Liberals mostly abstained and let the Labour man win in what had been a marginal seat in the previous general election. So there was a low turn-out even allowing for a wartime poll. The official attitude towards Communists as far as influencing public opinion was concerned continued as ambivalent. In mid-March, the 85 year old renowned Communist, Tom Mann, died. The *Daily Express* referred to him as *'a Communist with a sense of fun'*, and the regular columnist *'Peterborough'* of the *Daily Telegraph* paid his kind tribute. However, the Labour Party expelled a Manchester councillor who addressed a meeting to commemorate Tom Mann. Over Easter at some conferences of trade unions and that of the Co-operative Party, Communist supported motions obtained noticeable support.

Churchill of course remained profoundly opposed to Communism and Communists but he weighed their presence in society. Two Communists suffered internment, one fairly briefly, under the draconian regulation 18b.[xxxv] Churchill must have considered how the Communist Party of Great Britain (CPGB) might be used to further his project to mislead Hitler into a belief that Britain would side with Germany if and when Germany invaded the USSR. To have the *Daily Worker* banned and to intern a few Communists would give the right impression without endangering morale at home. In wartime Australia, the Communist party was already banned.

Because Churchill stood head and shoulders above his colleagues in the War Cabinet in his ability to discern and conduct the strategic direction of the war, there was a tendency to belittle his colleagues. Something of their abilities has been indicated above. The public conception of Churchill as a great wartime leader could not then or now be sensibly doubted. His capacity for brilliant rhetoric nearly always told. No one else could match it, though the more relaxed and homely style of J.B.Priestley came near in its broad appeal on the radio at a peak listening time. Churchill's presence mostly told positively for the relatively few who were in personal contact with him. The public were given images which survive in popular culture - the great statesman, patriot and orator with the disposition of a bulldog and as the man with the big cigar waving his hat on his stick. What was kept from the public was his often markedly poor chairmanship of the War Cabinet and related committees. His lisp he carefully converted into the famous slur. His time-wasting, prolonged monologues and ranting, adolescent propensities, and his failure to read documents properly were notorious in those exclusive circles[xxxvi] Yet clearly he was indispensable as a national leader. He knew it and exploited this knowledge.

Another characteristic of Churchill's was his ruthlessness in the context of his absolute defiance of Hitler and Nazi Germany. His positive incentive was the continued defence of the British Empire and Commonwealth, the preservation of the monarchy and Parliamentary institutions. He had no intention of challenging the Capitalist system as such but knew that at times it had to bend. He had the nous to respect, with whatever serious reservations for wartime, the principle of free speech. When the BBC took off the air musicians and actors who were supporters of the "People's Convention", the composer Ralph Vaughan Williams declined, as a gesture of protest, to allow his music to be broadcast. Churchill publicly regretted the BBC's ban, which was at once withdrawn.[xxxvii]

Some outstanding examples of Churchill's ruthlessness deserve citation. Early in July 1940, a French fleet in harbour in the French North African Empire, was devastated in a bombardment by the Royal Navy and some 1,300 French sailors lost their lives with many others wounded. A few weeks earlier France and Britain had been allies. The attack had been unnecessary as further negotiations would almost certainly have led to some compromise to prevent any pro-German use of these French warships. Nonetheless the onslaught showed the whole world that Britain was determined to fight Nazi Germany despite the fall of France. When Churchill, with his usual overwhelming oratory reported the incident to the House of Commons on 4 July 1940, he was jubilantly acclaimed by Conservative MPs for the first time as PM.[xxxviii]

Another example dates from two of the most crucial weeks of the Battle of Britain, ending August and beginning September 1940. The Luftwaffe was gaining control of the air over South East England by smashing vital airfields of Fighter Command. Many RAF fighter pilots were being killed, wounded or exhausted. Churchill reasonably surmised an imminent threat of German air superiority adequate to cover successfully an invasion of Britain. Churchill decided it would be better if the Luftwaffe were to bomb London heavily, thereby desisting from punishing Fighter Command further. There had been a small scale and indeed accidental bombing of London by the Luftwaffe on the night of 24/25 August. In retaliation the RAF raided Berlin. Practically no physical damage and few casualties resulted. However, several million Berliners were deprived of sleep, and Nazi prestige was hit. Goering, Commander-in-Chief of the Luftwaffe (second only to Hitler in the Nazi hierarchy), had been famous for his already tarnished promise that Germany would be safe from air raids.[xxxix] Further air raids on Berlin followed, and so on 4 September Hitler was prompted to make another impressive speech. He proclaimed that if the RAF continued to raid

German cities, the Luftwaffe would erase British cities. His audience applauded him wildly. In fact encouraging Hitler to make this public threat was a German appreciation of circumstances of which Churchill may well have been aware; that Fighter Command in Britain was on the verge of collapse and the heavy bombing of London would aim to break British morale to facilitate the invasion of Britain or a British capitulation. Churchill, with the aim of drawing fire away from Fighter Command, ordered the RAF again to raid Berlin on the nights of 5th and 6th of September 1940. More damage was done and more casualties resulted. Churchill believed his goading tactics saved Fighter Command. His admission of his own willingness to sacrifice London, which was heavily blitzed as from 7th September, is implied in his *Their Finest Hour*. This admission was not more blatant because a general election, that of 1950, was expected after publication.

Churchill's ruthlessness was complemented by his exceptional political and strategic guile. His historical knowledge and vision were narrow and centred on the role of the state. He had detailed knowledge of the great generalship of his ancestor the Duke of Marlborough, and of the prolonged warfare with Revolutionary and Napoleonic France less than a century before his birth. Amongst his favourite reading were novels by C.S.Forester about the fictitious hero, Hornblower of the RN.[xl] The career of Admiral Nelson was also personally compelling. Churchill's interest and career in politics covered more than forty years. His own father had been a foremost Conservative who had defied his own Party. Churchill had an edge of political experience over all other MPs except Lloyd George. Even when Churchill was in the political wilderness in the 1930s he was allowed access to top secret defence information. By 1941, Churchill was commandingly leading the Conservative Party, a feat in itself.

Churchill saw war as basically a contest of wills and must have pondered how Hitler might be deceived. His knowledge of stratagems of history as well as tricks on the battlefield provided background. In legend, most Trojans had greeted the wooden horse as a deserved gift from the gods; the few dissidents were ruthlessly crushed. The legendary Odysseus who planned the wooden horse could not have been overlooked by Churchill, who spoke publicly in favour of the study of the classics at Bristol University on 12 April 1941, when as Chancellor he awarded honorary degrees. The outcome of another great historic stratagem was the defection of a key part of King Richard III's army at the Battle of Bosworth Field in 1485, so that the Tudor dynasty ousted the House of York. As Churchill's *History of the English-speaking Peoples* shows, pre-war he studied this episode, relying partly on Shakespeare's *The Tragedy of King Richard III*. *(37)*

Further examples of the utility of '*a big lie*' to Churchill's knowledge included those of the Conservative Party during the inter-war period. The general elections of 1918, 1924, 1931 and 1935 were won by that party with huge majorities, albeit they were in formal coalitions in all but 1924. The encouragement of irrational hatred of Germany and reckless promises of post-war reconstruction were features of the 1918 election campaign. Nearly six years later, the forged Zinoviev letter provided fake evidence of an alleged Bolshevik plot against Britain. Shocked voters deserted the Liberal cause in droves for the Tories. In 1931 the Conservatives accompanied their intention to end free trade and defeat Labour with an insincere respect for the Liberal Party and the turncoat former leadership of the Labour Party. The 1935 election saw a reckless appeal to the voters to stand by the League of Nations. Churchill may have had little to do with the origins of these deceits, but he would have profitably learned from them. In September 1938, the Conservative government relied on a myth of German invincibility to manipulate public opinion to support the shameful Munich settlement. In the Spring of 1941 could Hitler's will be bent? Churchill must have considered this prospect.

The claim that Britain 'stood alone' has always been simplistic; the resources of the Empire were at its disposal, and the contribution of refugees from German-occupied Europe cannot be overlooked. Greece became an ally in the war against Italy. The 'white' Dominions of Canada, Australia and New Zealand gave vital help and expected to be treated virtually as equals. They provided army, naval and air force units, merchant ships and crews, war production, and the main safe training areas for the RAF under the Empire Air Training Scheme. Britain naturally enjoyed generous trading terms. In the Union of South Africa, a minority white population held a monopoly of political power. The country was led by General Smuts, an Anglophile as Prime Minister, who enjoyed a reputation as an Empire statesman, due not least to his Boer past and his status as an academic philosopher. He received firm support from his own Parliament for the deployment of several 'white' South African divisions and ancillary forces of blacks to liberate Ethiopia and neighbouring colonies from Italian rule. Stemming from bitter Afrikaaner memories of the Boer war, his support dwindled when it came to considering Germany as an enemy. The ratio of MPs in the South African Parliament in his favour was approximately eighty to sixty, though the opposition was divided. How long it would remain divided was uncertain. Part of the opposition was outrageously pro-Nazi, and of course widespread racism was a context to much of their politics.[xli]

Conventional lore has it that the neutrality in WW2 of the Republic of Eire was a deliberate slap in the face for Britain. Superficially that view remains common currency, but further consideration suggests that on balance Irish neutrality was for the best. Eire's entry into WW2 on the side of Britain would have caused serious unrest and active IRA hostility both in the Republic and the six counties of the North included in the United Kingdom. Bitter memories of British oppression preserved by many Roman Catholics and nationalists throughout the whole island would have inspired widespread sedition if not treason. Democracy in the six counties was considered as fake as far as the nationalists and most Roman Catholics were concerned.

In the Spring of 1941 the British government almost decided on an extension of conscription to the six counties but wisely the step was thwarted in time. In fact there were many volunteers for the British military and civil war effort from both the North and the Republic. The main disadvantage of Eire's neutrality was the absence of bases from which to fight the Battle of the Atlantic. The legal entitlement to British naval bases in Eire had been abandoned in 1938. However, Dublin turned a blind eye to British warplanes which overflew part of County Donegal. German spies who arrived in Eire were arrested. An attempted German invasion of Eire was generally regarded as improbable. Logically, it must have been calculated in London that Irish neutrality was on the whole desirable, but this assessment could not sensibly have been a public one.

Crown colonies were also supportive though most of their native populations suffered from appalling poverty and its consequences. Protests, assumed to be either Nationalist or Communist inspired, were ruthlessly suppressed. Malaya, under colonial rule in a framework of various constitutions, was an important source of rubber and tin, essential raw materials. Production was overseen by British planters and mine managers and engineers. Profits of the exploiting companies soared. A false sense of security prevailed in the adjoining port and naval base of the island of Singapore, as the Japanese threat was grossly underestimated,even scorned. India, with its 350 million population, was marginally reliable as the Nationalist movement struggled for independence.

Of the European governments in exile in London, the Poles remained nominally at war with the USSR and at peace with

Italy. A Polish brigade had moved from Syria to Palestine after the fall of France and formed most of the tiny strategic reserve in the Middle East. The open anti-semitism of many of the Poles in exile was an embarrassment, which British censorship only partly concealed.[xlii] The Czechs in exile in Britain were striving to receive formal recognition as a government, but progress was slow. There were a few Czech soldiers, but their airmen, and indeed, Polish airmen had fought in the Battle of Britain. Without them and other non-British pilots, Britain could have lost the war in 1940.

The 'Free French' who were under the leadership of General de Gaulle, provided a small military force in the Middle East. De Gaulle attracted less support in the Vichy controlled French Empire than he claimed, though some of central Africa had seceded to him. The British government had to maintain an uneasy balance between de Gaulle and 'neutral' Vichy in negotiations to gain diplomatic favours from the latter's proclaimed neutrality. Much sidelining of de Gaulle therefore featured, but it was not sought to disown the Free French completely. De Gaulle was at least a figurehead for the national honour of France, to date by far the biggest victim and prize of Nazi Germany. Before Marshal Petain sought an armistice, de Gaulle's relatively low substantive rank as a Colonel and his Under-Secretaryship of State of War for some ten days was more than compensated for both by his prescient public forecast years earlier of Blitzkrieg war and his vigorous leadership on the battlefield of Northern France in May 1940.

Two monarchs in London from occupied Europe, King Haakon of Norway and Queen Wilhelmina of the Netherlands, were acknowledged by their few compatriots also in Britain. Many merchant ships under their old flags and with their crews remained loyal to their monarchs and their governments in exile, as did their overseas Empires.

In the USA, the once strong cause of Isolationism faced an increasing surge of rational scorn from President Roosevelt and others, but what also played its part, was the evident recovery from the badly lingering effects of the Great Depression. Business and labour leaders felt the ongoing economic expansion for purposes of American rearmament and aid to Britain, to be both commendable and irresistible. The Isolationists had support from perhaps a quarter of the interested population, and a minority (though a vociferous one) of Congressmen and Senators. The American situation was only partly understood in Britain as far as public opinion went. The British journalists on the spot, among them Alistair Cooke for the *Daily Herald*, could hardly refrain from presenting an optimistic image. This led to a widespread - unfounded but highly comforting - belief that the USA would soon be fighting alongside Britain against Germany.

The "American way of life", through Hollywood's distorting prism of films formed part of the prevailing British culture. Entertainment and sport, although curtailed, remained vital for maintaining morale; probably as important as war news itself. The press, though often not too closely read, was vital. The BBC offered a choice to listeners between the Home Service and the Forces Programme and to some, the invaluable Overseas Service. The BBC fostered the urge to contribute to the fight against a foe seen as intent on destroying the British way of life; it also fostered a sense of community. Because the personal loss of so many of the usual sweeteners of life was inevitable, there had to be as convincing as possible as a compensatory feeling of "togetherness" or collective spirit. Even those of a sceptical or cynical mindset could not fail to be aware of the weight of public opinion backing the war effort, and therefore mostly felt impelled to comply with the specific military or civil tasks allotted to them, enforceable in the last resort by a state now vested with immense legal powers.

The outstanding example of crude 'hate' propaganda against Germany was a much publicised booklet, *Black Record*. The author was a top Foreign Office official Robert Vansittart (soon to be ennobled) and he portrayed the whole German race as inherently aggressive. Some controversy, including a debate in the House of Lords on 18th February 1941, inevitably followed publication. *Black Record* conveniently diverted attention from a more valid study of the causes of aggression, and by implication posed the allegedly benign racism of the British Empire against the detestable one of the *"Hun"*.

As part of the principle of collective responsibility at the top, the War Cabinet, the Defence Committee, the Chiefs of Staff and Joint Intelligence Committee had to make as realistic as possible their perceptions over the future of the war, and what should be done by Britain. Everyone at the top recognised that Germany held the initiative and knew that the German leadership was well aware of this; however this knowledge was distorted for British public opinion. The German options as viewed from the top in London seemed basically threefold, with the first one by far the most probable. There would be a German offensive from the direction of Bulgaria aimed at the conquest of Greece. There might be further German offensives against Yugoslavia and Turkey and through Spain aiming at the capture of Gibraltar and blocking the Western end of the Mediterranean. The Vichy French Empire in North Africa might be vulnerable. It was however weighed unlikely that the whole British position in the Middle East could be threatened. This view entailed a bad underestimate of the speed and efficiency of possible German offensives. The second and third options attributed to Germany were seen as an attempt at an invasion of Britain or an invasion of the USSR. In any event the Blitz and the Battle of the Atlantic continued. As regards a British plan to capture the Italian held island of Rhodes, the strength needed was never forthcoming, and initial offensives failed.

ENIGMA-the vital British enemy code -breaking apparatus-and other solid information, suggested an attack on Greece from Bulgaria as imminent in March. By the last week of March, a small army of British, Australian and New Zealand contingents and a few squadrons of the RAF were already in Greece with reinforcements on the way. They were to be reinforced. Germany knew the details of this. The British public only knew of the RAF in Greece although rumours were beginning to spread. Whereas some realists at the top in Britain believed disaster was looming, they could only express their fears privately. At the top facile optimism about defending Greece prevailed.

Though without specific knowledge, Lloyd George then aged 78 wrote on 11 March to his future step-daughter Jennifer Stevenson : '*I do not believe in the way we entered the war - nor in the methods by which it has been conducted. We have made blunder after blunder and we are still blundering. Unless there is a thorough change of policy, we shall never win. I do not believe in the way or in the persons, with which the War Cabinet is constituted. It is totally different to the war Cabinet set up in the last war... It is not a war Directorate in the real sense of the term. There is therefore no real direction*'.[xliii] Presumably, Lloyd George both assumed that American backing could prevent defeat but not assure victory, and that the USSR would either stay neutral or side with Germany. He sought, for the time being, no publicity for his assessment.

On 17 March, six days after Lend-lease became law in the USA, Sir Alexander Cadogan, permanent head of the Foreign Office and frequent attendee at meetings of the War Cabinet, wrote to Viscount Halifax, the British ambassador in Washington and nominally a member of the war Cabinet, '*We must expect a terrific opening of the Campaign of 1941, but I don't think we are ill-prepared*'. Though unwise, his confidence must have been sincere.

CHAPTER 3

Euphoria and Onwards

Ten days after the optimistic letter from Cadogan to Halifax came sensational news. In Belgrade, the capital of Yugoslavia, on the night of 26/27 March, officers led by a Serbian air force general overthrew in a bloodless coup, the pro-German government. This act, in effect, repudiated the treaty of only a few hours earlier under which Yugoslavia accepted the Tripartite Pact and therefore joined the Nazi New Order of Europe. The new government boldly declared that Yugoslavia would be a neutral state in WW2. The pro-German Prince Paul, the Regent for 17 year old King Peter, was immediately exiled, first to Greece, and then to Kenya under British supervision.

The effect of this news on Churchill was electric, and more good news was on the way. Two speeches of Churchill's on Thursday 27 March thrilled audiences, in whose company was the new American ambassador to Britain, John Winant. Churchill's theme was that '*Yugoslavia has found its soul*', a consciously inspiring formula which seems to have originated from Cadogan. The media was inspired to generate a wave of optimism which turned out to be unjustified, but which spread under its own momentum. Here it seemed was a whole nation of 18 million people refusing to be cowed by Hitler, and taking a resolute stand against the almost certain threat of German aggression. This was a new phenomenon in the Balkans. Slovakia, Hungary, Rumania and Bulgaria had all succumbed to the German demands for economic exploitation, and appropriate occupation by the German armed forces. It had looked as if Yugoslavia was similarly to be absorbed into the Nazi orbit, only to be miraculously saved at the last moment. Now Yugoslavia and Greece, which was continuing to thrash fascist Italy, and perhaps in addition Turkey (formally an ally of Britain), apparently barred Hitler's way further South.

Moreover, on the night of 28 March, the battle of Cape Matapan in the Eastern Mediterranean saw the Royal Navy triumph over an Italian fleet. This was publicly hailed at the time as a tremendous victory. Entries in private diaries[xliv] show the enthusiasm generated, with details of the numbers and types of enemy warships sunk and damaged. The British losses were almost nil. The press was gleeful for the next few days. In addition, in Italian East Africa, two land victories of strategic importance were won on 27 March. Keren, a strongly held mountain fortress in Eritrea, fell after a six week siege. The 4th Indian Division, comprising roughly equal numbers of Indian and British troops and commanded almost entirely by British officers, had suffered heavy casualties in failed attacks, but the Italian defences had at last crumbled. Simultaneously, in Ethiopia, Harar, a strategically important town on the road to Addis Ababa, was evacuated by the Italian Army, and fell without a struggle to advancing West African Units. The Italian Empire in East Africa was at last well on its way to total collapse.

Yugoslavia was depicted as having a powerful army ready to defend the mountainous terrain of much of the country. *The Times* waxed lyrical over the alleged strength of the Yugoslav air force, estimating it at 1,000 warplanes. The *Daily Mail* estimated 800 and the *Daily Telegraph* at first 500 and later 1,000. The army was claimed in the British press as *'Europe's best soldiers'*, estimates of numbers varying between 1 and 1$\frac{1}{2}$ million, and the *Daily Mail* optimistically informed its readers *'Slav tanks massing'* and *' the boy king in the event of war will lead his armies at the front'*. Churchill believed that the combined armies of Greece, Yugoslavia and Turkey would number seventy divisions and that these would either deter German aggression or prove more than a match for a smaller German army, should Germany take the offensive. For Churchill, the image of these seventy divisions became for a few days a fixation.

The new strategic situation looked so promising that it was made public. American newspaper estimates of the strength of the British army in Greece went as high as 300,000 and Graves stated in his diary for 29 March, after mentioning this figure , *'Actually, we have about 120,000 on the job…. The news of the Yugoslav coup d'etat is first class and bears out exactly the predictions of Lyndoe, the People's soothsayer'*. He like so many others was carried away. A top journalist at *The People* , Hannen Swaffer, opined on 30th March *'yes there has come out of the Balkans a great new hope'*. *Time and Tide,* a political weekly of liberal-minded opinion commented *'it has been the best week of the war'* and the *New Statesman* told its readers that *'The 27th of March stands out in history as a day of miracles'*. *The Observer* on Sunday 30th March bore headlines : *'Lift up your hearts…Good thoughts in bad times… Yugoslav revolution…'*. It toyed with the idea of *'an unconquerable combination in the Balkans'*.

Churchill's own unrestrained enthusiasm aroused acid commentary from one of his Secretaries, John Colville. He noticed that for much of the *'wonderful'* week-end of 29th and 30th March, Churchill was tripping up and down the Great Hall at Chequers to the sound of music from a gramophone *'playing martial airs, waltzes and the most vulgar kind of brass-band songs'*. The Junior Minister of Information, the literary minded Harold Nicolson MP, convinced himself that the capture of Keren and the coup in Belgrade would be decisive for winning the war![xlv] Adding piquancy to elation was the knowledge that Hitler himself was infuriated by the coup in

Belgrade. In the Beaverbrook owned *Sunday Express* of 6 April readers were told Hitler's fury is a *'controlled fury'*. Few may have noticed the reservation about Hitler's anger. After the German offensive had begun, the *Hamburger Fremdenblatt* commented that *'an irresponsible pygmy state had flung down the gauntlet to a mighty empire'*, and a foremost Nazi, Robert Ley, was reported in *Angriff* as saying it was a joke, though a poor one, that *'a man of the stamp of Adolf Hitler' was trifled with by a 17 year-old ragamuffin'*, meaning King Peter. Ley added in a remarkable mixed metaphor that *'the cesspool of Serbian intrigue and bloodthirstiness must be eradicated root and stem'*.

Jan Masaryk in his broadcast to the Czechs of 2nd April, rejoiced in the victories and successes of March as holding out hope for the future, but he sounded a note of caution that they did *'not mean that we should begin to be carefree and to think that victory is already in our pockets. On the contrary, we must redouble our efforts.'*

Whereas the alleged military strength of Yugoslavia was extolled, the press was more restrained about Greece and Turkey. Certainly, the Greek army over the previous five months had inflicted defeat after defeat on the Italian invaders of Greece, pursuing them deeply into Albania. However, without any publicity being forthcoming, there was grasping by some, of the forbidding reality that the Greek war effort was near to exhaustion.[xlvi] Greek soldiers were doubtless questioning the wisdom of fighting beyond Greece itself for the sake of a regime which was mostly loathed. Greece was emphatically not a democracy. Political parties were banned, and the Greek king was supportive of the continued military dictatorship of the successor to General Metaxas, who had died in January 1941. Although some Italian equipment captured in Africa the previous winter had been transferred to the Greek army, it was certainly not equal to the might of the

Wehrmacht. Yet it was customary to pay generous tributes to the Greeks for their courage and emulation of their heroic ancestors of classical times and to point to the publicly declared determination of the Greek government to resist any German invasion. Churchill's rhetoric was lavish. Radiation of his confidence continued after he himself entertained substantial misgivings over it.

The view on Turkey was constrained by diplomatic considerations. The *Daily Telegraph* referred to 2 million Turkish bayonets as '*a steel wall the Nazis dare not challenge*'. This praise left open the question as to where the wall was situated, and neglected also the facts that most Turkish soldiers were illiterate and Turkish military equipment completely inadequate.

However, the predisposition was there for the welcome events to make their impact. To some, this seemed a divine response to the National Day of Prayer of 23rd March. Others, such as Graves, were reassured by the predictions of the two foremost astrologers in two Sunday newspapers, Lyndoe in *The People*, which claimed he '*planned with the planets*' and R.H. Naylor in the *Sunday Express,* whose weekly column was entitled '*What the Stars Foretell*'. A study of the actual forecasts of these 'prophets' shows how inaccurate they were, and it is a fair, but perhaps surprising, inference that that they were advised by British Intelligence as to their alleged foreknowledge. It was essential both to maintain morale at home and, if possible, to fool the enemy. The upshot of Lyndoe's and Naylor's prognoses was that Germany was on the way to losing the war before long. It was also encouraging to the few who may have known, that the press in the USSR was enthusiastic about Yugoslavia's new stand.

Adding to the prevailing euphoria, was a claim on 1 April that a new much more powerful bomb had been dropped in an RAF raid on Emden. This was exaggeration, as it was only physically much larger than it was powerful. There was also the release of a threepenny booklet (with a sale on the first day of 350,000), claiming to be the official story of the Battle of Britain of the previous year. It contained exaggerated figures for losses of German aircraft given as at the time.[xlvii] The role played by Radar in the battle, understandably received no mention. In addition favourable publicity was given to new types of aircraft destined for the RAF; sadly misplaced, given the shortcomings that became apparent to those who were to fly them.

Churchill's then confidence that WW2 was at a turning point, could pray in aid the British victory over the Italians in North Africa and the Greek advances into Italian held Albania, despite the penetration of German power into the Balkans. That was the prompt for Eden to fly to the Middle East in February to muster support from Turkey and to offer an army to aid Greek resistance to any German invasion of Greece. He was accompanied by the Chief of the Imperial General Staff, Sir John Dill. There was also a possibility the USSR could be persuaded to add its weight to block further German expansion , as it was clear Moscow feared increasing German hegemony in the Balkans.[xlviii]

As regards Yugoslavia, Eden himself would appear at this stage not to have had a major role, but King George VI wrote personally to his cousin Prince Paul the Regent and there were diplomatic overtures asking him to desist from allying his country with Germany. It may be that there was bribery of Serbs so they might support toppling the pro-German government.[xlix] Yet Yugoslavia was a badly divided nation, a fact speciously ignored in Britain. Croats in particular favoured a pro-German policy in Belgrade. They ultimately hoped for independence.

However there was some truth in the publicised view that the coup in Belgrade was a popular uprising, originating in Serb antagonism to Nazism. The Serbs were Slavs and the intelligentsia had largely objected to the betrayal of fellow Slavs, Czechs, two and a half years earlier under the Munich settlement. Their profound rejection of Nazi racist doctrine was absolutely soundly based. Their portrayal by the British media as intrinsically patriotic was broadly true, but the calibre of the teenage King Peter was overestimated. His claimed initiative in broadcasting to the people after the coup was a myth. An actor had impersonated his voice. However, the new government took a significantly more lenient line towards the political left. Communists were released from prison. The Communist influence among workers and students was formidable. Many looked for support from the USSR, though hopes raised were soon to be disappointed.[1]

It remains uncertain to what extent Eden then recognised the risks of his mission to the Middle East. The Greek Government was persuaded to accept a British army in Greece. This operation (*Lustre*) was to serve as protection against a suspected imminent German invasion expected as coming from Bulgaria, which country the Wehrmacht began to enter in force on March 1. However, many Greeks considered British land forces as a provocation and many were favourably disposed towards Germany, which had taken a neutral attitude towards Greece, despite the German-Italian alliance. In Athens, Eden and Dill were assured of a substantial Greek addition to the proposed British forces. Too readily it was assumed that military co-operation from Yugoslavia and Turkey might be forthcoming.

Amazingly Dill and Wavell (who was also present in Athens for a while) failed to do their military homework. They recklessly advised Eden - and through him Churchill and the War cabinet- that there was '*a reasonable fighting chance*' a line could be held in Northern Greece against a German invasion. They submitted no detailed report but rashly judged that the mountainous terrain would be advantageous for defence. They either disregarded alternative opinions or these came too late to affect the British commitment. They did not anticipate reduced Greek military assistance, and that both British forces on the ground and in the air would be weaker than envisaged. Eden with his undoubted charm, persuaded Dill and also Wavell and the Greeks against their better judgement. Second thoughts on the part of Dill and Wavell came too late. Furthermore, strong argument at the time for sending an army to Greece stemmed from the pre-war British guarantee of Greek independence. It was accepted as highly undesirable to renege on this guarantee.

Eden's endeavours to persuade the Turkish Foreign Secretary that the interests of Turkey demanded that Turkey become an active ally of Britain and Greece, and Yugoslavia (if that country were to defy Germany) met only with politeness. Eden's mission was on one occasion facilitated by the presence of Stafford Cripps, the British ambassador to Moscow, who travelled to Ankara (then known as Angora) at first in a fast plane, helpfully provided by the Russians. The Russian expansion in the Balkans was intended to prevent Turkey aligning with Germany.[li] Indeed, on 25 March they reassured the Turks by treaty of a friendly stance towards Turkey, if Germany were to attack her. Stalin, however, was also fearful of too big an influence being wielded by Britain in the Dardanelles, a suspicion not without some cause. The Turkish government played a clever diplomatic game against the competitive jostlings of Germany, Britain and USSR, with the aim of Turkey surviving WW2 neutral and intact. They preferred realism to any sentimental alignment.

The leaning of Turkey towards Britain deceived Eden. The Anglo-Turkish treaty of the Autumn of 1939 gave a poor basis for confidence. Turkey and Britain were allies on paper only. Turkish national interests gained by a show of support for

Britain. This was foreseeably followed by German endeavours, which were a mixture of "carrot and stick", orchestrated by the German ambassador (the wily von Papen) to bring the Turks back to their senses. Eden could make capricious promises of armed forces and military equipment from Britain. These were dismissed by the Turks. The climax came at a meeting in Cyprus, when according to Eden the Turkish Foreign Secretary persuaded him that Turkey was on the brink of becoming a dependable ally, but Turkish hesitation persisted. Meanwhile the die had been cast because some of the new B.E.F. had already arrived in Greece.

So when the watershed of 27 March came, the next step was to secure the co-operation of Yugoslavia in the planned alliance. There was superficial friendliness on the part of the new Yugoslav regime, which must have resulted in MoI being given the go ahead to advise the British media to display wildly excessive and counter-productive optimism. What in fact was missing in the first few days of April was any willingness by the Yugoslav military seriously to discuss a joint defence against an imminent German invasion. The Yugoslav government was mobilising its army simultaneously with having to endure demobilisation on the part of Croat and other dissidents. The signs were that a German assault would happen shortly. The Yugoslav air force was in practice negligible. Belgrade was declared an open city. The government in Belgrade disregarded as reckless a plea from Churchill to attack the Italian armed forces in Northern Albania straight away, both to inflict another defeat on Italy and to capture armaments.[lii]

Before the Germans invaded Greece and Yugoslavia on Sunday 6 April, Churchill was aware his scheme for a concerted defence was on the road to failure, but of this there was no hint in public. Some 60,000 British, Australian and New Zealand troops and a RAF contingent were either already in Greece or on their way to arrive shortly. American correspondents reported and greatly exaggerated their presence, but the British press was censored until Monday 7 April. The arrival of the forces of the Empire in Greece then made a good story, with embellishments referring to a thousand tanks (ten times the actual figure) or more and non-existent flamethrowers. It was known that German diplomats and agents had observed in detail on the quaysides the landings of the new BEF The reticence of MoI had been utterly inept.

Euphoria about the Balkans continued to influence public opinion for some days after it had turned towards despair at the top in London. Unexpectedly, General Rommel at the head of the newly arrived Afrika Korps facing the Western end of British occupied Cyrenaica, struck and won victories. Benghazi fell to the Germans by 3 April. They then pushed eastward winning further victories. The British people were fed through the press misstatements oozing with complacency. The responsibility lay with General Wavell's GHQ Cairo and MoI. It was not the enemy, but the British public, which was misled!

The *Daily Mail* on 3 April claimed the Germans were in '*a Libyan trap*'. The *Sunday Express* reported on 6 April that there was heartening news and that, in words which soon became a classic of misstatement, '*the situation is well in hand*'. The *Observer* also used this soothing syrup. The *People* on the same day claimed the Axis advance was being held. The *Sunday Pictorial* : '*Here's good news. Wavell hits back in Africa. Nazis held. The situation is well in hand*'. Goebbels and Hitler later laughed at such press reports.[liii] Graves cheerfully began his diary entry on 5 April '*the German African Corps is only two divisions and will be cut off by the Navy. In any event, the crews of the German tanks will be fried alive in the heat of the Libyan spring*'.

With private realism, but not for public consumption, Colville recorded for Thursday, April 3rd 'We have been compelled to evacuate Benghazi in face of the German advance from Tripoli. The P.M. is greatly worried, but Pug General Ismay, Churchill's link man with the Chiefs of Staff refuses to take it too tragically........'. Harold Nicolson noted on 4 April that 'the Libyan news was worse than supposed'. Churchill knew by now that Turkey was bent on remaining neutral, unless herself attacked, and that Yugoslavia was in real peril - a frightening descent from his optimism of the previous weekend. Churchill later considered making Eden a scapegoat but prudently decided against it. The Daily Mail was to be highly critical of Eden, but he also had his defenders.[liv]

Once the German offensives against Greece and Yugoslavia had begun on Sunday 6 April, and the Afrika Korps proceeded to strike further towards the Egyptian frontier following the capture of Benghazi, the final remnants of euphoria at the top vanished. A feeling of dread set in which was to last for Churchill until the beginning of May.

Yet public opinion in Britain and the USA had been so dazzled that some pretences had to be maintained. This was becoming more difficult in Britain. Usefully, newspapers did not appear on Good Friday 11 April. American public opinion was better informed. German propaganda in the meantime, made striking headway in the USA. The expansion of German PR abroad coincided with a frustrating British reticence in providing firm war news, which attracted comment.[lv] At home, public opinion became increasingly marked by dissatisfaction with news presentation, as informants for MoI reported.[lvi]

Insofar as the media covered events in Greece and Yugoslavia, much was made of initial Greek resistance to German attempts to reach the Aegean Sea, east of Salonika. This resistance terminated after a few days, but a baseless claim was made that the German casualties were immense. *The Times* unrealistically suggested that malaria might slow any German advance. The insistence of the media that German casualties ran into many tens of thousands was fiction. *The Times* gave a final estimate of 75,000 German dead. *Picture Post* on 3 May referred to 'huge' German casualties. The German wounded were said to he overcrowding hospitals throughout the Balkans. There may have been a grain of truth in this, given the surely small number of hospitals involved. The actual German dead in Greece and Yugoslavia numbered probably about two thousand five hundred, and the wounded another six thousand , with over three thousand missing. There were fantastic claims of German losses of tanks and planes. The probability is that MoI believed this nonsense. Churchill himself went along with it in public for reasons of expediency, without committing himself unequivocally.[lvii]

The British, Australian and New Zealand forces, officially named as 'the forces of the Empire' were only peripherally engaged in the fighting for most of the first week. So it was publicly suggested that when the Germans came to confront them, the German attacks would be repelled. In the meantime, RAF action was credited with appreciably interfering with German supplies - the truth was that their impact was insignificant.

From Yugoslavia came only sparse news. The public learned of the terror bombing of Belgrade commencing on the first morning of warfare, the dead numbering about 17, 000, a mass butchery of civilians. German communiqués indicated German successes. Speculations about Yugoslav resistance and a claim of an advance into Albania amid Yugoslav rhetoric about the defence of their homeland,[lviii] were pathetically intended to stand for hard news. After a week there were some wild assertions of resistance increasing. However, it had to be accepted that Belgrade fell six days after the war began, and that the Yugoslav army officially capitulated at Sarajevo on 18 April. It was a bare solace that the young King Peter had a 'miraculous' escape in a British flying boat. A German plane fired on the craft and killed one of his ministers also aboard.

News from the Western Desert gave no cheer at all. The earlier optimism of communiqués was now badly rebounding. Benghazi had been officially described as a port of no use to the British. Within a few days, the Afrika Korps had taken it over along with local airfields. The Germans did not conceal the news, nor could its broad outlines now be concealed in Britain.

Much of the awful truth about defeat in Yugoslavia and Greece became clear towards the end of April. It was becoming obvious that retreat was the order of the day and that the campaign in Greece was being lost. On 15 April, a mere nine days after the initial German offensive had begun, the press in Germany gleefully claimed that the Greek Commander-in-Chief was asking the British to withdraw from Greece. *The Times* the next day reproved Dr Goebbels, the Minister of Propaganda in Berlin, for what it claimed to be one of his biggest lies. In a much more restrained way *The Times* criticised the Government for not making a more vigorous denial of the German claim. Unfortunately, the German claim was truthful. The news became official less than a week later. By then, the Greek Prime Minister had taken his own life. His death was reported-not the fact that it was suicide. Much was made of the Greek King for a few days heading the new government, as a mark of royal distinction.

As the Luftwaffe night-bombing of British cities became more intense in April than ever, here was another challenge to morale. What was lavishly claimed as part of the answer to the Blitz was retribution, the night bombing by the RAF of German targets. Ports and cities near to the North Sea were vulnerable. Kiel on the night of 7/8 April bore the heaviest RAF raid to date.[lix] Yet the destruction wrought was little, compared with that of the Blitz. Casualties inflicted on the ground numbered 88 dead and 184 injured. Two U-boat yards were put out of action for two days. Night shift workers were sent home in the middle of the raid. Houses were destroyed or damaged. One fire burnt for two days. 229 bombers took part, including a mere two four-engined Short Stirlings. Four aircraft were lost. Two nights later Kiel was raided again, this time by 160 aircraft including one Stirling. In this second raid the town was damaged much more than the dock area and 125 people were killed and 300 injured. 8,000 people were bombed out. Four aircraft were shot down but a further nine crashed in England. Two nights later Berlin was raided by over a hundred aircraft. Some public buildings were destroyed, about which Dr Goebbels whined. The German dead numbered some fifteen. The British press claim was 3,000! In the *Sunday Express* of 6 April John Gordon predicted the destruction of Berlin by the end of the year. The *Daily Telegraph* claimed equivocally on 14 April that British air raids on Germany were sometimes as big as German air raids on Britain. To give more credibility to belief in the imagined power of RAF bombing, it was announced on 18 April that if Athens or Cairo were bombed, Rome would be bombed. For good measure, it was alleged that an enemy squadron was ready to bomb the Vatican using captured British bombs!

The Battle of the Atlantic continued, and here the sinking of a few U - boats could be announced. German claims for shipping losses were exaggerated and easily ridiculed

By mid-April it became evident to Churchill and the War Cabinet that British morale was sliding, and that despite all the efforts of MoI and the media, these could not compensate for the growing feeling that the war was being lost in the Mediterranean and the Middle East.[lx] Though not for the ears of public opinion in Britain, Jan Masaryk in his weekly broadcasts to his homeland strove to be simultaneously courageous and realistic. His choice of themes for his three talks up to mid-April illustrate how the situation was deteriorating. March had *'been an extremely good month for us'*. The next talk on the 9th contrasted *'the great material superiority of the Germans'* with the moral superiority *'on the side of the small Balkan Davids'*, On 16 April Masaryk opened *'The news from the Balkans and Africa is not good'*, and ended *... I conclude by repeating my, our, your inflexible faith, the faith of all decent people, that Truth will prevail - must prevail. Good night - and onward'*. Here was drawing on moral capital and little else.

The Ministry of Information must have known it had to rely on the old chestnuts. Italy was the weakest point of the enemy. The collapse of the Italian East African Empire was encouraging but geographically and psychologically distant. The Italians had been soundly defeated on land, in the air and at sea, but the contrast between their vulnerability and German apparent near invincibility was painful. Yet it was worthwhile to take the line of Italian inability to fight for much longer. The *Daily Mail* as early as 5 April asked *'Will Italy throw out the Duce?'* A popular song already ran *'O what shall we do with the Duce, the Duce/ He's had no spaghetti for weeks'*. Cartoonists liked humiliating Mussolini, showing him for example as a pathetic looking jackal. During the critical week of 20 April the *Daily Telegraph* ran three articles by an American journalist who had been expelled from Italy, giving a picture of war weariness and economic strains.[lxi] Early in May, the *Sunday Pictorial* gloated that spaghetti in Italy was now a deep grey colour. One of the remarkable diarists of the war, Vere Hodgson, a social worker of Notting Hill London, was impressed by what she read in the *Daily Telegraoph*. Its nonsensical prediction of 16 April was that *'on April 26 Hitler will experience a serious defeat. Italy will seek peace soon'*. A myth persisted that some British paratroopers who in February had been dropped in Southern Italy to commit acts of sabotage remained at large.

From Italy's entry into WW2 on 10 June 1940 onwards, the Italian war machine went overall into decline.[lxii] Much of the detail increasingly became known to British Intelligence. For most Italians the war was deeply unpopular and Mussolini and Germany were blamed. The Labour MP Philip Noel-Baker in the Commons debate of 7 May called for *'a great air offensive against Italy'*. This was wishful thinking as there were few long-range bombers in the Middle East. However, Churchill congratulated him. Count Ciano, the Italian fascist Foreign Minister, recorded in his diary entries of 6 and 7 June and 14 July that supplies of coal, oil and scrap iron, all imported pre-war, were running short, the *'food situation'* was not *'brilliant but not very bad'*, and the Duce was being misled over Italian war output. The Galileo factory at Florence, intended to produce eight anti-aircraft searchlights a month, would have the first thirteen ready only at the end of 1941. As for the tens of thousands of Italian workers in Germany, they were engaged in fights there with Germans as *'a daily occurrence.'*

Whereas Italy seemed nearly out for the count, it was impossible to portray Germany in the same way. Hitler and the Nazis could always he ridiculed, but the idea the that German war machine was led by paragons of military efficiency could not be easily dispelled and had its dangers for morale. Certainly the essentially racist line of Vansittart that Germans were intrinsically wicked could always be pursued but diminishing returns had to be expected. Some of the press made much of St. George's Day, 23 April. There was a solemn editorial in *The Times* and there were sermons preached. The *Daily Telegraph* excelled in this field. *The Times* commented *'Wavell and Cunningham have not much to learn about the art of war'*, (copyright The Times/Sunday Times 23rd April 1941/nisyndication.com) neatly avoiding the unpublished fact that the RAF and land forces were desperately short of essential resources and that Wavell had already made grave misjudgements.

In his speech in the House of Commons of Wednesday 9 April Churchill's deliberate avoidance of any forecasting how the campaigns in Greece and Africa would go was a discouraging sign, as he gave the news that the Germans had captured Salonika, a key port and city in Northern Greece, that very morning. This news was exceptionally shocking. His praise for the peoples and regimes of Greece and Yugoslavia for their defiance of Germany could hardly pass as much encouragement. The blitz and the RAF bombing of Germany duly received his attention, but his ambiguity over combating the menace of the German night bomber and the damage being done to Germany by RAF bombers, could only arouse misgivings in his listeners. He was on surer ground over the Battle of the Atlantic and the vital help being given by the Americans, even though some details, of necessity, had to be withheld.[lxiii] He implied an olive branch to Vichy France by his reference to the British naval blockade being relaxed in her favour for cargoes of food, but this was a palpably defensive statement. His rhetoric centred *'on the constant flow of American supplies, which is being prepared for us'* but was preceded by his cold detached reference , (in the event taken by Stalin as a provocation and insult), to *'many signs which point to a Nazi attempt to secure the granary of the Ukraine and the oil fields of the Caucasus'*.

Churchill had moved a motion of congratulation in the Commons to *'the services of all ranks of His Majesty's Forces'* for victories won in the Middle East. MPs kept their reservations to themselves. Harold Nicolson privately thought that MPs were glum and sad to hear it[lxiv] . The few speeches which followed in support of the motion were intended merely as damage limitation. The Liberal Party spokesman Sir Percy Harris, MP for Bethnal Green, fudged by dwelling on war production. However, a virtuoso performance came from the theatrical Leslie Hore-Belisha (Secretary of State for War for most of the era of the previous Chamberlain government, but now out of office). His speech ingeniously parodied Churchill's while carefully avoiding giving offence. MPs increasingly felt that the gravity of the war situation was being hidden. However the reduced size of newspapers left little room for reports of Parliamentary debates, giving pride of place to Churchill's speeches. Pessimism spread among MPs and the journalists close to them.

Popular unease with the Government due to the loss of Yugoslavia and the imminent loss of Greece, and fears for Suez, became more marked during the week of 20 April. Two days earlier, Churchill had spoken in confidence to the editors of national newspapers with the aim of sustaining morale. Hannen Swaffer in The *People* begged Churchill to make a broadcast as soon as possible, but this did not take place until the next Sunday evening, 27 April.

It was true that the fairly well-informed Graves complained that it *'told us nothing about Greece'*, but A.P.Herbert informed him later that it *'was very smart piece of batting on a bad wicket'*. Colville thought the speech *'less (vivid) than usual'* and that it painted *'a sombre picture of the position in the East'* and bid *'us to turn our eyes westwards'* . Next day he wrote in his diary that the speech had been *'well received though there is inevitably some disillusionment after the brilliant successes of the last few months.'* The lance-bombardier diarist wrote that he *'heard very good speech by Mr Churchill on the wireless in the evening, while the Germans captured Athens & Corinth.'* Vère Hodgson gave her view at length, showing how seriously she took Churchill's message to the nation and though not mentioned by her, to the USA: *'Listened with profound attention to the Prime Minister's broadcast. He sounded a little weary. He does love to give us good news -and there is nothing to say, except that there is worse to come! He sketched fearful possibilities of Hitler extending in the Mediterranean.... and did not seem to think*

*we could do much about it. He did not explain lots of things we
should like to know. . . but I suppose we shall some day. If It
was inevitable the Yugoslavs should be defeated, why was he so
elated the other day when he announced they had declared for
us! Then how had the Germans got to Libya - and why did we
not know they were coming? He did not seem to mind his
responsibilities, and faced the future with equanimity; so we
must do the same. If he cannot win through - then no one can.'*
If anyone saw through Churchill's mendacious assurance of
Britain's immense power in the Middle East, they did not let
on.[lxv] A curious absence of logic was present when Churchill
spoke about the absolute need to defend Britain and the
Atlantic lifeline one moment, and then about an implied basic
importance of saving the Middle East the next.

The next weighty oration of Churchill's was his winding-up on
7 May of a two day debate in the House of Commons, which
ended in a vote of confidence for the Government by a huge
majority of 444. Again, Churchill dominated his audience with
his unrivalled command of spoken English. Again, his main
theme was that hope was linked with the prospect of increasing
American help and support for Britain, with the implication
that the USA would soon enter the war as an open ally of
Britain. The buoyancy and persuasiveness of his long speech
relied on his still-secret and growing confidence in the
possibility that Germany would invade the USSR. Supportive
information for this shining hope had come from ENIGMA on
4th May when it was revealed that the Afrika Korps was
basically switching to defensive tactics and on 5th May, that a
POW camp was being established in German-occupied Poland.
Listeners only heard him coldly repeat his formula that the war
might spread to the USSR.

MPs who took part in the debate were constructively critical
regarding the British war effort. The leading sceptics were
Lloyd George, whose 75-minute contribution could, from

Churchill's point of view, usefully be described as defeatist and the indefatigable Hore-Belisha, who soon afterwards was to claim *we were all duped by Winston's oratory*. Given that Hore-Belisha knew little or nothing of a possibility of the USSR as an ally in the near future, this comment was understandable. Churchill's speech about the future of the war was sparse, when analysed for actual content. The slenderness of the Government's case had been perceived by the extreme Left in the Commons. The ILP maverick, McGovern, gave an emotional pacifist speech, portraying Stalin as having the ultimate aim of inheriting a war devastated Europe. The Left MP D.N.Pritt (expelled from the Labour Party some fourteen months earlier for a pro-Soviet stand over the Soviet invasion of Finland) and William Gallacher, the sole Communist Party MP, had put down an amendment containing the demands of the People's Convention. It was not accepted for debate, and neither of them caught the Speaker's eye. They joined with two ILP members and the pacifist Labour MP Dr Alfred Salter to total five opponents of the motion.

Tuesday of the following week saw the morning papers give the sensational news of the arrival in Scotland of no less than Rudolf Hess, the Deputy Fuhrer of Germany, apparently as a fugitive from the Nazi regime. Euphoria soared because of the illusion this gave, of a total split in the Nazi leadership. Two days later (15 May) there was a sour element introduced. It was publicised that Hess had come to meet the Duke of Hamilton, who was suspected, however unfairly, of being a defeatist ready to negotiate a peace on German terms. The limelight soon shifted away from Hess. The earlier jubilation was replaced by bewilderment and dismay that there could be a new appeasement of Nazi Germany in the offing.

The German airborne invasion of Crete began on 20 May. German paratroops were falsely alleged to be dressed in British uniforms. Here was another example of Nazi perfidy! At first it looked as if the invasion might be repelled. A sea invasion of Crete was foiled by the RN, and there were claims of five thousand German soldiers drowned – the true count was about 300. A principal BBC commentator, Air Commodore Goddard, gave his seemingly authoritative opinion that airborne troops alone could not capture Crete. Amidst anxiety about the way the battle for Crete might go, came the unexpected shock of the loss of the battle cruiser HMS Hood, the pride of the RN. There were three survivors out of a crew of about 1,400. The *Daily Telegraph* called it 'bad luck' - evidently a shell from the new German battleship Bismarck had penetrated a magazine, causing the Hood to disappear in a vast explosion. Other newspapers blamed a design fault. A concentration of naval and air forces, including an American-made Catalina flying boat with at least one American serviceman clandestinely on board, led to the sinking of the Bismarck three days later. This gave a boost to morale soon tempered as Crete was lost to the German airborne invasion four days afterwards. Churchill announced the sinking of the Bismarck to compensate for his giving Parliament some limited news of heavy naval losses around Crete.

The defence of Crete had been initially presented as a recovery from the defeats of April, so its loss prompted more and fiercer criticism. A *Daily Herald* editorial of 6 June seriously warned that Britain could lose the war in the absence of real remedies for gross weaknesses. On 10 June a Parliamentary debate without a vote, revealed the deep unease. It ended with Churchill's speech, backed by a well disguised conviction that the USSR would be an ally within days, when he almost jauntily admitted a crucial and inevitable absence of air and land power.

Public opinion was hardly placated - it had been characterised by numbness for so long. The *Daily Mail* on 18 April commented that it was the Government which was '*spreading alarm and despondency at the moment'[lxvi].* Harold Nicholson's diary entry of 8 May refers to a general repression of defeatist feeling. MoI may have done its best, but it was the butt of jibes such as '*BEF stands for Back every fortnight*' and '*Give us the straw and we'll drop the bricks.*' The view that Germany was desperate and that in the not too distant future British and American armed strength would he overwhelming smacked too much of wishful thinking. The General Secretary of the T.U.C., Sir Walter Citrine, who had toured the USA to arouse support for Britain, curiously pronounced that his nation was like a boxer badly losing on points who would make a miraculous recovery, having regard to the invincibility of the forces of justice and democracy in which he had supreme confidence.[lxvii]

A new interest was taken in the shape of the post-war world, and this of course assumed a British victory. The idea was broached of the coalition government continuing post-war but this was not well received. The Foreign Secretary Eden came (or was propelled) to the forefront. There were multiple reasons for the choice of Eden as the right spokesman. He remained a darling of many Conservatives and a possible successor to Churchill as Prime Minister. He had to be given an opportunity to retrieve his reputation, which had suffered badly as a result of the Balkan disasters of April. Now he could prove his idealism to be of value. This would please the Labour Party, about to hold its annual conference. Labour hoped it would revive sympathetic public opinion following a very low poll of 21%. in the Hornsey by-election of 28 May.

In a much publicised speech on 29 May, Eden spoke of '*a World free from Want*'. There was to be social security at home and abroad. International co-operation would prevent starvation, anomalous rates of exchange, and mass unemployment. National autonomy for economies would survive as much as possible. To assist the rehabilitation of a Europe freed from Nazi tyranny, the British Empire, the USA and Latin America would cooperate. There would be no return to the chaos of the pre-war world. International trade would be encouraged, and a free Germany would be able to participate. The responsibility of *'the free nations'* of the world was emphasised. Significantly, Eden assigned no place in the post-war world to the USSR, or to a free India or China. A few days after the Labour Party's Whitsun Conference, Arthur Greenwood, a member of the War Cabinet with responsibility for post-war reconstruction, appointed Sir William Beveridge, a distinguished middle-of- the-road academic with a liking for welfare economics, to chair a new Committee to prepare what would become the famous report calling for a National Health Service.

Also addressing the issue of a better post-war world was a Conference at St. James's Palace which opened on 12 June. Leaders or representatives of fourteen Empire and allied governments in exile gave a pledge, described as *'historic'*, to fight on until the achievement of victory over Germany. King George VI attended and spoke, as did Churchill who ridiculed Hitler's 'New Order'. His speech concluded *'With the help of God of which we must all feel daily conscious we should continue steadfast in faith and duty till our task is done'*. Continuing in the background were the internal bickerings and divisions of the governments in exile. Eden, in his speech of two weeks previously, had specifically praised King Leopold of the Belgians, a virtual prisoner in his own country, as part of this new diplomatic flowering. The huge mineral rich colony of the Belgian Congo could not wisely be ignored, let alone occupied Belgium.

This new moral tone of politics was accompanied by declarations of leading churchmen at interdenominational Conferences. The atheism of Nazism was targeted, and Roman Catholics in particular were keen to label Communist doctrine as also highly objectionable. Roosevelt echoed this sentiment in his speech of 27th May, condemning both the Nazis and Communists for denying God. Calls by the Pope for an end to the war assumed the continuance of the Nazi regime, with inchoate statements on the need to honour Christian beliefs, principles and values. However, British Roman Catholics did not take their politics from the Vatican.

As a complementary development, the British desire to encourage resistance within German-occupied Europe took further shape. Broadcasts to Europe were stepped up. On 23 May transmissions purporting to be from a German pirate radio station began. The equivalent German transmissions directed at Britain were on a larger scale. The black propaganda from Britain was aimed to lower the morale of German servicemen. The core of the subject matter was the plausible self-aggrandisement, sexual antics and perversions and cynicism of Nazi bosses. The speakers were German nationals in Britain, refugees or genuinely converted PoWs, who had their own good reasons for hating Nazism. A Beaverbrook journalist and expert on Germany, Sefton Delmer, was the director.[lxviii]

A new campaign opening on 6 June was that of V FOR VICTORY. Broadcasts from Britain to occupied Europe encouraged the spread of the 'V' symbol. The opening bars of Beethoven's fifth symphony, as if the three dots and a dash of the Morse code for the letter "V", were repeatedly played. The symphony itself gained in popularity. Listeners were advised to trick Germans in small ways hard to detect, so as to show contempt for them. The considered opinion later, if not at the time, was that the exercise was virtually useless for encouraging resistance in occupied Europe, but it did arguably boost British morale as the public here were kept informed of these broadcasts. As for the V symbol, intended as graffiti, its value was reduced by Goebbels copying of the tactic with V this time standing for VIKTORIA. Beethoven's compositions were consciously absorbed into Nazi musical propaganda.

Nothing at this time (except demands for friendly relations with the USSR from some trade unions, the Co-operative Party and a very few individuals) implied any hope of the USSR becoming an ally.[lxix] After the arrival of Hess on 10 May, any such press comment was banned. The alignment of the USA as a fighting ally and not merely as a source of Lend-Lease goods, was regarded as imminent. Many events in the USA, combined with wishful thinking, provided irresistible hope for this.

Picture Post of 14 June showed a smiling Roosevelt on its front cover captioned *'Democracy's Other Champion'* quoting his words *'It can be done, it must be done, it will be done'*. The first article, by Walter Hill, was entitled *'All out Aid: And What it Means'*covering seven pages out of a rationed thirty-two.The previous week's issue had exaggerated the degree of unity of the Dominions with a tactfully sparse text and dull photographs. Shown smiling together on the front cover were 'Mr' Menzies and 'Mr' Mackenzie King, respectively PMs of Australia and Canada. Robert Menzies in particular was a severe critic of Churchill's Middle East strategy involving as it did high casualties suffered by Australian soldiers. This was known to the press but kept confidential. Each front cover also nicely publicised J.B. Priestley as the champion of a fairer society.

Roosevelt,although personally keen to give the British war effort maximum help, knew the limitations of his own political power. Opinion polls showed a good majority of Americans in favour of Lend-Lease, but significantly fewer prepared to run the risk of war entailed by escorting convoys to Britain. Yet American intervention in the Battle of the Atlantic was vital. Prominent Americans, including members of the cabinet, made forthright speeches advocating a convoy system to protect Lend-Lease deliveries. Others called for an immediate declaration of war against Germany. They, like the President, insisted that the cause of world freedom was at stake, but, unlike the President, claimed that American interests as well as ethics justified war straight away. There was a belief that Vichy-controlled West Africa would soon be seized by Germany to be used as a base for offensives against South America, where fifth columns would spring into action at Hitler's command. Given what was correctly known about Nazi ambition, it was tenable, if opportunist, to point to this unfounded danger.

The American isolationists were active over the whole political spectrum. Outright fascists and sympathisers with Nazism formed one wing. The mainstream of a traditional American disinterest in a disorganised world (always excepting the American continents) was the core of isolationism. There were also pacifists and on the Left, various groups including the much maligned and persecuted Communist Party, which was active and influential in some trade unions.

The main spokesman for the isolationists, though unpopular with the Left, was the anti-Semitic and world famous flyer Charles Lindbergh. Goebbels saw him as '*a man of honour*' and later '*a brave lad*' and ordered the German press for tactical reasons not to praise him. A mass rally which Lindbergh addressed was held on 23 April, when most Americans who took any interest anticipated an early German conquest of the Middle East. Why waste American wealth - and probably American lives - on succouring a doomed Britain was the message, when the defence of the USA should be the top priority. To which a logical response was: the best defence of the USA was the defence of Britain. The upshot was that Lindbergh had to resign his commission in the US Army Air Force Reserve as he outspokenly opposed American policy.

A grain of truth in Lindbergh's argument was that the US armed forces were still in a weak condition· About half of the army comprised draftees due to be released after a year's service. Their readiness for modern combat was non-existent. The officer material was of poor quality, so before long middle ranking officers of ability were fast-tracked to top commands. The tank force was to be greatly augmented, but at the beginning of April there were a mere sixteen modern tanks and these were light ones. Summer manoeuvres in Tennessee proved a disaster.[lxx] When the army was ordered by Roosevelt to provide a force to take over the occupation of Iceland at the end of June from a British garrison which had been there for nearly fourteen months, it refused on the grounds of incapability. Some 4,500 US marines belatedly landed in place of GIs.

The US Army and Navy Air Forces had started to receive modern planes in quantity but many had operational defects which had to be dealt with, and training for their use was bound to take time. The notion of preparation for war was hard to swallow. In 1941 the armed forces anticipated a total need for only 9,000 parachutes![lxxi] The US navy was in a better state of readiness but a weakness was its division into a Pacific fleet and an Atlantic fleet. This dilemma was not going to be resolved in 1941. Roosevelt's cabinet was divided on the issue but the Japanese threat in the Pacific was regarded as too serious for many risks to be taken. However, foolish racist assessments of the Japanese war machine permeated naval opinion. Information from diplomats in Japan was realistic, including knowledge of the superior Zero fighter plane, but was deficiently processed in the USA and Britain. Complacency ruled. For instance the *Daily Mail* stated on 22 April that '*Singapore is strongly held by the army*'. Misleading news of reinforcements (mostly Indians and Australians arriving in Malaya) was spread now and then.

However, American war production, financed by the US government and absorbing millions of previously unemployed workers expanded hugely. Prices and taxes rose. Trade unions made wage demands which big business, enjoying higher profits, often refused to meet. The government imposed various controls on the economy including enforced settlement of industrial disputes. Strikes lessened in this context. Some wage increases were granted, but the bitterness engendered led to at least one shoot-out , witch-hunting of Communists as alleged saboteurs, and one temporary official take-over of an aircraft plant. The British economist, J.M. Keynes, stayed for a while in the USA to advise the Government on combating inflation. America as a fighting ally remained the elusive prize for Churchill.

CHAPTER 4

Running on Empty

From April to June, Germany's punishment of Britain was the predominant theme of WW2. The Wehrmacht was demonstrating its supreme proficiency. The Luftwaffe took command of the air to support the Wehrmacht and to offset much of the power of the RN in the Mediterranean. By night the Luftwaffe heavily bombed British cities and ports. Together with U-boats and E-boats and surface raiders, it sustained a partial blockade of Britain primarily by sinking or damaging merchantmen and mining estuaries. Yet German superiority was only relative. Britain's resistance was far from negligible. The war seemed to be going Germany's way, but the German leadership could not forecast when constant defeats of British forces would lead to a German victory. At the time, any British victories were of secondary importance.

Hitler's mindset was clandestinely centred on Operation Barbarossa, due to commence in May or June, the date of 22nd June not being fixed until 30th April. So, for Germany, the Mediterranean and Middle East were sideshows, and after April, with the exception of the German attack on Crete, the absence of overwhelming German offensives in the Mediterranean and Middle East effectively saved Britain and the British Empire. The weaknesses of British forces did not spell disaster because the Germans simply did not exploit the victories they had won. Instead, Germany concentrated on the planned attack on the USSR in the near future.

The German victories were bad news enough even though they were not decisive. However, for some three weeks or more commencing in April to early May, the situation seemed to Churchill and his cohorts as desperate as that in any period during 1940. They were predisposed to this grim assessment by the defeats suffered and the dread of far worse to come, only aggravated by the continuing night blitz on Britain and the Battle of the Atlantic.

The blitz had lulled during January and February due to the inclement winter weather but had not vanished. Really heavy night raids recommenced in March. Up to a maximum of seven hundred bombers, based in occupied France and the Low Countries, could find their way to their British targets by means of a system of intersecting radio beams. The result was the destruction of city centres and more loss of civilian life, with added risks from delayed action bombs. The ARP services were able to cope and civilian morale was broadly maintained. The press reported visits by Churchill and the King and Queen to severely hit areas. If there were jeers amidst the onlookers' cheers, the media made no mention. It remained the case that any hope that counter-measures against the bombers would reduce the effectiveness of the raids, was not being fulfilled. These counter-measures were taking longer to develop than expected. Anti-aircraft fire, searchlights and a balloon barrage, if present, might make precise aiming more difficult for the bombers. They might sometimes have to dodge night fighters, but a night fighter could only occasionally close with an enemy aircraft, even with the help of moonlight and newly developed airborne radar. Relatively few of the raiders were shot down. The German rate of loss was never high enough to deter the Luftwaffe at night in 1941. That the RAF commanded the air in the daytime over Britain did not trouble Hitler.

'The Wednesday' and 'The Saturday' (April 16 and 19), as they were nicknamed were the heaviest raids London had endured since the previous September. In April and early May, Hull and Glasgow were heavily raided twice each, Bristol and Cardiff three times each, Portsmouth five times, Liverpool and Merseyside nine times, Plymouth eleven times. Coventry, Swansea, Birmingham and Belfast also suffered from heavy raids. The Luftwaffe now increasingly aimed at the major ports to further the Battle of the Atlantic. Bristol and Plymouth had sadly failed to arrange systematic evacuation of children. The Dublin Fire Brigade from neutral Eire rushed to help Belfast firefighters. Berlin claimed a later revenge raid on Dublin's Jewish quarter to be 'an accident'. The worst hit city, relatively speaking, was Plymouth, and the Government worried that local civilian morale would totally break. Cadogan's diary entry referred to Plymouth being 'wiped off the map'.[lxxii]

The last raid of the blitz proper, devastated much of London on the moonlit night of 10/11 May.[lxxiii] It was the heaviest suffered by the capital. Many public buildings were destroyed and even the House of Commons sustained damage. Although thirty three bombers were claimed to have been shot down, the actual number was sixteen at the most. It was the last big night raid because most of the German bombers were going to fly east for Barbarossa. It has also been plausibly suggested that the raid could have deliberately coincided with Hess's flight, so as to provide an additional "spur" to his projected peace negotiations. In any event, about 43,000 British civilians had been killed with many more injured, homeless and in shock.

Learning from bitter experiences the previous year, fire watching became compulsory and systematic. There was a growing campaign for the many local fire services to be amalgamated into a National Fire Service. Warehouse supplies of food were to be dispersed. More communal shelters, though far from enough, were available to the public. The abundant numbers of brick-built, badly designed and badly constructed surface shelters became increasingly discredited. There were large numbers by now of 'Anderson' shelters in back gardens. The Underground in London was organised to shelter 200,000 people using the stations with official approval. There were major tragedies when direct hits on shelters occurred. The most publicised of these incidents was when it seems two bombs (though one failing to explode) penetrated to the '*safe*' basement level at the *Cafe de Paris* in the midst of 'upper class' diners and dancers. Many were killed or maimed though some survived unhurt. Among the dead was 'Snakehips Johnson' a brilliant Caribbean jazz player and dancer, about whom the columnist Hannen Swaffer was to write as a tribute in the *Daily Herald* that '*he died the white man that he was inside*.[lxxiv] Such was the patronising racism of the time. After mid-May, a belief that the arrival of Hess in Britain was the cause of the end of the blitz was widespread.

The German leadership was inclined to take at face value exaggerated claims of sinkings of merchantmen with their precious cargoes; the German assessment of the battle became distorted. Goebbels' diary, as one example of doubt over these claims, had the effect of lengthening the estimated time which would elapse before Britain admitted defeat. No specific time span was foreseen or given, but the German people were certainly given the impression that British morale would eventually collapse and were told by Hitler that Germany would win the war by 1942.

In Britain, the shipping losses were recognised as serious. It was openly admitted that sinkings continuing at the rate of 6 million tons a year would exceed the rate at which new ships were being built. Nearly 3 million tons were lost in the first six months of 1941. The Germans officially claimed an annual rate of over 8 million and sometimes 12 million.[lxxv] Each side introduced new weapons and tactics into the ongoing battle. Fear of what the enemy might do next may have prompted Churchill's well-known comment that the Battle of the Atlantic provided his biggest single source of anxiety throughout WW2.

Yet he had cause for hope amidst the fear. The capture from a sinking U-boat on 10 May of its ENIGMA code book was one big step forward. The RN was as professional at sea as the Wehrmacht was on land.

American participation was vital in a number of ways. The fifty old US destroyers provided for Britain from the Autumn of 1940 onwards needed impractical refitting. Churchill, in his speech of 9 April, referred to the American promise to supply ten modern Coastguard cutters to operate in the Western Atlantic in liaison with the Royal Navy. President Roosevelt declared that American naval patrols in the Western Atlantic would give to the British information about U-boats, surface raiders and German supply ships, resulting from their sweeps. Some American naval presence in Greenland was to be forthcoming. By April, to Roosevelt's and Churchill's mutual satisfaction, informal arrangements between Britain and the USA for pooling intelligence and indeed other information in many fields were already far advanced. Neither Parliament nor Congress were informed.[lxxvi]

The great movement of the American economy towards formal entry into WW2 included a huge expansion of shipbuilding, warships and merchantmen, but this would take time. Meanwhile repairs of British ships were being undertaken in American shipyards, including the repair of the British aircraft carrier HMS Illustrious which had been badly damaged by the Luftwaffe in the Mediterranean.

RAF Coastal Command was expanded further to protect convoys and harass U-boats. Iceland was becoming exceptionally valuable as an air base. Bomber Command in April switched to attack, mostly by night, ports in Germany and occupied Europe - these targets were more easily identified than ones inland. German surface raiders worldwide scored some successes, but some of them were found, fought and sunk.

Meanwhile, during April, losses of merchantmen continued at an alarming rate.

The Luftwaffe made a substantial contribution to the German attempt to blockade Britain. Their fast bombers, flying at sea level, perfected off the coast of Britain the technique of skip bombing, which the Germans nicknamed the 'Swedish turnip'.[lxxvii] The escorts and guns on the merchantmen themselves, often manned by sailors from the RN in "plain clothes", were of only limited value as a defence. From the air, mines were laid which had to be swept. Some very long range German bombers, the Focke-Wulf Condors, (essentially adapted civilian airliners) operating from Norway and occupied France, added to German successes. These later became vulnerable to interception by Hurricane fighters catapulted from ships, who had to ditch when they had shot down or seen off the raiders.

At times whole convoys were attacked and badly mauled, but the German navy could as yet only operate fewer than twenty U-boats in the Eastern Atlantic at any one time. When Hess was interrogated by Lord Simon on 9 June, he boasted about hundreds of U-boats being constructed in Germany making use of the extensive river and canal system. The Admiralty at first took this boast seriously, but after checking decided it was without substance. The German plan for mass sinkings, as announced by Hitler in February, was not fulfilled despite the heavy losses suffered as a result of *'wolf pack'* tactics. German U-boats were not destroyed in large numbers, but five had been sunk in March and three of their ace captains were lost, two being drowned and one captured. Goebbels described this news as *'a very bitter drop of wormwood'*.[lxxviii] After May the U-boat offensive slackened due to the demands of Barbarossa, although it was to be resumed dangerously some months later.

The Whitehall appointment on 1 May of Lord Leathers as new Minister of War Transport, was proof that the civilian contribution to fighting the battle would be strengthened. The government had realised some months earlier that cargoes should be carefully rationed with essentials getting priority, and that their volume should be reduced wherever possible e.g. meat from the Argentine was boned prior to shipment. Troopships outward bound for the Middle East would return via Argentina if they had refrigerated holds for meat.

Allocating naval and air resources for the Battle of the Atlantic meant that fewer such resources were available for other fronts. Of course the warships and merchantmen of Britain's allies, including those whose homelands were in occupied Europe, were invaluable. Of all the war's participants, the merchant seamen were perhaps the most heroic. Their losses were immense. The risks for them at sea were constant. However it was the growing American involvement which favourably swayed the balance in the Battle of the Atlantic. It was in the Balkans and North Africa that German supremacy was going to be most evident, and seemed for a while the most dangerous development.

Extraordinary complacency at the Middle East GHQ in Cairo about the defence of Egypt followed the final victory over the Italian army in Cyrenaica. This was in February. By the end of the month it looked as if the remnants of Italian forces, which were protecting Tripoli some four hundred miles further West, were being strengthened by a few German units. However, Wavell's interpretation of intelligence suggested that no major Axis offensive from the West was likely before May. This was reassuring news because the new strategy of defending Greece was taking the best units away from the Western Desert. Less combat worthy ones replaced them. Benghazi was not used as a port - it was deemed unusable. Tobruk much nearer Egypt was chosen as the base for the forces in the front line, about a hundred miles south of Benghazi.

GHQ Cairo was the centre of an easy going life for the staff serving the C-in-C Middle East, the much lauded General Wavell. To him was attributed the land victories won over Italian forces. He was informed from London in code of the gist of ENIGMA intercepts. These showed no indication that the German-led forces, known as the Afrika Korps, under the leadership of General Rommel had any present intention of taking aggressive action in strength. They showed positively the opposite, therefore it seemed the mostly inexperienced British forces in situ would be adequate for skirmishes. The Empire forces included an armoured brigade and HQ unit of the 2nd Armoured Division, their strength in tanks about fifty of which only a proportion were operational. These consisted of light tanks and inferior Italian medium tanks which had been captured and to which British crews were not yet accustomed. Some armoured cars were also available. Many of the Cruiser and Infantry tanks which had won victories over the Italians during the winter were back in the Nile Delta undergoing repairs and refitting. This was taking an unduly long time. On the coastline a partly trained two-brigade Australian infantry division comprised most of the remaining frontline force.

Unexpectedly, on March 31st, Rommel began an attack in earnest. He was disobeying his orders to remain on the defensive. The Luftwaffe won temporary air superiority. The German tanks outclassed those of the armoured brigade. The German eight wheeled armoured car was superior to its British opposite number, not least in gun power. Rommel's surprise tactic of infiltration, caused a British retreat into the hinterland, and the Australians wisely rapidly retreated along the coast. Benghazi left undefended was captured by the Afrika Korps by 3 April. Due to mechanical breakdowns there was soon not much left of British armour fit for fighting the Afrika Korps.

The German force was certainly not overwhelming ; only one division with two Italian divisions. Again unexpectedly, while

GHQ at Cairo was pondering over the initial defeat which had come as a complete surprise, Rommel struck in the direction of the Egyptian frontier. Again he was disobeying orders. Tobruk was besieged by 10 April. Luckily, the retreating Australian division had got there first to serve as a garrison. Inland, the remnants of British armour were destroyed. A poorly equipped and trained Indian motorised brigade which had left Tobruk to reinforce the front line was routed. Three British generals and three brigadiers were surprised and captured in the desert by German patrols. The total German haul of PoWs was about 2,000. The War Cabinet in London received this alarming news on 10 April. To rub salt into the wound, it soon became apparent the *'unusable'* port of Benghazi was being used by supply ships for the Afrika Korps and the Luftwaffe was now using local airfields. Supply dumps were abandoned. All these facilities had carelessly not been destroyed.

Cairo GHQ had already decided not to send to Greece a further Australian infantry division. Reserves were rushed to the Western frontier or Egypt to hold an expected further attack by the Afrika Korps. In Cairo, the staff were starting to panic though, to his credit, Wavell kept calm and travelled personally to inspect danger spots. The veteran newspaper correspondent Alexander Werth wrote in his diary on 12 July, when he was in Moscow, '*Leonards, who was recently in Cairo, talked about the awful blunders that had led to the fall of Benghazi. I said: "In London people were in a foul stew, and thought the Germans might be in Cairo in a week." ..... "well, the trouble is that a lot of people in Cairo thought so too," he said. "It was a very unpleasant moment. Fortunately the Germans pushed on much further than they'd ever expected - and they exhausted themselves. The state of the German soldiers, without food or drink, was lamentable."*

Tobruk before it was besieged had had its prospective garrison supplemented by another Australian infantry brigade, by an

Indian contingent of about five hundred men who were able to terrify the Italian enemy and by miscellaneous units including some forty tanks brought by sea from Egypt. An airfield within the perimeter of the fortress initially served as a base for fighter planes but most were soon lost and the remainder had to be withdrawn to Egypt. German attacks on Tobruk were repulsed. Many fortifications installed by the Italians, before it had fallen to the Australians and British over two months previously, remained intact, and German losses in tanks and PoWs showed that the Afrika Korps was not invincible. The RAF was by now contesting the Luftwaffe's command of the air, but air superiority remained in the balance. There was doubt as to whether Tobruk could be held.

On the frontier, infantry and light armoured units formed a screen and faced the Afrika Korps which only occasionally attempted a further advance eastward. British and Australian forces remained far behind the lines in Egypt undergoing acclimatisation and training. Many tanks which had been in combat the previous winter were still not ready to be returned to the front, and the British tank force on the frontier was minimal.

The rational, though incorrect, expectation was that when Rommel received substantial reinforcements, the Afrika Korps would wield an overwhelming superiority. The enterprising British long range desert force, which remained intact, was small in number. General Wavell was not in a position to provide more than the minimum for defence. As far as tactics went, the whole German approach to warfare outclassed that of the British. The enemy were professional soldiers. Too few of Wavell's army could match the German enemy in contrast to the Italians. Rommel as a commander excelled, and had the skill to wring the maximum impact from his inferior Italian units.

While disaster threatened Egypt, some two thousand miles to the South and East the feudal kingdom of Ethiopia was about to be finally liberated as a result of the collapse of the Italian East African Empire. Addis Ababa was entered by South African troops and Ethiopian partisans officially on 6 April, five years to the day after its fall to the Italian invaders. The Emperor Haile Selassie, restored to his throne, was a friend of Britain, but he had to respect the power of feudal landlords. Social and economic backwardness made his government's alliance with Britain largely nominal. A loan from Britain and a British 'Resident' ensured his loyalty. Special measures were taken to protect Italian civilians from revenge attacks by Ethiopian patriots. Over the following months the remaining and isolated Italian garrisons surrendered. There were two immediate valuable results; the opening of the Red Sea and the Persian Gulf to American merchant ships by declaration of Roosevelt on 11 April that they were no longer war zones, and the freeing-up of two Indian divisions and a South African division for sending to the Western Desert or elsewhere. This transfer and training for desert warfare was to take more time than desirable, but by mid-May the 4th Indian Infantry division was again in the Western Desert, where it had been until the end of 1940.

The strategic advantage for Britain of the conquest of the East African Italian Empire could not, however, compensate for the danger coming from the Axis forces in and around the Mediterranean. On 3 April, there was a palace coup in Baghdad resulting in a new Iraqi government. This, unlike the new government of Yugoslavia of a week earlier, was pro-German. For the time being it concealed its sympathies but soon an immense strategic advantage now seemed to be opening for Germany as was realised with fear in London.

The defeat of Yugoslavia, accomplished by the Germans in eleven days, came as a disheartening shock. This defeat was so quick that American war supplies promised under Lend Lease could never be delivered. For a few hours a British armoured column had penetrated into Yugoslavia from Greece to engage a German vanguard. This onslaught was merely a pinprick and whatever small casualties and slight delays were caused the Wehrmacht, many of the British vehicles broke down. The poor roads and rocky terrain proved too much for British tanks and other vehicles, and the more appropriate mules and donkeys were in short supply.

Meanwhile, Turkey remained staunchly neutral, and Germany was eventually to benefit from further imports of Turkish chrome, and also from the right under treaty of merchant ships to travel from the Danube into the Black Sea and through the Dardanelles into the Aegean and the Mediterranean and Adriatic.[lxxix] Turkish neutrality facilitated the German occupation of the Greek islands in the Aegean, which fell like dominos in the course of the next few weeks. These could be bases for further German offensives, as London soon realised.

The Empire forces in Greece intended to defend a line against the Wehrmacht. After a first week of bad weather, they were heavily strafed by the superior Luftwaffe. About eight hundred combat aircraft overwhelmed eighty RAF planes. The very first night, German bombers attacked the key port of Piraeus. An ammunition ship exploded. Consequently, many merchant ships were sunk or badly damaged, and the port was devastated. The British press reported only the loss of a Greek hospital ship. Soon after the capture of Salonika a mere three days after the German offensives began, panzers and Alpine troops were pouring into Greece from Southern Yugoslavia. German pressure and the regrouping of the three Greek divisions of poorly-equipped and poorly-trained soldiers forming part of the allied line, saw the line disintegrate. The under-strength Australian Division, the New Zealand division, what remained of the 1st brigade of the ill-fated 2nd Armoured Division and miscellaneous British units, were outwitted and outflanked and by 14 April were beginning to retreat towards a new line at

Thermopylae a hundred miles further south. Three weeks later, Lloyd George in Parliament told how thrilled he had been to hear on a BBC news bulletin how splendidly the area of Mt. Olympus was being defended, only to learn shortly afterwards of the German claim that they had captured Mt Olympus. Churchill could only lamely and probably truthfully reply that London had not been receiving much information from the front.[lxxx] Cadogan wrote in his diary on 16 April, '*in Greece German forces broke through our right down the coast...(This) was considered by our General Staff nitwits to be impossible...*' The presence of Bavarian and Austrian Alpine troops on the mountain slopes had not been foreseen.

The retreat down the peninsula of Greece proceeded often in a disorganised fashion. The RAF in Greece was being obliterated. The Greek army of the Epirus, which had proved its capability against the Italians since the previous October, capitulated on 21 April. The Germans, who initially accepted this surrender, arranged humiliatingly for the victory formally to be Mussolini's. The captured Commander-in-Chief was shortly to become the first 'Quisling' Prime Minister of a Greece under mostly Italian occupation. Evacuation by sea of the Empire forces, without all their heavy equipment, took place between 24 and 29 April. This contingency had been in fact secretly planned weeks in advance.

The Luftwaffe sank, among others, two RN destroyers (HMS Diamond and HMS Wryneck) laden with seven hundred soldiers on their way to Crete or Egypt, from which there were about fifty survivors. About 80% of the Empire Forces were evacuated, over 50,000 out of over 62,000. Over 9,000 PoWs, including some 7,000 Australians and New Zealanders and about 2,000 British, were taken by the Germans. The Greek PoWs were mostly soon released and went home. Militarily, the campaign had been a disaster. By contrast, in terms of politics and strategy, the advantages far outweighed the disadvantages.

Against German aggression, a self-sacrificing stand on moral principle had been taken based on the formal British guarantee to Greece of 1939. This rallied sentiment in the USA for Britain. The resistance also contributed to delaying Hitler's further plans. Although the German casualties were light (some 1,500 killed), their Panzers suffered wear and tear.

Rommel's successes in North Africa and the victories over Yugoslavia and Greece encouraged the pro-Nazis and the waverers in neutral and occupied countries to see a German victory in WW2 as imminent. Even Mussolini felt able to claim, ridiculously, that the Italian role had been decisive. Hitler generously declared that the Italians should be given credit for preoccupying the attention of British forces, which otherwise would have inconvenienced Germany.

Indeed, with Italian participation, Axis bombers pounded Malta from January onwards. Malta withstood almost continuous air bombardment, but its value as an offensive base was reduced. Its airfields under heavy attack could not sustain any large RAF bomber force; only one squadron of Wellington bombers was there, but had to be withdrawn to Egypt for part of April. Too few warships were based on Malta. The British aim was to prevent Italian supply ships from reinforcing the Afrika Korps. Although on the night of 15/16 April a whole enemy convoy escorted by Italian warships had been sunk by British warships while on its way from Italy to Libya, this kind of victory was not to be repeated for many months. For the rest of April, most British warships had to concentrate on rescuing from Greece as many of the Forces of the Empire as they could, and on running supplies to besieged Tobruk, Malta and Crete. Moreover, the route taken by Italian convoys on their way to Tripoli took advantage of a short sea passage across the Mediterranean to the Libyan coast. Some submarines uneasily based on Malta sank enemy ships but it became obvious that most Italian ships could travel safely to Tripoli with reinforcements for the Afrika Korps. British seapower in the Mediterranean had been badly frustrated.

A second kind of British attack, which in Churchill's view would gravely weaken the Afrika Korps, was to strike at the port of Tripoli itself. The Admiralty demurred at the sacrifice of a battleship, which Churchill wanted for a blockship. As a compromise a heavy naval bombardment was to take place. This was carried out in the early hours of 21 April. Soon smoke and dust obscured the target. The port was out of action only for a day or so. It was soon realised that the bombardment had essentially failed and it was ruefully seen as good luck that the fleet had not been attacked by the Luftwaffe. The Admiralty was not prepared to repeat the venture, and advised air raids. However, a mere five squadrons of Wellington bombers were stationed in the whole of the Middle East including Malta, and these aircraft did not take kindly to the daytime heat and the ever - present sand. Churchill, proving he had his wits about him, responded to this advice scathingly.[lxxxi]

Vichy France leaned increasingly towards taking the side of Germany, despite the assurance of Marshall Petain that France would not take up arms against Britain, its former ally. The price for the neutrality of Vichy France was a British relaxation of the naval blockade, so there was sizeable commercial traffic between Southern France and the French Empire across the Mediterranean. Britain would be powerless to ask for French neutrality if the RN were driven from the Mediterranean. When there was an occasional gun battle at sea between British and French warships, Vichy could conveniently point out to Berlin how it was defying *'perfidious Albion'*. Such was the clandestine diplomatic policy of Churchill's government towards Vichy France, facilitated by the American ambassador in Vichy, Admiral Leahy. Some sharp American warnings to Petain were calculated to ensure that the French fleet was not handed over to Hitler, and in addition to this stick was the carrot of allowing more trade with the USA. A more acute crisis was to arise by mid-May over Syria as the Luftwaffe was allowed to use air bases there. An RAF raid on Sfax in Tunisia towards the end of May was a warning to Vichy that Britain would not tolerate French help for the communications of the Afrika Korps.

Spain also presented a problem. The cruel and oppressive fascist regime of General Franco was ideologically on the side of the Nazis. Because of the damage done to the economy during the Civil War, the country was too weak to align itself with Germany in WW2 except as a non-belligerent. However, Spain's entry into WW2 remained a possibility. The British response was diplomacy at its most proficient. A commercial agreement ensured that Spain could import supplies of food and oil, which was yet another partial lifting of the RN's blockade. There was a British loan to Spain. A blind eye was turned to limited Spanish succour of U-boats engaged in the Battle of the Atlantic, and increased Spanish trade with Germany, not least in valuable minerals. However, the " iron fist in a velvet glove" was the preparation in Britain of a rapid troop-carrying convoy to seize the Canary Islands and Madeira, should Spain join Germany as a belligerent. If that were to happen, German forces might be able to capture Gibraltar and take control of the Western entrance to the Mediterranean. The Chiefs of Staff were to ponder over these contingencies for many weeks. The British ambassador in Madrid, Sir Samuel Hoare (a possible successor to Chamberlain as Prime Minister), displayed acumen in negotiations. His sympathy with the fascist regime was evident. In London, the Spanish ambassador, the Duke of Alba, was honoured. This was an official gesture, painful if limited, of hostility to Spanish Republican refugees in Britain.

Beyond Syria to the East lay oil-rich Iraq, under its pro-German government since 3 April, and oil-rich Iran under a pro-

German Shah with the presence of many Nazi agents. Iraqi protestations of loyalty to the British cause - pursuant to a treaty which Iraq saw as having been imposed - were evidently insincere. Wavell declined to take any military precautions, truthfully claiming he had nothing to spare to protect British interests in Iraq. The British forces in Palestine under the Mandate which were intended to deal with any Arab restiveness consisted mainly of a cavalry division on horseback-Churchill did not conceal his anger at that state of affairs! They were deemed unfit to move to the East into Iraq. So, on 18 April, a brigade and more of the Indian army landed at Basra. Basra was already earmarked as a major base and supply depot for future Lend-Lease cargoes carried in American ships. Near to Basra was a British airbase at Shaibah. This arrival of these troops was a precaution but hardly decisive. During the last two weeks of April, Iraq was coming nearer to the boil, eventually with military dispositions to menace the big and important British base at Habbaniyah, fifty miles west of Baghdad. This base was cut off from Basra and Shaibah, air traffic apart, because of floods. The location of Habbaniyah below a plateau made it a poor fortress. By the end of April, in addition to some 9,000 civilians present, came over 200 women and children from Baghdad. The base included a flying school with nearly eighty planes. Of these, only four were modern warplanes, the remainder biplanes from the 1930s and trainers. There was a garrison, however, and the aircraft were hastily but effectively prepared for combat.

The government of Iraq decided to become openly aggressive. Iraqi artillery and infantry appeared on the plateau overlooking the base. The Iraqi general in command presented an ultimatum: without his prior permission no plane should fly and no one should move from the base. The prospect of withstanding a siege seemed doubtful. The besieged took the initiative and early on 2 May without prior warning bombed the prospective besiegers. The Iraqi retaliation was largely ineffective. RAF support from Egypt was forthcoming. After three days the siege was lifted, with carnage inflicted from the air on Iraqi forces, but there was as yet no prospect of capturing Baghdad or the Northern oilfields. The Iraqis expected German support. It came later in May, but only amounted to indecisive intervention by a few German and Italian warplanes via Syria. It did not help that the head of the German military mission was killed apparently accidentally by "friendly fire" as his plane was about to land at Baghdad airport.

There remained some risk that German forces might arrive through Syria in strength. The hostile government of Iraq continued to control Baghdad and the oilfields near to Mosul. Iran under its Shah, unfriendly towards Britain, took no part in the conflict. Egypt was restless but under firm British military and indirect political control. The corrupt regime of King Farouk was duly propped up by Britain. By mid-May, a military column some two thousand strong did go to Iraq from Palestine by command of General Wavell and by the end of May, all Iraq was back under British control and the 'rebel' leaders had fled the country.

By the end of April the mainland of Greece and many islands were in German or Italian hands. Cyprus presented a major source of anxiety to the Chiefs of Staff. An invasion via the island of Rhodes could scarcely be resisted effectively. There was a poorly trained and equipped local defence force - perhaps four thousand strong - and about a thousand British commandos. There was little heavy equipment and virtually no air power.[lxxxii] The commandos had come to Cyprus to form part of a force to capture two Italian islands near Crete, and, if all went well, Rhodes itself. An initial attack had failed. Later the plan was abandoned as impractical. In Cyprus the mix of the population, two thirds Greek and one third Turkish, with an uncertain loyalty to Britain, did not augur well. The municipal elections due to be held earlier in the year had been cancelled. To make matters worse it was known both in London and Berlin that British warships in the Mediterranean could in daylight barely defend themselves against German dive bombers. Italian torpedo bombers and light craft were also a menace. Despite the inferiority of the Italian navy, some of its submarines sank British ships and on 26 March an Italian speedboat had rammed and fatally holed British cruiser HMS York at anchor in Suda Bay, Crete.

From the beginning of May, it became practically certain as a result of ENIGMA information that Crete would be the next German target. Signs of an imminent airborne invasion were detected. Churchill publicly and privately expressed confidence, shared grudgingly by Wavell and General Freyberg, the Commander-in-Chief in Crete, that the island could be held. The garrisons in Crete were weak, the RAF contingent the merest handful of modern warplanes. The mountainous terrain of the island meant poor communications between the garrisons which included Australians and New Zealanders who had been evacuated from Greece. Crete had been occupied by British forces under five successive commanders as from November 1940, but little had been done to prepare defences. Invasion had been assumed to be only a remote possibility. About ten thousand British troops were in Crete and the Anzacs brought the total to over thirty thousand. The native Greek contingents were poorly trained and barely equipped. The defenders had to rely for their links with the outside world on a few harbours on the North coast of the island, the South coast 400 miles from Egypt having virtually none. The North coast was vulnerable to air attacks from Southern Greece and islands a short flying time away.

One advantage enjoyed by Freyberg was knowledge through ENIGMA of much of the German battle plan. The Germans would attempt to seize the three primitive airfields of Crete. These at least could be defended even though the Empire forces were weak. It seemed to Freyberg, however, that a seaborne invasion should also be guarded against, which meant an unfortunate dispersal of his forces. Another misjudgement was not to deploy units further west in the belief that if this were done it could suggest to the Germans that ENIGMA was being cracked. Air cover was not going to be possible. The four remaining Hurricane fighters flew away from Crete to Egypt the day before the invasion. There were few anti-aircraft guns, field guns and tanks. An alarming deficiency of such equipment and other essentials was barely addressed during the three weeks before 20 May, the day of the invasion.

The first day of OPERATION MERKUR - the German name for the invasion- suggested all could go well for the defence of the island, as most German paratroopers were picked off by defenders, who also destroyed many troop carrying gliders, despite complete German air supremacy. However, the invaders siezed one significant foothold and this was duly exploited. This was the airfield of Maleme towards the west of the island. Freyberg's caution had not paid off. It is not clear even now why some pretext could not have been found for strengthening the defence of Maleme.

The second day at Maleme the Germans landed many JU 52 transport planes carrying mountain troops on board. It was too late to prevent this, even though further heavy casualties were inflicted on the invaders. The impossibility of movement by day due to overwhelming air attacks, the absence of a counter-attack the first night and the inadequate success of one on the next led to the crumbling by 22 May of the defence of the West of the island. That second night a seaborne invasion was foiled by the RN but it failed to prevent ever-more German troops and equipment landing from the air. The fact that the rest of the island was being held was deceptive. Only one of the two principal Northern garrisons was rescued by the RN. There followed an agonising retreat of the remnants of the defenders, mostly by night and on foot to the South coast of the island. This allowed the evacuation by the RN of about half of the British and Anzac defenders. Nearly twelve thousand became PoWs. Alarming numbers of British warships were sunk or damaged by the Luftwaffe, mostly during the first three days of the battle for Crete.

German losses were high, although not as high as claimed at the time. About half of the airborne invaders were killed or wounded or missing. Strangely it was assumed in Britain that up to 50,000 German airborne troops might remain to be deployed imminently to Britain's disadvantage somewhere.[lxxxiii]

The loss of the island of Crete was a bitter blow. Not only was it shocking in itself with no more than half the defenders escaping, but it seemed to confirm a systematic pattern of significant land victories won by Germany from the beginning of WW2. Churchill had proclaimed the importance of Crete and Tobruk as fortresses and sally ports for offensives. Now Crete had gone and it was natural to worry about the same fate overtaking Tobruk. The RN in the Mediterranean was in a dangerously weakened state.[lxxxiv] The strategic importance of Crete was also notable for the control of the Eastern Mediterranean. From Hitler's point of view, it was a safeguard against British bombing of the Rumanian oilfields. Unknown to Churchill, (let alone the public in Britain), this had been the principal motive for the German invasion of Crete.

Crete had fallen by 1 June. At last, seven days later, the forces of the Empire entered Vichy held Syria, including the Lebanon. From the end of April onwards it had seemed possible that Syria would soon be occupied by German forces.[lxxxv] Small numbers of their aircraft were using Syrian airfields for flights to Iraq, although they were often attacked by the RAF from mid-May. Vichy was adamant that any British land attack would be resisted. They hoped that open defiance of Britain would weigh with Hitler and at last put the French in his good books. They were playing a clever game. By resisting any British attack on Syria they believed they would both strengthen their influence on Germany and protect their own Empire. It seemed Petain could be persuaded by outspoken pro-Germans in his government, such as Admiral Darlan, the more to align Vichy France with Germany.

On 18 May, just before Crete was attacked, General Catroux, the C-in-C of the Free French in the Middle East, mistakenly concluded that General Dentz, the Vichy C-in-C in Syria, was on the brink of agreeing a Free French takeover. Catroux asked Wavell to provide three hundred lorries and air support for his six Free French battalions. London ordered Wavell to agree. He refused as he could still not spare anyone or anything. Churchill insisted, and Wavell offered to be relieved of his command! Given Wavell's prestige, this was a serious threat to Churchill's own position. However, a disastrous collision between Churchill and Wavell was averted when Catroux learned at the last moment that Dentz would remain loyal to Vichy.

A full-scale German entry into Syria seemed likely to the Chiefs of Staff although Churchill himself was by now practically convinced Germany was about to invade the USSR. OPERATION EXPORTER was decided upon. Empire forces would enter Syria from Palestine and Iraq and crush any resistance. A distinctly modest Empire force was assembled as Wavell's resources were still limited. It consisted of two brigades of Australian infantry, a brigade of a second Indian infantry division which had come from East Africa, two cavalry regiments based in Palestine, one battalion of the Commandos from Cyprus and a small Free French contingent (most of the Free French not wanting to fight other Frenchmen). Some sixty RAF aircraft, provided an air component. If the Germans had landed en masse in Syria, this Empire force would have been wholly inadequate. Within a week, a limited advance was accomplished. Then stalemate. A Vichy French force counter-attacked and captured hundreds of soldiers. Reinforcements came to the Empire force and a third phase of the skirmish led to an armistice on 12 July; effectively a British victory. Syria was now safe for the immediate future.

Empire forces casualties in Syria included about 1,000 dead and over 3,000 wounded. The French casualties were fifty per cent higher. The French PoWs were released for repatriation to France. Only about 6,000 of them opted to join the Free French. Some hard negotiations took place for British PoWs to be released back to the Middle East from Vichy France. The five week conflict did not end the running sore between Britain and Vichy France. Under the terms of the armistice, many able-bodied Germans who had been fighting in the French Foreign Legion were allowed to return to France and thus to Germany.

Although Iraq was finally subdued by the end of May, with Baghdad and the Iraqi oilfields captured, it seemed that German forces might mobilise through the USSR, with Soviet permission, to enter Iran from the North.[lxxxvi] This extravagant hypothesis was entertained in all seriousness by the Chiefs of Staff, who took the decision that if this were to happen the RAF would bomb the oilfields of the Soviet Caucasus. In March and April 1940 such bombing by the RAF (and also by the L'Armee de l'Air based in Syria) had been planned. RAF Reconnaissance planes had taken photographs on at least two occasions, and one had been driven off by Russian anti-aircraft fire. There was talk at the top of setting the oilfields ablaze.

In the Mediterranean area the Luftwaffe remained a threatening force. Alexandria was severely bombed on the night of 4 June. Mining of the Suez canal had been a grim reality since January. While the invasion of Greece was ongoing, some German aircraft had left Sicily to take part. Then remarkably, on 7 June,

Rome Radio announced that the Luftwaffe was leaving Sicily. In fact this had happened a few days earlier, and the units had departed to take part in Barbarossa later in the month. As a result of having to face only Italian air raids, Malta was going to be a more viable offensive base.

By the end of May, a defensive victory had succeeded in stabilising Iraq as an area free from German influence. The German threat of conquest of the Middle East remained a risk however, considered sure to materialise whether Barbarossa was aborted or was successful. Tobruk and the Egyptian frontier would be uncertainly defended in the contingency of any massive strengthening of the Afrika Korps. So the Iraqi campaign, and then in June and July the Syrian one, were of limited value only. The daring German conquest of Crete also evidences this conclusion. If Barbarossa were successful then it could be expected there would be sweeping German offensives from the direction of the USSR. Nor could the possibility of a German invasion of Turkey be ignored, although this increasingly became perceived as less likely if the Wehrmacht could bypass Turkey.

After ENIGMA information of 4 May which essentially gave notice that the Afrika Korps was going on the defensive, Churchill, though not the public, could feel with renewed confidence that Egypt and Tobruk could be held. Merchantmen had set out from England on 26 April to sail through the Mediterranean with a cargo of 295 tanks and 57 Hurricane fighters. They were to be convoyed but the Admiralty considered the risk of their loss as appalling. Although the Chiefs of Staff did not want Home Defence to be deprived of these tanks, Churchill insisted, and on 20th April the decision was made to rush them to the army of the Nile - OPERATION TIGER. In the event, one ship hit a mine and was lost, but 257 tanks and 43 Hurricanes arrived in Egypt on 12 May. Twelve of the tanks were sent to Crete where they were lost in battle. The other tanks had to be prepared for action in the Western Desert, and their adaptation for desert warfare was going to take three weeks or so. The time had come, as Churchill believed, for offensive action on the Egyptian-Libyan frontier, and particularly because these tanks nicknamed by Churchill *'tiger cubs,'* had arrived in Egypt.

On the poor supposition that there was an opportunity for the Afrika Korps to be smashed, Churchill hustled Wavell into a premature attack against the latter's better judgement. Rommel on the other hand, was prepared. In OPERATION BREVITY, fifty five British tanks and infantry attacked. Some 500 German prisoners were taken, but the defence was vigorous and then the Afrika Korps counter-attacked. They had a superior number of tanks and handled them effectively. British casualties increased and the offensive had to be called off with the front line more or less restored to its original position. This battle lasted for three days.

Churchill, unlike Wavell, was satisfied with the outcome of this limited offensive. He was impatient for a further attack, for which his *'tiger cubs'* would be ready. Suddenly, the Afrika Korps attacked on the frontier and the British force had again to retreat. The prospect of a successful British offensive was clearly further reduced. Although Wavell foresaw failure Churchill displayed optimism about the new planned offensive, BATTLEAXE. It seems that Churchill, with the aim of raising morale in his colleagues, grossly underestimated the risks. The British heavy tanks, known as Infantry tanks, were too slow and had inadequate gun power. The British Cruiser tanks, as they were called, were only about as powerful and fast as their German counterparts, no better. In comparison with the Afrika Korps which possessed *'flying garages and workshops',* maintenance and repair facilities for British armoured vehicles were inferior. In May, command of the air in the Western Desert had fluctuated, which was an ominous sign in itself.

BATTLEAXE commenced on 15 June. By then, Churchill knew that the Germans would shortly invade the USSR. He must have wanted the utmost pressure to diminish the German war effort. About 25,000 British and Indian troops participated. The first day was promising. British tanks and infantry went on the offensive and several hundred PoWs were taken, but by 16 and 17 June the Germans were clearly winning the battle. Rommel also sprang a new tactic. German anti-aircraft guns of 88mm calibre and of high velocity were dug in with their muzzles barely above ground level to act as effective anti-tank guns. British casualties over the three days exceeded 1,000 and about half the tanks were lost. At the price of sustaining heavy losses, the RAF eventually took command of the air, which covered the British retreat but with some British units being strafed in error. The official communiqué with an economy of truth stated that the *'troops having accomplished their purpose withdrew slowly to their base'*. Churchill was deeply depressed by the failure of BATTLEAXE. Further, he had learned of the surrender of three battalions in Syria, which succumbed to a Vichy counter-attack. So he must have felt increasingly inclined to pin hopes on the USSR becoming Britain's new ally.

In the Western Desert, the numerically inferior Afrika Korps had proved marginally superior to the forces of the Empire, in fighting and surviving in readiness in the filthy and oppressive conditions of the desert. The Germans were finally beaten in the Western Desert more than eighteen months after their arrival there, due to their then gross inferiority of material and supplies. In Churchill's eyes, the high reputation of Wavell diminished sharply from April onwards. The gross errors of GHQ in Cairo and Wavell's disobedience were bound to become intolerable for Churchill. Though Churchill himself was far from blameless and modern weaponry was lacking, he felt increasingly compelled to protect his own authority. The RAF Commander-in-Chief in the Middle East had earlier been replaced though not disgraced.[lxxxvii] Significantly, an Inspector General for logistics was belatedly appointed.

Wavell was effectively sacked on 21 June by his exchange of commands with General Auchinleck the Commander-in-Chief in India. The changeover was announced ten days later and was masked by news of the German invasion of the USSR. The scapegoating of Wavell diverted attention from the weakness of the Empire forces in the Middle East. This weakness was concealed from the public until ten days before the invasion of the USSR. Churchill in his noteworthy broadcast of 27 April referred to 'vast Imperial armies' and in his Parliamentary speech of 7 May claimed that nearly half a million men were in the Middle East. The truth was that 132,000 were East or West Africans or Sudanese who were in East Africa, many in supply services. They were not going to be used against the Wehrmacht as a matter of policy. There was a fear that training and experience would encourage them to revolt against Imperial rule. When they were armed, it was mainly with rifles. The justification for their not fighting Germans was that they could not become acclimatised to the 'cold' of the Western Desert at night. Another 20,000 men were in garrisons as a safeguard against any explosion of Arab nationalism. The actual number of combat fit units was few. When Washington was told that the army in the Western Desert was $4^1/_2$ divisions strong, the exaggeration must have been found pathetic. It was not until the Autumn that a much reinforced Middle East seemed secure, but the future was to bring new German threats and sporadic German successes until the decisive battle of El-Alamein was won in the Autumn of 1942.

CHAPTER 5

Pride before the Fall

"Blond like Hitler, slim like Goering and tall like Goebbels", was a standard joke about the Nazis but it was one which a majority of Germans shared with resignation as they had no choice but to accept the cult of the Fuehrer and his acolytes· Luckily for civilisation, the deep flaws in Nazi ideology and thought processes were at all material times inconceivable to the criminals themselves. Although the history of Germany during the vital few months with which we are concerned is only a fraction of the twelve years of Nazi power, these months see the zenith of that power. For Hitler, a sense of imminent triumph prevailed. The prospect of world supremacy beckoned as never before.

The personality of Hitler as the dictator whose decisions could not be challenged, must hold centre-stage. We may colloquially assess Hitler as a 'mad evil genius', but knowledge of his mental processes and their origin is invaluable. Hitler's mindset was immensely destructive, with his absolute commitment to militant racism and a corresponding absence of humanity. It is however as necessary to emphasise his profound faith in the pre-destined global power of a "Master Race" under the auspices of a divine providence, and with planned architectural monstrosities as its most obvious manifestation.

Hitler's traumatic personal past, linked with the traumas of Germany's past, formed and sustained his single-minded determination to fulfil his ambitious political aims. That these were broadly consistent with the needs and claims of the big landowners, the militarists, the nationalist intention to reverse the Treaty of Versailles, the monopolists in the economy, the principal churches and many of the disaffected including much of youth, was to his advantage. His *National Socialism* was intended to replace the appeals of Marxism and Liberalism. To him, those ideologies were fit only for the decadent, and were the prime cause of the degeneration of the Aryan race. To him they meant loathsome international perspectives, claims to a one-sided social justice, and a disparagement of loyalty to the state, an inclination to ruinous philosophical materialism and pollution of Aryan blood. It seemed logical there should be support for them from Jews, Slavs and others of deemed inferior races, who would have to be conquered.

The Nazi Party with its *Weltansschauung* (world view) as set out in the biblical solemnity of Hitler's book MEIN KAMPF fortified by the marked hypnotism of Hitler's rehearsed, manipulative oratory, and an urge to commit acts of brutality, won the loyalty of much of the youth. Much emphasis was placed on pageantry with martial music and grandiose films, with privileges available for conformists. Preparation for victorious warfare, (at low human cost until the invasion of the USSR), intoxicated the mass psyche and stimulated further mass dehumanisation. The use of radio and film for propaganda was marked and innovative. One human touch was conspicuous in the form of the Sunday 'Request Concert' linking troops with the Home Front.

Nazi philosophy emphasised endless struggle in life and could be seen as a form of social Darwinism. The Nazi ideal of the victorious male warrior served by accommodating females ran the risk of morally alienating masses of the population. However, the record of Nazism and Hitler of brilliant diplomatic and military success coupled with revival from the effects of the worldwide economic depression, weighed heavily in the contemplation of many Germans who otherwise distrusted Hitler and Nazism. So long as Hitler continued to be hailed as a political and military genius, their misgivings and even disgust, counted for relatively little. Mostly, they prudently kept quiet, lest they too become victims serving time in a concentration camp, shopped to Himmler's feared Gestapo.

Hitler's resolve was strengthened by the often frenzied adulation afforded him by many of the young. In his own mind he had become a new and secular saviour. For millions of people, loyalty and hero-worship were strengthened by a legal obligation founded on a personal oath of obedience to Hitler. Hitler also found in the operas of Wagner a constant source of inspiration and encouragement. The Valhalla of Nordic myth could have been a metaphor for Hitler's own most deeply felt convictions. By 1936, the Swiss psychologist C.G.Jung had publicly identified Hitler as Wotan, though understandably not naming Hitler, as *'a god of storm and frenzy,* (who) *releases passions and the lust of war, moreover* (who) *is a paramount magician and a conjurer who is versed in every occult secret".* There was an industry of research and performance in support of racist doctrine, often cruel and bizarre, but which contrived to give further credibility to the Nazi regime. The Swastika emblem, the standardised greeting 'Heil Hitler' and its associated salute were outward signs met with every day.

In his capacity as leader and with recognition of his 'genius' mandatory, Hitler had virtually the sole responsibility for deciding the strategy which would win WW2 for Germany - preferably in 1941. He chose to invade the USSR. It was inspiring for Hitler to look forward to the crushing of hated Bolshevism and Soviet power by force, once and for all time. *Lebensraum* (living space) in vast areas of Soviet territory for future generations of Aryans was to be one outcome. It was arguably appealing to seize Ukraine and the Caucasus for their wheat and oil and mineral resources. Yet economists and the

German Foreign Office doubted whether a German invasion of the USSR would make sense. They preferred further bargaining with Stalin for more trade. They did not get their way. Hitler presumed (contrary to diplomatic advice from the supporters of the traditional line of alliance with Russia, pursued by Bismarck) that Stalin could not be trusted to refrain from breaking with Germany at some time in the future. However, none of these critics challenged the notion that Germans would win any war with the USSR, if there were war. Hitler also saw the alliance with the USSR as subversive of the Nazi creed itself, and for that reason, it was profoundly unsettling for him and many Nazis.

Hitler was so sure of German military - and racial - superiority that he ordered, as far back as July 1940, the plans for the invasion of the USSR, later known as *Operation Barbarossa*. These plans were prepared in the utmost secrecy. A successful invasion of Russia had to come not later than midsummer, as a total surprise, and in overwhelming force. Also required, as ordered by Hitler, was a disciplined orgy of blood lust to kill innumerable Communists, Jews, Gypsies and others deemed sub-human, which would violate normal conventions of warfare.

There were Nazi leaders and professional servicemen at the top who were fearful of extending WW2 to an invasion. They wanted to avoid a war on two fronts and the horror of the Russian winter, and who bore in mind the sheer size of the terrain. The common sense doctrine of no war on two fronts, which had been emphasised in *Mein Kampf,* had been flagrantly disregarded in WW1 with disastrous results for Germany. Hitler overruled these objections - yet he failed to make a true evaluation of Soviet strength. He gave undue weight to reports of Soviet economic and administrative deficiencies. He had no adequate grasp of Soviet skill and popular enthusiasm, and exaggerated the factor of unpopular ruthless coercion in the USSR. He relied, perhaps inevitably, on blitzkrieg tactics, which had worked so well against other nations, France in particular.

The apparent innate superiority of German arms spoke for itself. Stalin's purges had badly damaged the armed forces of the USSR and Hitler estimated the Red Army as comprised of masses of poorly trained Slav peasants of poor morale and technical standards, led by officers of a proficiency far inferior to that of the Germans. The huge superiority in numbers of Soviet tanks and planes was more than offset by their inferior quality. He failed to note the awareness of such weaknesses by the best Soviet military leaders, and their intentions - and some measures - for significant improvements. These were being inaugurated when plans for Barbarossa were at an advanced stage. Meanwhile, Hitler, led onwards by his fanaticism, formed the expectation that the devastating offensives planned would, in a few weeks, topple Stalin's rule and the whole political structure of Soviet power. Goebbels envisaged that *the entire fabric of Bolshevism will collapse like a house of cards.* Hitler himself told General Jodl *We have only to kick the door and the whole rotten structure will come crashing down.*[lxxxviii]

The nature of the Nazi dictatorship made it impossible for Hitler to doubt his own genius or for his lieutenants to question his judgement to his face. For the most part, they were relieved not to have to accept the burden of responsibility. Where there was dissent, it carried no weight. The structure of power in the state apparatus which usefully strengthened Hitler's own absolute authority as dictator, inevitably encouraged a deficiency in his own judgement. Did his own professed doubts about Barbarossa have any depth? Or was it only for calculated melodrama and for the record when he said *"I feel as if I am pushing open the door to a dark room never seen before, without knowing what lies behind the door".*

In deciding on the invasion of the USSR, Hitler must also have considered certain perceived images: the urge for the war to be over and won soon, the risk the German economy might fail if the war were prolonged, the desirability for the peoples of occupied Europe to be won over to Nazism by an anti-Bolshevist crusade, and the hope Germany's enemies would ultimately choose to align themselves with Nazi Germany.

The elaborate plans for Barbarossa and the preparations on a huge scale meant that the option of an alternative Mediterranean strategy leading to the conquest of the Middle East became increasingly difficult to revive. This alternative had come onto the agenda after the loss of the air Battle of Britain in September 1940. An elite unit secretly rehearsed the capture of Gibraltar. However, Hitler relied on the threefold co-operation of Franco, Marshal Petain and Mussolini. Though amicable, he offered unacceptable terms. Spain with its wrecked economy needed more financial aid than Germany was able to offer. Franco's claims for an enlarged Spanish African Empire clashed with French and Italian interests. Petain found Hitler's insistence on France as a downgraded and humiliated nation, unacceptable. Mussolini was too proud to rely on much German military aid. In addition, the palpable failure of the Italian attempt to conquer Greece spoiled hopes of a peaceful German domination of the Balkans. By March 1941, the only vestiges of the Mediterranean option which Hitler chose to retain were the eviction of a British military presence from Greece, the capture of Crete, the defence of Tripolitania, and useful practice for the Luftwaffe in bombing and mining Malta, ships and the Suez Canal.

Also off the agenda as from September 1940 was an invasion of the British Isles. Only the Channel Isles were under German occupation. The blitz of British cities and the Battle of the Atlantic continued in the hope that the infliction of such huge punishment would lead eventually to a de facto British capitulation. The blitz and German attacks on shipping were harmful to the British war effort, and Hitler asserted *that Germany was slowly choking England to death.*[lxxxix]

Germany's industrial base was subordinate to the Nazi regime. A huge and powerful segment was state owned under Goering's auspices, but principles of private profit and ownership had been guaranteed and were enhanced by Hitler's triumphs. Nazis held many key positions in the big monopoly enterprises. It seemed marvellous to their directors that the whole trade union movement had been replaced by a Nazi dominated 'Labour Front'. Up to the invasion of the USSR, the war brought great gains and non- Nazis at the top of industry had only secondary reservations about the regime. The wizardry of financial policy had facilitated huge accumulations of raw materials. Nonetheless these stocks were being run down, prudently but surely. The naval blockade of Germany and occupied Europe, whatever the peripheral exceptions , served as a further warning of the danger of a prolonged WW2. The organised plunder which followed the victories in Western Europe in the spring and summer of 1940 added to stocks, but this a was one-off event. Raw materials and oil and wheat purchased - mostly on credit terms - and punctiliously delivered from the neutral USSR - considerably aided the German war machine. Other adjoining neutral states were also trading with Germany to perceived mutual advantage.[xc]

The much trumpeted Nazi *New Order* became the theoretical framework for the German economic hegemony of mainland Europe with the exception of the USSR. The propaganda line was that prospects were bright. However, the fact that Britain remained at war and maintained its naval blockade combined with a small but growing fear of American backing for Britain, handicapped the evolution of the New Order. The acute shortage of skilled labour, apparent at the time from press advertisements, did not bode well if the war were to last long.

The Wehrmacht with increasing demands upon it (there were some 300,000 soldiers in occupied Norway alone), needed increasing numbers of technicians, as did the other armed forces. There were over five million men under arms. In speeches in 1941, Hitler expressed his pride in the strength of the German armed forces and their modern weapons, but the stark fact was that industry was deprived of many skilled workers. Machine tools were ample and the fact that mainly only single shifts were worked was due to the shortage of skilled labour and the need to conserve raw materials,

The conscription of women for industry was rejected as a danger to morale, but despite the Nazi ideology of 'Church, children and kitchen', they were in employment in manufacturing and service industries and agriculture. Agriculture also relied on some 1.8 million French and 400,000 Polish PoWs and slave workers. The Poles were deemed racially inferior and were persecuted and had few amenities. In Berlin, around 30,000 Jews were employed in war production, notably at Siemens, about which Goebbels grumbled in private.[xci] There were temptations for foreigners to move to Germany to work. A higher standard of living was held out for them and their families, with opportunities for them to enjoy leave at home. There were in the Spring of 1941, 1.5 million foreign 'voluntary' workers in Germany from all over Europe in addition to 1.5 million PoWs employed in the German economy. Coercion and intimidation for the 'voluntary' workers did not inflame significant reaction for the time being.

Productivity was generally falling and central planning of the economy was poor. Only now did Hitler begin to recognise the need for standardisation and mass production for the war effort. Given his faith in blitzkrieg warfare, 'total war' was not as yet state doctrine. Production was just about sufficient both for warfare and to maintain living standards for civilian Aryans. Germany was now producing fewer warplanes than

Britain but the Luftwaffe was still stronger in number than the RAF. The present was endurable if uncomfortable, but unremedied depreciation of vital fixed capital could not be sensibly ignored. Economists were acutely aware of the reasons for the collapse of the German home front in 1918, including the notorious 'Turnip winter'[120] . One academic (Banse) concluded that "From the point of view of war economy it is impossible to win a modern war unless the warring party can lean on one of the great empires, namely Great Britain, Russia or the U.S.A".[xcii] Whereas armaments and ammunition needed for the next blitzkrieg were in plentiful supply, due not least to pre-war planning and the absorption of Austrian and Czech heavy industry, the shortages of skilled labour and raw materials for the long term and the absence of rationalisation for war production weighed badly. On the other hand, commercial agreements with Swedish and Swiss industry were rewarding, and payment when necessary was in gold, most of which was looted from banks in the occupied countries, and from Jews. Industry in the occupied territories was exploited to the uttermost by various novel and unfair legal measures, often with the collaboration of the foreign industrialists themselves. They were often allowed a minor share of profits as a reward for helping the German war effort. Ultimately such collaborators would try to cover their tracks. German industrial might could look near impregnable but professional economists were divided about future prospects if the war were to continue. The only safe assumption for strategy (which one may presume was Hitler's way forward) was that within a year or two negotiated peace in Nazi Germany's favour, if not outright victory, was essential.

Meanwhile, a superficial optimism reigned, with negative features hopefully confined to the gaze of the discerning and loyal. The economic pride of the New Order was the innovative and sophisticated replacement of natural products by artificial ones, nicknamed, though not by Nazis, Ersatz. Oil was a vital example. Romanian and other oil wells produced up to about half of the needs of the German war effort. Some further oil came from the USSR. Synthetic oil production in Germany relied on brown coal, and alcohol from potatoes. Synthetic rubber *Buna* was also manufactured in large quantities. Highly developed networks of railways, navigable rivers and canals provided a viable system of transport. Of course, crises arose which had to be resolved. A well publicised one was the introduction of *a coke fence*, a North-South line dividing Germany. Invaluable coke was forbidden to cross this line. For the sake of efficiency of management, experienced businessmen replaced Nazi Party officials. However, to a disconcerting extent, coal, oil and food were in short supply outside Germany. Prior to German occupation, all of these and feed for cattle and poultry had been imported from parts of the world, now cut off due to the British naval blockade.

Any discontent among German workers, many of whom would once have had Social Democrat or Communist loyalties, did not cross a dangerous threshold. In the first few months of WW2, draconian measures had been superimposed on an existing tight system of labour discipline. It was officially admitted that *"it was especially the loss of extra pay for night, Sunday and holiday work that the workers found unjust"*. Their 'spontaneous' widespread protests were in fact discreetly organised. Obviously mass suppression would have been counter-productive. At the end of 1939, Ley, the Nazi Minister of Labour, declared that the earlier restrictions were no longer necessary. It may be recalled that after the German conquest of Poland in September 1939, *the phoney war* allowed Germany some breathing space. It continued to be a theme of Nazi propaganda that the regime was no longer Capitalist but on the side of the workers. A rosy post-war future was a propaganda theme. With coercion and patriotism, the latter fortified by news of impressive military victories, there was an atmosphere of sulky compliance, with demands for more intense labour and longer hours. The families of many in the armed services had their incomes supplemented by vouchers for necessities as a result of state measures.

Beginning in the Spring of 1940, the successive German conquests gave rise to a huge import of consumer and luxury goods brought back to Germany for civilians by servicemen of all ranks. It was policy that they should take advantage of the artificial exchange rate, fixed by the Nazi occupation authorities, to facilitate plunder. Clothing, shoes, food and wine in large quantities were purchased by German soldiers for their families and friends. Customs officers relaxed enforcement for soldiers on leave laden with booty. So in this way WW2 raised on occasion a low standard of living.

Berthold Brecht, then in exile, wrote in one poem culminating in widow's weeds coming from Russia :

And what did the soldier's wife receive
From Paris the city of light
She received from Paris a silken gown,
'Twas the talk of the town, the silken gown
She received from the city of light.

In Spring 1941, Hitler continued to assert in his speeches that *National Socialism* was pro-worker. Britain was mocked for its allegedly poor social services and the absence of a state Opera. The USA was considered a cultural desert. There was an absence of any public mention by Hitler of Russia and Communism prior to 22 June, but he boasted that all would-be revolutionaries were behind bars.

Some production of unnecessary consumer goods continued at least until the Russian campaign began. Travel by rail over long distances to visit evacuated children was still possible. Small businesses, although reduced in number under pre-war regulations intended to make life difficult in that sector, were far from disappearing. Pensioners up to the age of 75 and the partly disabled were not yet being forced to re-enter employment. Domestic service in middle and upper class households continued. It seemed to Hitler that there was adequate war production for his blitzkrieg strategies. Although huge and more powerful armed forces for the future were envisaged, plans were on paper only, perhaps simply intended to impress.

Food rationing, not too much reduced from pre-war austerity standards, was bearable for the Aryan population. The armed forces were conspicuously privileged for generous food supplies. A thorough rationing system ensured that children and young people did not suffer, though some commodities like genuine coffee and tropical fruits almost entirely vanished to be replaced by 'ersatz' products. Although meals in restaurants were on the ration, the wealthy and privileged could eat at a price more or less as they wished. Howard K.Smith, a solidly pro-British American radio correspondent in Berlin,was disappointed by the relatively high standard of living of German workers there until, as he noted, there was a marked decline after the invasion of the USSR. As for smoking, Goebbels notes in his diary his opinion that a policy would have to be decided upon as to whether cigarette advertising should be banned, as supplies of cigarettes - and alcoholic liquor - were for civilians sometimes totally inadequate.[xciii] There was a joke about one result of Rommel's conquests in Africa being the use of camel dung for tobacco, such was the fame of ersatz. The normal meat ration of 500 grams per week was due to be temporarily reduced but was in fact permanently reduced.

Meanwhile, everyday life retained some sense of normality for ordinary Germans. Hope that the war would soon end victoriously seemed to have some substance. The well organised mobilisation of youth was a feature which found a milder counterpart in the Parliamentary democracies. But, in Germany, militaristic content abounded in education. This had been the case from soon after the inception of the Nazi regime. A commitment to Nazi ideology was standard and when this clashed with religious affiliation, the Churches had to accept the new dispensation. Provided the Churches were compliant, they were left alone, much to the disgust of Goebbels, whom Hitler ordered to continue his subscriptions to the Roman Catholic Church. Occasional protests from Church personalities about specific Nazi measures were tolerated. There was palpably nothing too systematic or forceful about these adverse criticisms. A very few outspoken churchmen were sent to concentration camps; the Lutheran Pastor Niemoller, a U-boat ace in WW1, surviving to become a peace campaigner in the 1950s.

The militarisation of youth meant a far from voluntary conformity but it was a substantial encouragement for those who found an emotional outlet in war games both on the ground and for study.[xciv] At one extreme were the elite of the SS, a relatively small number of mostly young, keen, fit, obedient and brutalised Nazis whose loyalty and proficiency were exceptionally reliable. There were special schools for those picked as likely future leaders, with high casualties incurred in battle training. There were arrangements for sexual intercourse between males and females, selected for their alleged racial purity, fitness and political fanaticism, to breed *supermen* and *superwomen*. The progeny so conceived failed to fulfil expectations, but this only became apparent after the Nazi era. In contrast, the mass of youth had to endure, not enjoy, Nazi practices and exploitation without daring to complain. Many in their twenties had no living father, which inclined them to accept Hitler as a father figure.

The Hitler Youth included most young males between the ages of ten and sixteen and their culture was shaped by the need to condition them for warfare. Sport was in this spirit. Anti-

Semitism was endemic in culture, including the German cinema. The annual Nuremberg rally up to 1938 was a high point. Some of the films produced by German studios were intended to appeal particularly to war-minded and racist youth.[xcv] Airmen and crews of U-boats were singled out for praise as aces and daredevils. The competence of the Wehrmacht was seen as legendary, and relations between officers and other ranks evidenced a perceptible mutual confidence, vital for modern warfare.

The solemn emphasis on the importance of healthy indoctrinated and dehumanised Aryan youth involved enmity towards the congenitally weak, backsliders, opponents of the regime, and the "racially inferior". Although the literal mass extermination of German Jews was scarcely begun until the Autumn of 1941, complex lawful discrimination originated in 1935 with various provisions for those of part-Jewish descent. Quite often persecution became murder. Already the systematic murder of an estimated 70,000 "Aryan" people, chronically mentally ill or physically disabled and sterilisation of deemed inferiors occurred.[xcvi] Publicity which defeated the censorship aroused some public anger, but Nazi indoctrinated youth were inclined to see these atrocious measures as euthanasia and as necessary for the war effort. In the concentration camps were held political enemies, tens of thousands of Jews, Communists and others including Jehovah's Witnesses, gypsies and homosexuals. Periods of detention varied and there were releases. Many inmates, however, were murdered or died from disease, exhaustion, torture or suicide. Organised infliction of cruelty on the prisoners strengthened the bonding of SS guards with the Nazi regime and creed. It seems that the paratrooper step-son of Goebbels took part in a gang rape, which was hushed up, one interpretation of his diary entries of 12,13 and 20 February 1941.

Amazement at the grip of Hitler and Nazism on the German people fails to take account of some features of the evolution of Germany into a united nation state within the living memory of many grandparents. Anti-semitism had been furthered by Martin Luther, the original Protestant, and racism generally was a cultural outlook shared with other European nations and justified by pseudo-science and eugenics. The undue emphasis on obedience to authority was a cultural trait, which had been a prop for the regime of the 18th century monarch of Prussia, Frederick the Great. Hitler had a particular admiration for this brilliant leader and harsh disciplinarian. The contribution made by the 18th century German Romantic movement in philosophy, literature, music and painting was of world significance. The operas of Wagner, with their reliance on Nordic legend and German traditions, provided inspiration for Hitler's vision of a Greater and Nordic Germany ultimately to be the centre of a new World Empire. The philosophy of Nietzsche with a cult of the *Superman* was ripe to be distorted. It was easy for many Germans to despise other national cultures out of ignorance. As for German science, it had been a world leader in the 19th century and later. Although German Jews had contributed immensely in these fields, the Nazis forbade any mention of them and their achievements.

The defeat of Germany and huge casualties in WW1, the myth that the German army had been stabbed in the back by a Marxist home front, the ensuing burdens of the Treaty of Versailles, reparations, disarmament and later wild inflation provided fertile soil for Nazi ideas. Much political turbulence and the subsequent failure of the democratic political parties to overcome the great slump of 1929 provided the main impetus for the Nazi rise to power. Older Germans, often cherishing cultural values at odds with Nazism, felt that Hitler and his regime had something to offer, however distasteful some of the detail. The Communist Party, which had peaked at over 6 million votes a few months before the Nazi party came to power, had some members willing to risk their lives for the cause, and a few of their units contrived to survive despite the harshest suppression. A few undetected men in high positions secretly gave information about the German war machine to Moscow. One of these was Richard Sorge, a popular Press attaché at the German embassy in Tokyo, who had access to vital information.[xcvii] Pre-war, some Aryan Germans of worldwide fame, the best known being Nobel prize winning novelist Thomas Mann, emigrated out of disgust. Many better-off Jews, including the world famous Einstein, emigrated, some Nazis profiting from their flight. Pre-war international efforts got many Jewish children away legally.

Within the 'Greater Germany' comprising Germany according to its 1914 boundaries, plus Austria and the Protectorate of Bohemia and Moravia, some normality of economic life persisted. In the occupied territories much muddle prevailed behind a veneer of order, cruelly maintained in Poland and with some harshness in the North and West. A ruthless and clever extraction of wealth, goods and services for the benefit of Germany and the occupation authorities, was a priority. Works of art were looted systematically, such actions being authorised by Goering.

No overall monolithic structure was in place. In the East, a rule of terror was imposed on the supposedly inferior Poles and Jews. Personal relationships between Poles or Jews and their German conquerors constituted a criminal offence, with capital punishment among the penalties. Forced labour became commonplace for the development of roads, railways and airfields for Barbarossa. Already there were more than a million Poles in Germany, nominally 'volunteers', mainly engaged in agriculture, and living in destitution. The standard of living for Poles in Poland fell with appalling results. As far as the Nazi creed went, this was punishment for their military resistance in 1939 and for their sub-human status as racial inferiors. Many of the pre-war intelligentsia perished. The Catholic Church was tolerated, but clearly as a subordinate authority. Higher education ceased. The universities and secondary schools closed for Poles. As a further infliction of indignity and as a diversion, pornography, drinking and gambling were encouraged. Nearly one quarter of pre-war Poland was incorporated into Greater Germany. The minority of Poles deemed to be Aryans, gained the doubtful privilege of compulsory German citizenship. Polish children considered eligible to be Aryans were kidnapped and reared as Germans. Another quarter of pre-war Poland, including badly damaged Warsaw, was under brutal colonial rule, directed from undamaged Krakow. By the Spring of 1941, up to 100,000 Poles had been murdered by the German authorities, of whom about half were Jews. Vast involuntary shifts of population occurred. The remaining part of pre-war Poland was incorporated into the USSR as a consequence of the Nazi-Soviet pact.

Especially barbaric measures affected over three million Polish Jews who remained in German occupied Poland. The principle of 'divide and rule' added to German motivation. More than 300,000 Jews had migrated to the Soviet occupied part of Poland in 1939 with German encouragement. Virtually all remaining Jews were herded into the existing ghettoes of Warsaw, Krakow and Lodz. These became closely guarded, isolated and badly overcrowded enclaves suffering gross food shortages and other deprivations. Death rates rose steeply as the Nazis desired. Nazi cunning ensured some co-operation from Jews as 'prefects', who predictably faced agonising dilemmas. The Lodz ghetto, as a result of pre-war industry, became a centre for textile production for the German armed forces. The illusion of survival was nurtured for its exploited residents. While no plan of extermination was as yet formulated, a predisposition to murder Jews on a huge scale was unquestionably generated.

Elsewhere in occupied Europe, the Nazi policy was to win over populations to willingly accept German hegemony, whilst persecution of Jews and Communists took place. The anti-

Bolshevik crusade arguably appeared as a future turning point in favour of domestic collaborationists. The potential for genuine friendship with Nazi Germany was publicly and loudly acclaimed but, at this time, there was no hint of the forthcoming invasion of the Soviet Union.

Meanwhile, the cold and hunger of the Winter and Spring and the obvious and draconian commandeering of most of the available fruits of such production as could be maintained, bred resentment. The demands of the military occupation were inevitably bureaucratic. Ordeals arising from queuing, identity papers, permits and rationing told. The French were aware of the indignities. France (less Alsace-Lorraine annexed by Germany and a North-Eastern industrial strip separately administered) was divided into two mostly self-contained zones, occupied and unoccupied. Nearly two million French PoWs remained in German hands. Political numbness was the norm, but patriotic feeling did not totally vanish. General de Gaulle in Britain presented a symbol of resistance, even if seen as futile.

With the aid of collaborators, propaganda through the German controlled radio and press sought to overcome hostility. In the first place a typical preoccupation was getting enough to eat. The pitiful official rations were often not honoured. Most motor vehicles had been taken away to Germany, and there was little petrol available, so bicycles served for visits to the countryside where town dwellers could obtain food at a price and through personal contacts. The occupation included a huge requisitioning of crops but excessive bullying of the wily peasantry was absent.

So long as hunger prevailed, it was possible to blame Britain under Churchill for prolonging the war. No anti-German protest was lawful. So most people, absorbed in their personal problems, took refuge in detachment and cynicism. For some people, memories of the massacre of French sailors by the

Royal Navy in Africa, and the earlier evacuation of Dunkirk, allegedly leaving French armies to their fate, weighed heavily. By the end of April 1941, what was presented as the invincibility of the Nazi cause was for some a good argument for an early negotiated peace.

It required a rare and exceptionally courageous patriotism actively to oppose German domination. Receiving BBC broadcasts was barely tolerated and spreading news from them was illegal and dangerous. Ridicule and cheek at the expense of the occupiers was a safer method of raising morale. For example a poem published in a Paris newspaper in April read as if it were an eulogy of Hitler, but when the text was read as if a vertical line went down the middle, a contrary meaning was apparent! Was this inspired by a clandestine British Republican poem of the 1790s?[xcviii] The Germans soon became wise to such moral resistance. They fined and imprisoned, and imposed press bans but death sentences were the exception until after the invasion of the USSR. The Jews in France and the Low Countries had been specially registered by the end of 1940. This and some discrimination seemed the limit of oppression. As such, it seemed it could, with ingenuity, be endured. Vichy France - an authoritarian regime under the 86 year old Marshal Petain - was perceptibly worse for anti-semitism. Mid-May saw some five thousand foreign Jews in occupied France being interned in concentration camps.

In Holland, German moves to discriminate against Jews were for a while frustrated by huge public protest including a general strike in Amsterdam, led, by among others, a Communist roadsweeper. Goebbels noted 78 demonstrators as shot in the ensuing suppression, but some delay in extending anti-semitic policies resulted.

In occupied France, some trade union activity was allowed by the Germans both to facilitate production for the German war machine, and arguably to show how opportunistically reactionary was the Vichy regime with its ban on trade unions. Nazism was claimed to be both anti-revolutionary and anti-reactionary. Some former Socialists aligned themselves with Nazi politics by openly favouring a negotiated peace with Britain on German terms. Notably in Paris, a centre of recreation for German soldiers on leave, there was the most sustained attempt at economic and cultural reconciliation - on German terms. German behaviour was intended to be polite and correct. The sophisticated French film industry survived. Some of the intelligentsia made a show of collaboration, partly convinced of ultimate Nazi triumph. The once powerful French Communist Party (PCF) was beginning to organise sabotage. It was already suffering the loss, beginning as early as September 1939 of many officials and activists imprisoned.[xcix] Many of these in Vichy France were sent to labour camps in Africa. The line that the USSR was developing as an impregnable Socialist society, that ruling classes were facing deep crises and a prospect of a Socialist France worth struggling for gave hope. The PCF, showing gumption, and at great risk participated in organising a miners' strike in the Pas de Calais in the Spring of 1941. The indigenous fascist movements earned little respect. They enjoyed a monopoly of local political power, Denmark excepted.

The division in Belgium between Flemings and Walloons, allowed the Nazis to play off the two communities against each other. However, as in Holland, only a tiny fraction of the population became openly pro-Nazi. In Norway and Denmark (the latter treated very leniently by Nazi standards as a neutral under German military occupation) pro-Nazi sentiment was rare.

According to Goebbels' diary, the Protectorate of Bohemia and Moravia saw the best results for Nazism.[c] The Czech Communist party, illegal and harassed, acknowledged that while Germany seemed to be winning the war against Britain, its influence on the working class remained largely nominal. The demoralisation sown by the Munich Agreement of 1938, when Britain and France had wilfully abandoned Czechoslovakia to its fate, was clearly reaping a bitter harvest. Yet, positive pro-German feeling was distinctly limited.

In the summer of 1940, Churchill had instructed the Minister of Economic Warfare, Labour's Hugh Dalton 'to set Europe ablaze'. By the Spring of 1941, there was only sporadic military action. In Norway, agents kept German warships under surveillance. In the Low Countries and France locals had begun to help RAF aircrew to escape to neutral Spain. In February 1941, British paratroops temporarily damaged an aqueduct in Southern Italy. They later had to surrender. One of them, formerly a caterer in Soho of Italian origin, was shot by the Italians as a traitor. Another British landing, on the Lofoten Islands off Northern Norway, lasted for a few hours on 4 March and may have included as a motive, the proposed seizure of ENIGMA equipment. Fish oil stocks, installations and shipping were destroyed. Some Norwegian volunteers, a few quislings and Germans were taken away to Britain. The Germans punished the islanders for their alleged disloyalty. They also maintained more watchfulness over the long Norwegian coastline and kept significant units from participating in Barbarossa. British disinformation continued to suggest a British invasion of Norway as probable.

In the Balkans, Slovakia, Hungary, Romania and Bulgaria were German satellites to a greater or lesser degree. They were sources of products, mainly raw materials and foodstuffs, for the German war machine. Puppet governments were installed in Belgrade and Athens by the end of April. Croatia became an Italian satellite.

Whilst occupied Europe presented no immediate problems for Germany, Hitler was aware that this might not remain the case.

He certainly entertained hopes that the success of Barbarossa could generate participation in his anti-Bolshevik crusade.

Some causes of concern for Hitler in early 1941, were diminishing. Though the official hope of total victory the previous summer had been dashed, fresh victories in April in North Africa and the Balkans came as a relief. Yugoslavia and Greece were subjugated in campaigns of far less duration than the two months planned for, and the British forces in Greece had been severely punished. The Luftwaffe proved its superiority in the Mediterranean. The blitz on British cities and the Battle of the Atlantic gave further reassurance. The RAF night raids on Germany were usually bearable. That they took place at all was a blow to Nazi prestige because of Goering's pre-war promise to the German people that Germany was immune, but there was little serious damage done. The RAF oil bombs were nicknamed Churchill's dirty socks. Howard K. Smith in Berlin found arrogant Nazi intrusion into his reporting of the war intolerable and gave in his notice. Goebbels was anxious lest Germans should become too optimistic about the prospect of early victory.[ci] He insisted that expectations should not be unduly raised, but he remained confident, as did other Nazis, that eventually Britain would agree a peace with vital German gains intact. It seemed rational to believe that there was a latent peace movement in Britain and that Churchill's defiant leadership could be broken.

The last week of April saw a massive German propaganda campaign against Churchill personally.[cii] He was vividly portrayed as an immoral statesman, a liar, a warmonger, a servant of the Jews and plutocrats, a drunkard, a heavy smoker, a desperado, a pervert glorying in pink underclothing and dictating from his bath, and with a past of failure as a statesman and strategist. Duly cited were the military disasters of Antwerp and the Dardanelles in WW1, and in WW2 the fiasco of Dakar and the evacuations from Norway, Dunkirk and now Greece. Hitler in his triumphalist and sarcastic speech of 4 May once again scorned Churchill; a theme which had given him pleasure ever since the war began. These tactics at such a time may also be perceived as consistent with Hess's forthcoming attempt to prepare ground for peace negotiations aimed at unseating Churchill.

Hitler knew that preparations for Barbarossa could be only partly concealed. At the end of April, German troops arrived in Finland. Transit rights for German troops and supplies over Swedish territory were agreed. White émigrés in Germany, including Ukrainian nationalists, were being trained as interpreters and administrators. The May issue of the Wehrmacht's house magazine reminded its soldier readers that Bolshevism had been the first enemy of the Nazis. Currency was being printed for use in an occupied USSR. Much of this was publicised in the world press, partly as hard news. One Nazi counter to such dangerous revelations was to prove the most effective. It was suggested in April that Hitler and the German General staff were at loggerheads about the wisdom of a German invasion of the USSR. It was implied that there was a fear both of a war on two fronts and of the hard Russian winter, which had doomed the great Napoleon. Such disinformation was convincing for the few well-informed people worldwide who came to learn of it. How could Hitler be so mad as to go to war with the USSR, when German-Russian trade relations were obviously so advantageous to Germany, and when Germany was mostly in the ascendant in WW2? This question seemed to most observers to have only one rational answer: Hitler could not be so mad. He would press Stalin only for more economic aid and possibly for a military alliance to open a route to India. What could be more natural than that the pressure for such negotiations would include much of the Wehrmacht and the Luftwaffe near the Soviet border, arguably safe there from RAF raids.

Many German diplomats in Moscow were keen for peace between Germany and the USSR to remain the norm, and said so. They sent reports to Germany giving their interpretation of the potential military strength of the USSR which Hitler chose to reject. German agents were shown something of industry, so they could see the USSR was a force to be reckoned with, but not, it seems, the factories behind the Urals beginning to produce up-to-date tanks and warplanes. Few, if any, of these German diplomats knew of Barbarossa. They were encouraged both by Berlin and in Moscow to look forward to a rosy future for German-Soviet relations. It was hoped that the considerable volume of trade in Germany's favour would expand, even as deliveries of machinery from Germany to the USSR were being delayed. The German diplomats believed in the likelihood of German offensives continuing in the Middle East, with more victories to come. They talked to other diplomats in Moscow along these lines.[ciii] When the Soviet government expressed its anxiety over a possible threat of war by Germany, the German ambassador in Moscow, Count von Schulenburg, advised a formal Soviet letter to Berlin asking for reassurances. This was sent early in May. A rumour of 26 April to the effect there would be war between Germany and the USSR within 14 days, which Cripps forwarded to London, was probably a German plant. Reports must have been sent to Berlin that Stalin and Molotov were cold-shouldering Cripps as a provocateur who wanted a German-Soviet war. The German diplomats in Moscow took the view that, given the new world situation, the USSR was on the brink of a realistic re-assessment. Germany was about to triumph in WW2 and Stalin would seek a new understanding with Hitler accordingly. They believed they were farsighted. A new phase seemed to open on 6 May when Stalin became PM, formally Chairman of the Committee of Commissars. The same day Goebbels noted in his diary that Stalin, for his apparent indifference to German war preparations, was like a rabbit before a snake.[civ]

When Hitler weighed the pros and cons of proceeding with Barbarossa, before finally fixing its date on 30 April for 22 June, he must have taken into account the likely reactions of Britain and the USA to a German invasion of the USSR. There were three possible scenarios. Choosing between these on empirical grounds must have been difficult because the data was patchy. Much of it could be assessed as from or through the agency of British Intelligence. In respect of its likely veracity, one must recall the Venlo incident of November 1939. This was when two British agents in then neutral Holland had been tricked into meeting German agents claiming to be from an anti-Hitler German peace movement. These Germans were in fact from the Gestapo and the two luckless British agents were kidnapped across the border into Germany. Here was a conspicuous success for Nazi political warfare, but British Intelligence was arguably at that time, as practised in deceit.

The first of the three scenarios would have been that Britain and the USA would side with the USSR. This was supposed to have been the desired outcome for Churchill and Roosevelt. They were deemed the arch warmongers, and Hitler had said publicly after the conquest of Poland that there were those in Britain who longed for a conflict between Germany and the USSR, and he would not be obliging them. The second (diametrically opposed) scenario would have been the very desirable prospect for Hitler that, on the invasion of the USSR, Britain and the USA would align with Germany to destroy forever the USSR and the Bolshevik menace. This could not have been less than a hope for Hitler, and as will be contended, a ruse of Churchill's was to trick Hitler into believing this would happen. Was Hitler deceived? We do not know. He himself perhaps could not be sure whether the message at the heart of the scam was authentic, but evidently he considered at least an intermediate scenario. This was that Britain and the USA after a few weeks observation of the speedy conquest of the USSR, would make peace as he wished; Churchill being ousted from power in Britain and Roosevelt's presidency fatally undermined. This third scenario was for Hitler almost as good as the ideal second one.

Goebbels' diary entry for 22 June relating to the previous day reads *'the Fuehrer has high hopes of the Peace party in England'*. The diary entry for 18 July 1941 of the Italian foreign minister Count Ciano is supportive: *'Anfuso (*i.e a senior aide*) has had an intimate and very interesting conversation with Frau Mollier, the wife of the German press attaché (*i.e in Rome*), She revealed that the Russian campaign has caused a deep crisis in the German ruling classes. Hitler went to war believing that the struggle against Bolshevism might lead the Anglo-Saxon countries to end the conflict. Von Ribbentrop did not agree; in fact he was convinced that Churchill is ready to make an alliance even with the devil himself if only he can destroy Nazism. And this time he was right.'*

On the 31 January 1941 Hitler himself said: 'I have offered Britain a hand time and time again. It was the very essence of my programme to come to an understanding with her'. In his speech of 4 May, Hitler had referred to a 'small clique' in England, which was preventing peace, consisting of 'British warmongers' and 'Jewish capitalists'.

On 3 October 1941 Hitler declared ; *"Unfortunately the nation whose friendship I wanted most - the British – did not join in "*. He went on to qualify his disappointment by blaming *"a few"* in Britain, supported by *"international jewry"*, for this frustrating state of affairs.

This deluded outlook was one which effectively suited Churchill's aims and was one that he would in due course deviously seek to encourage.

We can be sure there was a predisposition in Hitler's mind to foresee Britain and the USA coming to terms with Germany once Barbarossa was seen to be succeeding.

In Hitler's long letter to Mussolini of 21 June 1941 notifying him of Barbarossa (the letter was purposively not delivered until after the invasion of the USSR had begun), he declared he felt *'spiritually free'* after nearly two years of simulated friendship with the USSR. He implied that in reaching his decision for the invasion, he had taken all conceivable factors into account.[cv]

So we are left uncertain whether the British disinformation, which is later postulated here, decisively affected Hitler's decision to postpone further German offensives in the Mediterranean and the Middle East. This alternative German strategy was pressed for most zealously by Grand Admiral Raeder, the chief of the German navy, up to the end of May. He advised Hitler the way forward for Germany to win WW2 in 1941 was the German conquest of the Middle East. Raeder, when the German victory in Crete would have reinforced his case, was disappointed to be assured by Hitler that it was necessary for Germany to dispose of the USSR first.

So Hitler's gamble of Barbarossa relied on processes of reasoning which seemed to him to be almost impeccable. History was to expose them as fallacious. The deficiencies of Hitler's mindset have to be emphasised. Were he - and Hess - duped by a trick of Churchill's? The case for arguing that this deception was decisive relies on Hitler's determination to eliminate the USSR having as a *vital* component his belief as indicated by Goebbels and Ciano as mentioned above, and as implied in his speeches of 31 January, 4 May and 3 October 1941. Nobody can be sure as to the extent Churchill's "Trojan Horse" entered Hitler's mind, but the circumstantial evidence is present.

CHAPTER 6

The Deadly Embrace

Stalinism in the USSR, the self-proclaimed 'Land of Socialism', was at its height in the Spring of 1941. Whatever the shortcomings of the Soviet Union, peace, if uneasy, was preserved amidst the turmoil and destruction of war elsewhere. Neutrality seemed to pay. The loyalty of Soviet citizens, whatever the unarticulated reservations, was primarily guaranteed. Memories were strong and vivid of the enormous cumulative calamities of WW1 and the civil war following the Bolshevik revolution, famine and disease. Then there were the dislocations which accompanied the First Five Year Plan, including the pains of forced collectivisation and yet more famine and shortages. Politically, the 'great' purge of 1937/1938 was intended to advance the building of a Socialist society whose paper rights and liberties, as laid out in the 1937 Soviet constitution served only to consolidate Stalin's grip on society. Millions perished in labour camps, the Gulags, in remote areas. The historical truth began to be publicised only after the death of Stalin in 1953.

The notorious pact between Germany and the USSR of August 1939, which preceded Germany's invasion of Poland, surprised and shocked the democracies. This inevitably caused uneasiness among progressives, however they might seek to justify to themselves that Stalin had no choice as Britain and France refused to reach a sensible agreement with him to defend mutual interests against Hitler. It spelled complicity with fascism, even though there were practical advantages - as events showed.

Absorbed into the USSR was first the Eastern half of the old Poland, which commonsense recognition of ethnicity suggested should never have been stripped from the Soviet Republic some twenty years earlier. Here was a buffer zone as a useful defence against a German invasion. *Mein Kampf* and other ideological and political onslaughts against Communism and the USSR , threatened such an invasion. The Baltic states of Lithuania, Latvia and Estonia provided bases for the Red army from October 1939 onwards, and by mid-1940 were occupied as part of the Soviet Union. The ensuing elections were at best of shaky validity, but Jewish people felt relieved by annexation as an alternative to Nazi domination. Many Jews were skilled artisans who were to prove valuable for the Soviet economy. The winter war of 1939/1940 against Finland was at first an almost unbroken series of military disasters for the Red Army, but in March 1940 Finland, after initial victories followed by more than a month of defeats, was forced to accept Soviet demands for the security of Leningrad. The Red Army lost as many as 200,000 soldiers. Whether the war against Finland, which aroused a wave of prejudice against the USSR in Britain, France and the USA, was wisely embarked upon, remains to this day controversial. The case that Soviet hostility antagonised so many Finns that Finland later allied itself with Germany could not be openly argued until well after Stalin's death.

Summer 1940 saw a Soviet takeover of Bessarabia and Northern Bukhovina, parts of Romania, intended to strengthen the defence of Ukraine. Just as
Finland had been antagonised so now was Romania. Soviet aggrandisement was motivated chiefly by considerations of self-defence and the intention to recover what in part had been included in the Czarist Empire; the USSR now claimed to be stronger as a result of its undoubtedly ruthless defensive measures.

The Soviet army, navy and air force were purged of huge numbers of senior officers prior to WW2. They had been shot or sent to the Gulags. Those in the Gulags were later mostly returned to the forces, but the purges continued on a smaller scale. In spite of this, the Red army won defensive victories in the Far East, where large scale Japanese attempts to advance the frontiers of Manchukuo were repelled in the Summers of 1938 and 1939. The future Marshal Zhukov was in command there. The purge had also taken many victims from industry at a time when Soviet tanks and warplanes were becoming obsolete. Soviet war games at the end of 1940 showed the danger if Germany should attack the next summer. Many officers of all ranks, to the consternation of Zhukov for one, appeared not to understand German Blitzkrieg tactics. Too many of the old methods of warfare lingered for study and training, despite the shock of the initial failure of the Red Army in the war against Finland. No wonder many outside the USSR held a poor opinion of Soviet military strength in 1940 and the first half of 1941.

Stalin and the Politbureau knew that Soviet fighting forces were not yet ready for combat and chose in the Spring of 1941, appeasement of Germany as the best policy. Though it was deemed necessary to modernise the fighting forces and industry in case neutrality should be impossible to sustain, dangerously complacent grandiose propaganda about the invincibility of the USSR prevailed.

It was important that the Soviet economy should not be overstrained by war preparations. The popular cause of neutrality should not be prejudiced. Above all, Germany should not be provoked by any military build-up. Some risk of Britain and the USA menacing the USSR could not be excluded, even if for the time being this seemed unlikely. The balancing acts needed to maintain Soviet neutrality certainly presented new challenges.

After the fall of France in the summer of 1940, a wave of fear at the top regarding German prowess had led to the introduction of a standard eight hour day (replacing a seven hour one) and a standard six day working week. Labour discipline became much tighter. The right for a worker to change his or her job was much curtailed. Failure to comply with the new Labour code could result in severe punishment. These new measures raised production marginally but emphasised a risk of war. In February 1941, a much publicised 18th Conference of the Soviet Communist Party took place. Here was discussed what could be done to improve the efficiency of industry and public transport, particularly the railway and waterway systems. The grain problem was somewhat opportunistically deemed to have been *'already solved in the main'*. The Conference was intended as a call to Party members and organisations to commit themselves further without delay, and much more attention was to be given to personal responsibility for exact achievements in the fulfilment of the third Five Year Plan. The armed forces and the defence industries were to become increasingly important in an economy where bottlenecks of materials were conspicuous for interfering with production overall. Simultaneously, a fifteen year plan was envisaged for Soviet industry to advance in peace towards supremacy over world capitalism. Statistics were cited to show the progress made,but these were plausible rather than truthful. The President of the USSR, Kalinin, who enjoyed a reputation for *'Communist education'* was insisting on *'a conscientious attitude to work'*, the *'faultlessness'* of *'the quality of industrial goods'* and *'higher productivity'* to satisfy the test of *'From each according to his abilities, to each according to his work.'* He also called for patriotism, a collective spirit and *'vigilance to meet any eventuality.'*[cvi]

New models of aircraft and tanks were already being produced but much output had to be scrapped as defective. The ground attack aircraft, later nicknamed the Stormovik, the Pe-2 twin-engined light bomber, the all-wood fighter the LaGG-3 and the fighters Mig-1 and later Mig -3 were to replace the outmoded models, of which there were many thousands. A few of the new aircraft appeared in massive air displays, but would not have impressed the German servicemen diplomats present. It was going to take time for pilots to train to use the new aircraft, however much morale might be raised by the popular depiction of airmen as the '*Stalin hawks*'. Tanks such as the KV1 and T34, the best in the world at the time, were similarly only just coming into service. Of the many thousands of older tanks - far outnumbering the better German models - only about a quarter were serviceable.

After March, publicity was given to the reinforcing of the armies on the Western frontier. Here was a show of strength which gave Hitler in due course a pretext for his false claim that Barbarossa forestalled a Russian offensive. The bulk of the Red Army defended Ukraine, with fewer divisions to defend the central sector - the route to Moscow - six hundred miles to the rear, where the main fury of the German attack was to come. Stalin, backed by the Politbureau, and to the consternation of Zhukov among other top military, insisted that readiness should only be partial to avoid any suggestion of provocation. This was a titanic misjudgement, as was the placing of dumps and depots close to the frontier. The plans for defence were sloppy and their implementation incomplete. The defence line to safeguard the old frontier fell into disrepair. It was blithely assumed that warnings, such as a propaganda 'hate' campaign or at least an ultimatum would precede war, and that if war came Soviet counter-attacks at the frontier could be mounted. It was disastrously assumed that so long as Britain remained in WW2, Nazi Germany would probably not risk extending the war to the USSR.

One sensible diplomatic precaution was taken. Mid-April; a pact of non-aggression with Japan served as some protection for the Far Eastern borders. It seemed to Stalin that this step would render German aggression improbable, given German reliance on action by their Japanese ally. This pact was negotiated despite a ban in March on war materials for export (from Germany passing through the USSR for Japan). But the USSR did recognise the Japanese puppet state of Manchukuo. Of course the Japanese could not forget their heavy defeats by the Red army in 1938 and 1939. Moscow had to declare that Soviet support of Nationalist China led by Chiang Kai-Shek would not be prejudiced, and Japan did not protest. This was because the benefit to Japan of the pact was to facilitate war in South East Asia and the Pacific. In Moscow, Stalin bade an emotional farewell to the departing Japanese Foreign Secretary, Matsuoka, then hugged the German military attaché and colloquially insisted on USSR-German friendship as in the mutual interest. The Moscow correspondent of the *News Chronicle* was a lucky witness. He also reported in full to the Foreign Office in London.[cvii] Soon he was to be expelled from the USSR for his journalistic expertise and outspokenness...and doubtless for being an agent..

Soviet plans for the evacuation by rail, in the event of war, of industry and civilians to the industrial base East of the Ural mountains were prepared. Steps were taken to ingratiate the Roman Catholic Church in what had once been Eastern Poland, so as to enhance the loyalty of new citizens to the Soviet cause.[cviii] Townsfolk and peasants were far from won over to the Soviet cause, despite literacy campaigns and land redistribution in favour of many peasants. There was much acclaimed help from the state for agricultural development. Collectivisation was encouraged but was not obligatory. In the former independent Baltic states, much pro-German feeling persisted, despite or because of mass deportations to Gulags.[cix] Anti-semitism grew beneath the surface as a response to Soviet rule. In what had formerly been part of Romania, likewise only a portion of the population felt loyalty to the USSR.

The German planning for Barbarossa was too clandestine for it to have any significant effect on the surface of Soviet-German relations until April 1941. During the second half of 1940, and even later, it was only an option for Hitler, and not a certainty. There were disputes between Germany and the USSR, particularly concerning frontier adjustments and exchanges and shifts of population, but these were settled by negotiation. One apparent climax of good relations was the visit of Molotov, the Soviet Prime and Foreign Minister to meet Ribbentrop and Hitler in Berlin in mid-November 1940.

The Germans sought the entry of the USSR into the Tripartite Pact (Germany, Italy and Japan), and in return offered the USSR an opportunity to help itself to parts of Asia South of its borders. The Soviet response was a courteous but total refusal. The British Empire remained undefeated, so there was no point in any dealing which assumed otherwise. There were some bon mots uttered by Molotov. For instance, when Ribbentrop assured him that Britain was already defeated, Molotov asked why, if that were so, they were talking together in an air raid shelter with RAF bombers overhead. Hitler himself decided he could no longer endure the presence of Molotov, who in their two meetings had dared to grill him over Germany's future intentions and to demand neutrality in the Balkans and Scandinavia. Ribbentrop was at least able to continue dialogue until it eventually ended inconclusively. Hitler's resolve for Barbarossa was strengthened, but the USSR remained a commercial source of raw materials for the German war machine. Trade relations continued and improved despite the diplomatic stalemate. In mid-January 1941, the Soviet press complacently hailed a fresh trade agreement as a great new landmark in Soviet-German relations.

With some artfulness, the Russians repudiated any suggestion of a convergence of Communism and Nazism. Some favourable comments about the defence of London against the German blitz appeared in the Soviet press. There was a friendly description of the lifestyle of gunners at an anti-aircraft battery, including mention of their ample diet and a faint hint that some of them might have Communist sympathies. Certainly the Soviet public was encouraged to feel antagonistic towards the German bombing of civilians in Britain. A dig at German racist culture was Eisenstein's production of Wagner's opera *Die Walkure* at the Bolshoi Theatre. Nazi guests regarded some of the innovative stage effects as a desecration - '*deliberate Jewish tricks*'! In March, a Stalin prize was awarded to Eisenstein for his magnificent and anti-Teutonic film *Alexander Nevsky* for which Prokoviev composed the music. Other patriotic works of art received awards. At the end of April, Stalin was on the telephone to the patriotic Jewish Ilya Ehrenburg to indicate to him his anti-Nazi historical novel *The Fall of Paris* could now be published. Until then, Ehrenburg, although at liberty in Moscow and a committed Communist, had been disallowed any publication following his return to the USSR from occupied Paris in July 1940.

In March and April, Soviet-German relations underwent a new severe strain. An attempt had been made by the USSR to secure the integrity of Bulgaria so it would be immune from German occupation. The Soviet offer of a treaty to facilitate Bulgaria's continued neutrality was spurned by the King and his government although much public opinion in Bulgaria beyond the illegal Communist Party would have welcomed it. When the Wehrmacht entered Bulgaria from Romania on 1 March, Moscow sent a strong note of protest to Berlin. The German reply was bland and an obvious snub to Molotov. On 25 March, the USSR and Turkey entered into a treaty of friendship, a sign of goodwill in the face of possible German aggression. Following the coup in Belgrade two days later, better relations between the USSR and Yugoslavia came into sight. Diplomatic relations dated from some nine months earlier. It was surely no coincidence that Stalin must have authorised a joke intended to be at Germany's expense; *Pravda* commented that if the Soviet Government had failed to congratulate the new administration in Belgrade it must have been due to forgetfulness.[cx] Within days, a Non-Aggression pact was signed in Moscow between the new Yugoslav government and the USSR. It was a friendly gesture towards the new Yugoslavia, a warning to Germany and a reminder to Bulgaria that it could have enjoyed a like facility, if it had so chosen. However, within literally a few hours the tide turned. The Luftwaffe was devastating Belgrade, Yugoslavia was being invaded and so Molotov was snubbed again. The Soviet-Japanese Non-Aggression Pact of 13 April restored some degree of confidence but the Politbureau soon decided, in the light of German victories, a new and emphatic line of appeasement of Germany should be pursued. On 6 May, Stalin was appointed the equivalent of Prime Minister in succession to Molotov, who continued as Foreign Minister,

The day before Stalin became head of the government as well as continuing as General Secretary of the Communist Party, he gave a speech to a private audience of new officers of the armed forces. No absolutely reliable report of this speech now exists. It may be safely surmised that he warned of the danger of a German attack on the USSR during the summer, and admitted that effective resistance could prove difficult. The answer: there would be diplomacy intended to delay German aggression. By 1942, the Red Army would be much stronger. Britain, with American help, was continuing to fight Germany. Japan would probably remain neutral. The USSR had to prepare for the eventuality of war. Stalin, without committing himself, envisaged as a possibility that the USSR would have no alternative but to make war on Germany in 1942. The audience would have been aware that the buffer territories West of the old peacetime frontier of the USSR were a valuable acquisition for defence. In public, early in May, the Commissar of Defence, Marshal Timoshenko, spoke of the need for more defence preparations, but the Soviet public was being simultaneously lulled into a false sense of security.

The distasteful new appeasement of Germany began. Norwegian, Belgian, Yugoslav and, later, Greek diplomats lost their status as their governments in exile were deprived of recognition. The pro-Nazi rebel government of Iraq was recognised. Moscow and Vichy exchanged ambassadors.

Soviet relations with Britain were not straightforward. The neutrality of the USSR was recognised, but how long would it endure and what would then happen? One grouping of opinion wanted the USSR to become the enemy either in addition to Nazi Germany, or alone. Churchill was most definitely not of this grouping. While he upheld anti-Communism, this was far from his priority. The second grouping of opinion categorically preferred that the USSR become the enemy of Germany, but it did not seem to many that Britain could do anything to bring it about except by an intolerable sacrifice of principle in recognising Soviet territorial gains resulting from the Nazi-Soviet Pact. In a third grouping were those who wanted friendly relations with the USSR and thought this was an achievable aim and a way forward towards winning the war. Isolated was the small but intellectually influential Communist Party of Great Britain which officially simultaneously wanted the USSR to remain neutral, and for both fascism - and essentially capitalism worldwide - to be overthrown by mass popular movements.

In the British government, the second grouping of opinion was broadly predominant. The Christian Socialist, Sir Stafford Cripps, (Britain's ambassador in Moscow since June 1940), was quietly predisposed to outright friendly British-Soviet relations, but he learned by bitter experience that Stalin insisted on Soviet neutrality to the extent of showing him few favours. His firm belief that Hitler was hell bent on destroying the USSR was treated by Stalin as a way of provoking Soviet entry into the war, which meant that Cripps was in danger of becoming *persona non grata*. Yet enough realism persisted in the Soviet leadership for Cripps to remain acceptable.

The Soviet ambassador in London, Ivan Maisky, of nine years standing, continued to display his usual charm. The snobbish Cadogan noted privately '*I rather like Maisky although or perhaps because he is such a crook*'. Cadogan, an inveterate anti-Socialist, classed *Daily Herald* readers as unintelligent, and crowed when the Secretary of the Greenock Trades Council, believed to be sympathetic towards Communism, misspelt '*foreign*' in a letter proposing more trade with the USSR. From January onwards, Eden as the new Foreign Secretary was Cadogan's superior, and Eden, unlike his predecessor Lord Halifax, saw no basic objection to the inauguration of good relations between the USSR and Britain.

The stumbling blocks, however, were real. Britain refused on principle to recognise *de jure* the three annexed Baltic states as part of the USSR. Their elections of the previous summer were regarded as phoney. Soviet claims to their gold reserves at the Bank of England were rejected, as were their claims to Baltic merchant ships detained at British ports and their crews. Whilst Halifax had worsened the friction, Eden perceptibly eased it. A further difficulty under the auspices of Halifax had been the unnecessary British refusal to acknowledge the USSR as having an interest in the German dominated Danube Commission. This soon became history as Soviet objections to German expansion in the Balkans became manifest early in 1941. However, another cause of dissatisfaction arose when early in 1941 the Minister of Economic Warfare Hugh Dalton publicly protested about allegedly increased Soviet imports of raw materials finding their way to Germany. An exchange of views based on conflicting statistics was inconclusive.

An attempt by Churchill to warn Stalin of the coming German invasion backfired. His brief written message of 3 April for Cripps to give to Stalin immediately and personally was that three German panzer divisions had been about to be repositioned to attack the USSR, when the order was cancelled so that they could remain in situ to attack Yugoslavia. Cripps procrastinated. He foresaw the communication as potentially fuelling Stalin's fear that Churchill was aiming to provoke a German attack, and Cripps was already giving ample personal warnings. Eden took the side of Cripps when Churchill complained. When Stalin belatedly received Churchill's warning, *Pravda* was already denouncing Britain as working for the USSR to enter the war.[cxi] Stalin's misjudgment led to the further cold-shouldering of Cripps so as to impress Germany that the USSR had no wish to align itself with Britain.

The arrival of Hess in Britain proved to be a big setback for Anglo-Soviet relations. Stalin, and Russians generally, treated it as a serious attempt to forge an Anglo-German alliance against the USSR. This attitude was totally contrary to Churchill's own wishes and intentions but was a reasonable interpretation given Churchill's previous attempts to *'strangle'* Soviet Russia in its infancy. As sinister-looking was the British plan at the end of May for the RAF to bomb the vital oilfields of the Caucasus.[cxii] The British apprehension of a German army travelling with Soviet connivance through the Southern USSR to invade Iran could easily have been misinterpreted by Stalin as only a cover. It seems that German disinformation led to British suspicion. In May, Eden was doing his best to convince Maisky that Britain had no evil designs on the USSR, and he partly succeeded subject to the proviso that Maisky remained certain that Churchill's aim was to provoke a German attack on the USSR. However, Maisky was sure Hitler would not dare to do this. Maisky partly convinced Eden that the USSR and Germany would not become allies. This was not too hard a task as Cripps personally envisaged Germany and the USSR becoming enemies. Maisky's reports home did not succeed in dispelling Stalin's growing suspicion that a British, American and German plot to destroy the USSR was in the making.

Churchill himself hoped that there was a good chance that in the summer of 1941 Germany would be at war with the USSR, and that it would be in the best interests of Britain and the Empire. He had opposed the dismemberment of Czechoslovakia of September 1938, as did the USSR. In the summer of 1939 he firmly advocated without success, an Anglo-French-Soviet alliance to deter Hitler from further aggression. Other political initiatives of his had historically been unpopular with many ordinary Conservatives. For example, he had narrowly survived a "no confidence" vote from his local Constituency association in 1938 over his opposition to appeasement. These experiences were a factor leading him to exercise the greatest discretion in seeking an Anglo-Soviet alliance. Despite his confidential attempt to warn Stalin early in April, he spoke icily in public about the possibility of a German invasion of the USSR. He had only limited disagreements with Cripps, whom he himself had appointed the British representative in Moscow the previous summer, but considered it expedient in the presence of colleagues to call him ' a lunatic among lunatics'in December 1940. During the Battle of Britain, Churchill had publicly suggested that the presence of the Soviet air force was restraining the Luftwaffe, and Bevin later publicly gave his opinion that eventually the USSR would have to join with Britain and the USA for its own defence.[cxiii] The American commercial attaché in Berlin was given by a German staff officer, in the darkness of a cinema, secrets of Barbarossa. When Harry Hopkins was in London in January and February 1941 as the most trusted confidant of Roosevelt, he must have verbally informed Churchill.[cxiv] So he was further predisposed to speculate that the USSR could become an ally.

Churchill, by his own account, did not form his suspicion that there would be a German invasion of the USSR until just before the end of March 1941, but he was certainly at that time, isolated in his view. Not until Mid-May did the JIC share this suspicion. Principally he relied on ENIGMA information. It is also possible that he took account of reports from Prince Paul of Yugoslavia and General Antonescu who believed that a German invasion of the USSR would be welcomed in Britain and the USA. Nor would Churchill have ignored Hitler's purpose as set out in *Mein Kampf.* Benes and Masaryk were predisposed to the belief that there would be a German invasion of the USSR and they had a mole in the German high command. None of this evidence could be classed as reliable. The competing view at the top in London was that either there was German disinformation or there was to be increasing German pressure on the USSR for a closer relationship backed by a threat of force. Harold Nicolson notes at the end of March that only he and R.A."Rab" Butler, the junior Foreign Office minister, believed there would be a German-Soviet war.

In early May the ENIGMA information was far from conclusive according to the best professional assessments. Despite Churchill's request at the end of March, nothing was done by the Joint Intelligence Committee (JIC) to prepare a report about what might happen if there were a German invasion of the USSR.[cxv] Its report in June followed a much later request for an opinion in this field.

ENIGMA information about German preparations for an invasion of the USSR was ambiguous.[cxvi] It was known that a few miscellaneous units were moving into German occupied Poland, but the Luftwaffe's blitz on Britain intensified and information suggested the Mediterranean and Middle East remained the German priorities. A large army across the Channel, was still ostensibly poised to invade England. While it was known to British Intelligence that this army was supplemented by twenty one divisions of older soldiers whilst able-bodied and better trained men were being transferred to the East, the significance of this redeployment was missed.

On 10 April, the JIC advised the case for believing a war between Germany and Russia was near as *'unimpressive'.* On

Tuesday 22 April there was indecision about the probability of a German invasion of the USSR soon. This was the outcome of a meeting, with no details extant, of representatives of the Foreign Office, Military Intelligence and JIC. Only the FO thought there was a possibility of invasion in the near future. There was an appreciation of some build-up of German forces facing the USSR, and this was seen as supporting likely German pressure on the USSR as mentioned above.

On 24 April it was learned through ENIGMA that a Luftwaffe signals regiment was moving from the Channel area to the East. On 26 April, the three panzer divisions about which Churchill had sought to warn Stalin over three weeks earlier, were known to be moving East as planned. On 1 May, the arrival of the Wehrmacht in Finland was reported in newspapers. On 3 May, Luftwaffe units were moving from Greece to Poland. On 5 May, British Intelligence learned of, and attached great significance to, the installation of a PoW cage near Cracow. On 6 May, fresh information came through Yugoslav sources of the probability of a German invasion of the USSR by mid-June – as Cripps advised. Messages from Cripps about the prospect of a German war on the USSR were equivocal from mid-April onwards, so inevitably must have been taken with a pinch of salt in London. MI advised of a German build-up but was inclined to the view that this was for intimidation, not war.[cxvii] On 8 May, the day after one of Churchill's great orations, Bletchley learned of the codename 'BARBAROSSA' and on 14 May, advised war between Germany and the USSR as probable. On 16 May, (certainly after the arrival of Hess in Britain), Churchill notified Smuts in South Africa that it looked as if Hitler was massing against Russia. Churchill's original hunch had by now become, to him, a probability.

Two days before the meeting of 22nd April, a Foreign Office dispatch was sent to Cripps in Moscow, which included the paragraph: '*There have been indications that German General*

Staff are opposed to war on two fronts and in favour of disposing of Great Britain before attacking Soviet Union but everything of course depends on Hitler's decisions.' An addendum refers to a possibility of a new agreement between Russia and Germany for increased supplies of Russian oil for Germany.[cxviii]

The source of the information passed to Cripps that there was a division of opinion between Hitler and his generals is not known. It may have been German disinformation designed to conceal Barbarossa. It may have originated in a message from Benes to Churchill when they met at a review of Czech troops on the Saturday 19 April. Whatever the explanation for the falsehood, it was taken seriously at the time. At first sight it provided grim confirmation that the German war machine intended the conquest of the Middle East and beyond.

Churchill's confidence that the USSR would soon be attacked by Germany, was qualified by his realisation that Hitler might change his mind, abort Barbarossa and stick to the conquest of the Middle East. The successful German attack on Crete in the last ten days of May was a disturbing reminder of this risk. There was a general expectation that Stalin would simply negotiate around the further demands of Germany. This was the view taken by most of Churchill's intimate circle, despite Maisky's denial that there were any negotiations at that time between Germany and the USSR. Eden was inclined to accept the truth of Maisky's denial, but many of his officials simply could not imagine the USSR as the next victim of German military aggression. On 31st May, Cadogan expressed the opinion that the Germans would not be "such fools".

However, Churchill must have remembered that Hitler had on at least two occasions changed his mind about commencing invasions. The massive German land offensive of 10 May 1940 was to have commenced six months earlier. Its postponement to the Spring led to an awe-inspiring German victory. Secondly, in the midst of the Battle of Britain, the invasion of Southern England planned for a date in September was postponed.

It remained essential for Britain to maintain a front of coldness towards the USSR, whilst not spoiling any prospect of an Anglo-Soviet alliance. This was partly accomplished by MoI given an easy task amidst the willingness of much of the media to express dislike and suspicion of communism and the USSR, if not ignoring the topic. It should borne in mind that Lord Beaverbrook had a major role in guiding the content of the press, either directly or indirectly or through the MOI for this purpose. Many directives to the press were of course highly confidential. That Beaverbrook had the ability and will to carry out this operation may be gathered from his book POLITICIANS AND THE PRESS. He had been Minister of Information in 1918 and his closeness to Churchill was well-known.

Time and Tide gave an extreme view: Stalin was destined to become a '*super-quisling*'. The Sunday *Observer* and the leftist weekly *New Statesman* remained avowedly non-committal. The *Manchester Guardian* featured frequent commentaries from the distinguished scholar Sir Bernard Pares implying the desirability of an Anglo-Soviet alliance. The *News Chronicle* for one, gently shepherded its readers towards accepting the possibility of Russia as an eventual ally.

The *Sunday Times* left its readers in some doubt by presenting opposing interpretations of German-Soviet relations. Specifically Tilea, the former Romanian minister exiled in London, stated his belief on 30 March that Germany would invade the USSR. However he accepted that 'many people' believed that the German threat would remain just that. In the event of invasion, odds were generally placed on a quick German victory. This climate of opinion provided a source of satisfaction for Churchill. The initial poor showing of the Red

Army in Finland in 1939/1940, the purge of senior officers, and the then obsolescence of Soviet tanks and war planes, must have figured in his reasoning. Nothing much was to be aired in the British press to give Hitler the impression that it would be folly for Germany to invade the USSR, or that the USSR would be welcomed as an ally by Britain and the USA.

At the Whitsun Labour Party Conference in the first week of June, where many delegates would be unwilling to follow an anti-Soviet policy, Clement Attlee openly wondered whether Stalin was about to conclude an agreement with Hitler. He wondered whether, at rumoured new Soviet-German talks, the Russians were to be guests at the dinner table or on the menu! The astute MP, Philip Noel-Baker, wisecracked that Hitler was disappointed that Hess flew to Britain, '*Damn the man, I told him Moscow not Glasgow*'. No one was publicly reported calling for the USSR to be an ally. The time was not yet ripe for this.

In late May, the Communist periodical, *Labour Monthly* for June went to print. An article detailed how the Red army would definitely repel a German invasion of the USSR. The Soviet use of huge numbers of paratroops was contemplated. The main conclusion to be drawn by readers was that Hitler would not be so mad as to make war on the USSR. The author was a retired British officer, Major Hooper, who post-war said privately that he was glad he had only signed the article with a pseudonym 'Mark Four', so unrealistic did its conclusions turn out to be. Readers assumed that it represented the official Soviet view.[cxix] If the article were noted by German monitors, as had to be expected, its Communist complacency would have delighted the planners of Barbarossa.

A distinguished admirer of *Labour Monthly*, was the 85 year old George Bernard Shaw, the dramatist of worldwide fame. His interest in politics went back sixty years. He had never ceased to hold socialist convictions. His greetings to the journal for its twentieth anniversary must have predated 22 June, and he partially supported the Communist view of the war as 'imperialist'. Referring to the popular mood in Britain about the war and most people's support for Churchill's leadership, he reflected: *'Their British freedom may be a delusion and an imposture; but if an imposture is successful we must reckon with it even in our efforts to expose it'*.

Shaw believed Stalin to be a true Fabian Socialist guiding the development of Socialism in the USSR. If he were ever inclined to believe in the truth of the widespread allegations of Soviet crimes and atrocities, he would have seen the Soviet vices merely as transitional phenomena.

The relationship of the USA with the USSR could not be ignored at the top in London. If the USSR were to become an ally of Britain, as Churchill hoped, it could not be at the expense of Anglo-American links. His expectation that a German invasion of the USSR would be forthcoming within a few weeks must have been imparted to Roosevelt. Neither, however, could sensibly notify more than a handful of colleagues, as a leak might result in Hitler changing his mind and cancelling Barbarossa. What was to be done to keep Hitler satisfied that Britain and the USA would align themselves with Germany against the USSR once the invasion of the USSR was underway? How could they ensure that dislike of the USSR would not simultaneously propel it into the arms of Germany?

Roosevelt increasingly dwelt on the importance of the USA arming and helping Britain and defending the Atlantic and its environs to the maximum. The USSR seemed an irrelevance. The patronising tones directed at the USSR had been reduced at the beginning of the year when President Kalinin congratulated Roosevelt on his re-election as President and the ban on the export of American machine tools to the USSR was lifted. This was not least because American interests in relation to China and the Far East were antithetical to a Japanese-Soviet alliance, on the lines of the Nazi-Soviet Pact. However, in line with Churchill's political strategy, Soviet assets in the USA were partly frozen in June. Exports of machine tools from the USA to the USSR were again banned.

What Roosevelt had to take into account as potentially dangerous, was the strong anti-Communism of the powerful American Roman Catholic Church. As a result, the issue of an imminent German invasion of the USSR was largely evaded by him. Roosevelt could not predict the Roman Catholic reaction to the invasion. Would they be prepared to subordinate their ideological loathing to the defence of the USA? Like Churchill, Roosevelt would not be deflected by their innate anti-Communism. Yet it was perilous that little could be discussed in advance. Most likely, it was hoped that Churchill's oratory would once again sway American public opinion. On June 15, the private message from Churchill that he did not expect any *'class reaction'* must have been intended and received as encouraging. A short radio broadcast by Churchill was heard in the USA as a forerunner of his great appeal of a few days later, when he accepted an honorary degree. He referred to *'the world witnessing the birth throes of a sublime resolve'* and the need for unity to destroy Nazism.

The American political tradition made it easier for liberal-minded Americans to accept the Realpolitik though not the totalitarianism of the USSR. Considering the lingering harm of the great slump, the proclaimed social development of the USSR at whatever cost was grudgingly admired.

CHAPTER 7

Prelude to Desperation

What motivated Churchill to protect at all costs and by all means, British hegemony over the Mediterranean and Middle East? His military and diplomatic strategy throughout 1941 to the Nazi invasion of the USSR, must be seen through the prism of the significance of this region to the preservation of the British Empire through the Suez Canal short sea route to India and beyond. Vital telephone communications used cables on the bed of the Mediterranean. An adage dating from before WW1 had it that Alexandria was the key to Islam, and that (an accommodation with) Islam was the key to the British Empire in Asia and Africa.[cxx] But it was the oilfields of Iraq and Iran, oil pipelines and the refinery at Abadan on the Persian Gulf, that were truly vital to British interests. Had the Mediterranean and the Middle East fallen under German control, all air travel across it would have become impossible. As it was, already by January 1941, it had become extremely risky for merchant ships to cross the Mediterranean.

The dread, which afflicted Churchill and his closest colleagues whether in the War Cabinet, its Defence Committee and the Chiefs of Staff , had at its root the basic weakness of the British and Empire forces in the Middle East, the practical impossibility of reinforcing them quickly, and the perceived overwhelming German strength and their apparent readiness and willingness to launch immediate and even simultaneous powerful offensives. Day by day from early April the situation worsened sickeningly, until not earlier than 4 May.

The way Churchill himself deals with the crisis of the period in *The Grand Alliance* suggests that he felt unsure how to record it for posterity. In the first place the narrative threads are not pulled together in the book as they must have been by him in reality. Secondly, it looks as if passages were drafted and then superseded by more discreet editing. For example, the break in the narrative on page 209 of the first edition of the book in itself not unusual, but then a date a week later is strangely given for his great broadcast of 27 April! The possibility (or as this author sees it the overwhelming probability) of an ingenious stratagem intended to overcome the Middle East crisis, must warrant exploration.

The previous summer, after the fall of France, the principal threat to Egypt had come from the Italian armies in Cyrenaica, with some risk that the armies of the Italian East African Empire might also be a menace. In October 1940, Smuts had sent a telegram to Churchill expressing his fear of a German offensive against Egypt through Turkey and Syria. It would be *'grandiose enough to appeal to a mind like Hitler's'*. If it succeeded, as Smuts feared, *'it would open the way to Baghdad and Persia and the oil, and it would cut vital empire communications and give Mussolini hope.'* His idea as a preventative was for the securing of two then neutral states, Greece and Turkey, as allies, and a strengthening of Wavell's army in Egypt. With further misplaced inspiration he foresaw a German bribe to the USSR of Constantinople to ensure the USSR as a full ally of Germany.[cxxi] Smuts appeared not to have considered Spain or the Vichy French African Empire. However, his sense of dread and his unreal appreciation of Greece and Turkey, could have led him to bring them too into his adverse equation.

The situation was much worse by April 1941. Alan Bullock some fifty years ago adjudged 'Even a quarter of the forces being concentrated (by the Germans) for the attack on Russia could if diverted to the Mediterranean theatre of war in time have dealt a fatal blow to British control of the Mediterranean.' Post-war, Field-Marshal Montgomery told the American Defence Secretary Forrestal that 'the failure of the Germans to appreciate sea power, and therefore the strategic importance of the Mediterranean, lay at the root of the decision they made in 1941 to abandon the Mediterranean campaign, just as they were about to win it completely, for the adventure into Russia.' Major-General J.N. Kennedy, Director of Military Operations at the War Office in April, remarked bluntly 'If it had not been for Barbarossa the Mediterranean would have been lost.'[cxxii]

Churchill was well aware both of the dangers and consequences of such a loss. In two of his telegrams to Roosevelt, those of 29 April and 3 May, despair and desperation are apparent.[cxxiii] To quote from the first: '*I feel Hitler may quite early now gain vast advantage very cheaply and when we are so fully engaged that we can do little – nothing to stop him spreading himself.*' On 29 April the first editorial of *The Times* included '*If such a calamity as the loss of Egypt were to occur the struggle might become almost interminable accompanied by destruction on both sides which would set back the clock of civilisation for many years.*'(copyright The Times/Sunday Times 29th April 1941 /nisyndication.com) This view reflected Churchill's directive to the Chiefs of Staff of the previous day, and he emphasised that it was a "matter of honour" to defend Egypt.

The second of these two telegrams went into more detail about the future of the World balance of power if Germany should conquer the Middle East. It would appear to have been largely drafted on 2 May. The telegram commenced by expressing gratitude for Roosevelt's support for Britain's cause. This was truly diplomatic as Roosevelt had cabled Churchill (to the latter's consternation), that the USA could take no step to stop Germany seizing the Azores and Cape Verde Islands. This statement of American unwillingness implied that the USA would take no action to prevent a German take-over of the Vichy French African West coast of Africa including the naval base of Dakar, less than 2,000 miles from Brazil.

This second telegram also included Churchill's agreement that the USA should "look after" Vichy France – meaning particularly that the latter should remain neutral and that its fleet should not fall into Axis hands. Churchill desired the USA to act to prevent French Morocco from being taken over by Germany. That then seemed an imminent possibility. Churchill anticipated perhaps as *'the supreme turning point'* a broadcast which Roosevelt was soon going to make to the American people. This was delayed by his indisposition which lasted for ten or more days. Some commentators thought this delay was due substantially to his deep anxiety and depression over the awful course WW2 seemed to be taking. His speech was on 27 May.

In his second telegram, Churchill mentioned only some of the domino effects of a German conquest of the Middle East. More of the truth would have been just too depressing. South of the Nile Delta, a defence of the Nile valley would have raised difficulties of supply, while the Germans would have had internal lines of communication. Ethiopia would have been hard for the Germans to penetrate, but the vast and raw material-rich areas of the Belgian Congo and the Portuguese colonies, Angola and Mozambique, would have become vulnerable. Neutral Portugal under its fascist dictator Salazar could easily have reneged on its traditional friendship with Britain, if its neighbour Franco's Spain, joined with Germany. That had to be expected if Suez fell,(as Hoare the British ambassador advised). The government in exile of Belgium, nominally in control of the Belgian Congo, might soon become an unreliable ally of Britain. The risk of Africa as a whole coming within the German orbit was augmented by the less than firm grip of the Smuts government on the Union of South Africa.

Churchill specifically pointed out to Roosevelt that the loss of the Middle East would have *'grave consequences.'* Neutral Spain, Turkey and Vichy France would probably be motivated to side with Germany, and likewise Japan. He could have added to this list Portugal, Sweden and Switzerland. His message continued with the prospect that most of Asia and Africa could fall into the German orbit. Winning WW2 would become at the least, exceedingly difficult. Despite Roosevelt's cable of a few days earlier, Churchill begged for an immediate American entry into the war. He must have known this was an unrealistic prospect, however expedient his request.

The evidencing of his "bulldog" determination was politically defensible, but the advice Roosevelt got from his own top military men rebutted Churchill's *'personal'* optimism that the Middle East could be held. Roosevelt relied more on *'a remarkably prescient memorandum'* of April from Admiral Richmond Kelly Turner of the Navy Department. He foresaw that by June the Germans might be in control of the Mediterranean and that the Germans might invade Syria and *'the end will then be in sight'*. Turner feared that the morale of the British government might be lowered if the US were to express alarm. So he recommended that British courage and self-sacrifice in sending troops to Greece should receive praise. (He overlooked, it seems, the ANZAC contribution). He thought it wiser however for such a eulogy to await the final outcome of the Greek campaign, though he could have had no illusions about its failure. Averell Harriman, then in London as a personal representative of Roosevelt, wrote to Vice President Hopkins feeling *'as if living in a nightmare'* and that *'real confidence in victory'* might disappear.[cxxiv]

Nor could the effects in Asia of a German domination of Syria, Iraq, Iran, Palestine and Turkey be overlooked. Iran had many German agents who influenced a pro-German Shah, whatever his caution to date.[cxxv] On 3 May the outcome of the warfare in

Iraq could not be predicted. It looked as if Syria were vulnerable, and also the islands of Cyprus and Crete. Would a land route to India soon be available for the Wehrmacht? This seemed possible. All the more so if Hitler were to proclaim himself a *'Protector of Islam'*. A nightmare vision of WW1 as imagined in John Buchan's novel GREENMANTLE might now be coming true in WW2.[cxxvi] The top Egyptian general later fled his post, due to hatred of the British occupation of his country. The Arabs of Palestine were restive with their dislike of Zionism.

That Hitler had generally only a lukewarm interest in the Middle East pending the conquest of the USSR was not known in London. A powerfully worded directive of his in support of anti-British Arab nationalism came too late, on 23 May.[cxxvii] Given that preparations for Barbarossa were a top priority and the invasion of Crete was underway, these were empty words.

India was in ferment, a poor situation if the Wehrmacht were to mass on its Western borders, perhaps with Afghanistan as a further enemy of the British Empire. The Raj commanded the loyalty of local Indian Royalty not least by means of longstanding systems of mutual corruption, but their peoples might show hostility to British rule if Hitler were to play his hand well. The Hindu, Subhas Chandra Bose, a charismatic Nationalist politician, (arguably second only to Gandhi in the Congress movement), had after all, arrived in Berlin. He had fled there early in 1941, escaping from arrest in India, and later travelling westward on the Trans-Siberian railway. It could not be known in London that he was received merely with courtesy by Hitler and Mussolini, but it was frightening that he should broadcast to Indians calling for them to revolt en masse against British rule. He was later to find refuge in Tokyo and to die in an air accident in 1945.

Of course Indian war industry was not negligible. The financial backers of Congress, the Tata family and its networks, dominant industrialists, juggled their interest in production for the war effort with their politics of nationalism. Small manufacturers followed suit. Midst all the complications and the confusion implied by official statements and the press in Britain, it could be understood by the discerning that if the Wehrmacht were to come to the Western frontier of India, with Soviet and Afghan complicity, it would be alarming in the extreme.

Beyond India lay the colony of Burma where deeply felt nationalism also simmered, and that of Malaya. The loyalty to the British Empire of its Chinese and native Malayan inhabitants was shallow. Japan and Germany were allies under treaty even although Japan remained neutral as yet. The Japanese role as mediators in frontier warfare between Thailand and Vichy-ruled IndoChina, was leading towards the establishment of Japanese military and naval bases in Southern IndoChina, an ominous development. Japan was pressing for improved commercial relations with the Dutch East Indies so as to obtain more oil necessary for its war machine. American opposition was becoming definitive in objecting to Japan receiving more oil from that or any other source.

The American aim was for an early end to the Japanese invasion of China to facilitate American trade and investment in a Nationalist-run China. The Chiang Kai-Shek regime might swing towards Germany. Meanwhile Chiang fought against the Communists, its nominal allies within China, and relied on Soviet supplies transported by road across Central Asia. American support for Chiang was significant and included American volunteer pilots with American fighter planes. The Japanese would have liked a negotiated end to their exhausting war against China, but preferably by means of their existing puppet regime in occupied China, coming to terms with Chiang. With a German conquest of the Middle East, there could be an opening for tripartite negotiations between Japan, the Japanese puppet regime and Chiang's regime. The Japanese aim to expand their Empire in the whole Pacific region, was already recognised in outline in London and Washington. This ambition would have received a boost given a German conquest of the Middle East.

What of the specific balance of forces in the Middle East? Of the RAF, RN and British and Empire armies, mention has already been made of the loss of the eighty up-to-date serviceable fighters and bombers of the RAF in Greece in April. That loss represented about half of the total serviceable modern fighters and bombers in the Middle East. Towards the end of April 1941 there were merely two or three squadrons of Hawker Hurricanes stationed in the Western Desert of which on any one day as few as thirteen aircraft might be serviceable. What was left of the Hurricanes (based on an airfield within the perimeter of Tobruk), had to be withdrawn, leaving the fortress of Tobruk deprived of immediately available fighter cover. By the end of May the number of fighter squadrons had been increased to five, still prospectively grossly outnumbered if the Luftwaffe were to mass in strength.

There were five Wellington bomber squadrons in the whole Middle East including one based on Malta. These aircraft were only of effective use at night. They were exaggeratedly claimed as scoring hits on enemy targets; both sides were by this time using decoys and dummy aircraft to blunt enemy attacks. Doubts about the aircrafts' serviceability were increased by their vulnerability to the heat and sand of the Western Desert. The relatively modern Bristol Blenheim type was also at risk in the presence of German fighters. There were a few squadrons of these available for the Western Desert, but it is noteworthy that Halder, a leading German general, believed on 6 May that the RAF was running short of aerial bombs in the Western Desert.[cxxviii]

Useful modern American warplanes included reconnaissance planes and several squadrons of Tomahawk fighters. The

Royal Australian Air Force first flew them in action over Syria after 8 June. The RAF was able to struggle for air supremacy over the Western Desert in May 1941, but had there been a German presence in strength, the odds against the RAF would have been too great.

Some figures of reinforcements *arriving* in the first half of 1941 in the Middle East - including Malta - for the RAF, also indicate its weakness. From January to March little additional strength came, though some Mark 2 Hurricanes replaced the Mark 1 type. A mere 13 came in March 1941 but by June the number arriving soared to over 200. Losses were nonetheless barely compensated for. From March to May, 58 Wellington bombers actually arrived along with 111 new Blenheim bombers in that same period. Until the summer, problems of maintenance and lack of spares were a constant source of concern, combined with the slowness of progress in establishing Takoradi as a transit base. Far more aircraft are recorded as sent than actually arrived and were serviceable, and it is hard to believe that Churchill was unaware of this.

Reinforcements of Hawker Hurricanes to Malta were flown direct at great risk from aircraft carriers in the Western Mediterranean, 35 in April and 47 in May. They only compensated for losses. To keep fighter squadrons operational in Malta was a top priority.[cxxix]

Takoradi on the Gold Coast (now Ghana) was only in its early stages as a valuable sea and air base. Vital reinforcements of aircraft could arrive there either crated on board merchantmen or flying from aircraft carriers. Then, assembled, they could fly four thousand miles to Egypt. If all this looked easy on paper, in practice it was a series of operations which needed far more organisation and resources than were at first anticipated, and in April there were still appalling delays and bottlenecks. The presence in crates of American warplanes, which had been shipped direct by the USA, caused assembly problems, as mechanics from Britain lacked the expertise and the tools. Many Tomahawk fighter aircraft were for months in need of improvements and spare parts so they might be fit for combat. The alternative supply route, round the Cape of Good Hope, was an intolerable distance.

It was feared that the RAF in the Middle East was going to be overwhelmed as had happened in Greece in April. In the event, the expected massive German offensives did not materialise except for the invasion of Crete , where the Luftwaffe enjoyed total air superiority. In support of the British entry into Syria of 8 June, only about sixty RAF aircraft took part and not all of these were modern warplanes.

The victory of the RN at the Battle of Cape Matapan on 28 March had been much celebrated, but the Luftwaffe had been absent! What became exceptionally frightening particularly from 6 April onwards was the menace of the Luftwaffe in the Eastern Mediterranean.[cxxx] Malta in the central Mediterranean was already suffering from German bombing raids, and as from January Alexandria and the Suez canal had been seriously mined from the air and ships bombed. From the outset of the German invasion of Greece, the lurch towards maritime disaster became pronounced. The air raid on the port of Athens, Piraeus, on the night of 6 April had caused immense destruction to the port, shipping and supplies. When ships of the RN went to the rescue of many of the Empire forces in Greece after mid-April, it was found too dangerous for them to be in range of German bombers in daylight. Navy losses were painful in the last week of April.[cxxxi]

By 20 May, when Crete was invaded, those losses continued during the last ten days of May around the island. The strength of the RN in the Mediterranean after the Battle for Crete was reduced by about two thirds, but by then the German invasion of the USSR was only days ahead.

The effective strength of General Wavell's armies in the Middle East, (which was greatly exaggerated by Churchill in his rhetoric of 27 April and 7 May), would have been inadequate to stem any substantial German offensives in the region. The losses in Greece were bad enough. Those in the Western Desert particularly in the first half of April were dispiriting and the strains on General Wavell's resources were too great to be endured easily, if at all. His defiant refusals initially to provide contingents for Iraq and later Syria, have already been mentioned. The main priority for defence was the Western frontier of Egypt, including the defence by 10 April of the isolated fortress of Tobruk, well behind enemy lines.

At the end of April the few defenders of Egypt against the Afrika Korps consisted of units not formally incorporated into divisions of infantry; the 22nd Guards Brigade, 2nd Rifle Brigade, and 1st Durham Light Infantry. The 11th Hussars and the Kings Dragoon Guards manned light tanks and armoured cars inferior to those of the Afrika Korps. There were a mere two squadrons of the Royal Tank Regiment with some thirty cruiser and heavy tanks including some captured Italian types. By mid-May, the number had arisen to about fifty. Some artillery was present, but the whole force amounted to little more than a screen were there to be heavy German attacks, which were expected soon. For the time being, the Afrika Korps and the British units were about equal in strength. However, the expectation in London and Cairo - and Washington – in late April, was that the Afrika Korps would soon be immensely reinforced. It was feared Tobruk could fall and its garrison be lost. Meanwhile, keeping Tobruk supplied by sea put a further strain on the RN.

In reserve and undergoing final training in the Nile Delta were more Australian infantrymen, the Polish Brigade (which was forbidden by the Polish government in exile to fight the Italians), the British 6th Division, described by the historian

Barrie Pitt as '*motley*', and during April the 'Desert Rats', and the 7th Armoured division, whose tanks were in the workshops for maintenance and repair. In due course, substantial reinforcements would come to Egypt both from Britain and from liberated East Africa, but all that arrived by mid-May was the Indian 4th Division from Eritrea. It had fought in the Western Desert in December. The tanks which came to Egypt on 12 May in OPERATION TIGER could not be ready for action until June. A hundred thousand depot troops in Egypt and elsewhere under General Wavell's command constituted the tail of the fighting machine. The presence of various units was very evident to casual observers in Cairo, but most of them were non-combatants.

These dreadful weaknesses of British and Empire forces were known to Churchill, and in the light of events, the normal reaction among the Government in early April 1941, was one of rising panic. The main source of information about the likely next moves of the Germans in the Middle East came from ENIGMA. The depressing tidings were heard amidst news of actual defeats and severe losses in the Balkans, the Western Desert, the Blitz, and the Battle of the Atlantic.

It is worthwhile looking at the almost day- by- day course of events as known to Churchill during the nearly one month commencing 6 April 1941, (the date of the German invasions of Yugoslavia and Greece). As early as 10 April, Admiral Cunningham, the C-in-C of the RN in the Mediterranean, warned Churchill about the vulnerability to Luftwaffe raids of the principal naval base of Alexandria and the lesser base of Haifa, if German aircraft were to use bases in Western Egypt and Syria. On 14 April, no doubt with this in mind, Churchill advised in writing the Chiefs of Staff that it looked as if '*superior armoured forces*' might be invading Egypt '*with consequences of the most serious character*'. On 18 April, he warned newspaper editors about the forthcoming evacuation of Greece.

That same day, ENIGMA indicated that German transport planes, (250 Ju 52s), were massing in Bulgaria with the implication that an airborne offensive was looming somewhere in the Eastern Mediterranean. On Sunday 20 April, when Churchill was at Ditchley Park for the week-end, fear reached its height. Rumour abounded regarding the possibility that the German General Staff were voicing doubts about the feasibility of invading the USSR, but a terrifying report from Wavell was received also. Wavell admitted that British tanks on the Egyptian-Libyan border were inferior in number and quality to German ones. His 'stop press' was even more disturbing. He understood that a whole new German Panzer division had landed at Tripoli earlier in April and could be in action in days. Such a division could include over four hundred tanks. He could have added they alone would outnumber British ones by nearly ten to one, assuming the report were true!^{cxxxii}

By 20 April the part suspension of Malta as an offensive base was another very serious anxiety. Not only was the Luftwaffe reducing its usefulness, but the immediate priority for the RN was to evacuate the Empire forces from Greece and. no longer attempt to sink enemy convoys on their way to Libya. Only submarines and a few other warships were left in Malta for that purpose. Moreover, Malta had to be kept supplied by sea and this grew ever harder to accomplish.

The meeting between representatives of MI and the Foreign Office on 22 April has been commented on. An anonymous typed note was attached to the tersely worded minute evidencing the mixed conclusion of this meeting, which reads *'If Germany can beat us, Russia is in the bag. Russia does not represent an obstacle to Germany in her battle with Great Britain. A pincer movement against Suez is the most likely course'*. ENIGMA information for late April / early May seemed to confirm this terrifying prospect.

On 23 April the Chiefs of Staff tended to the belief that poorly defended Cyprus was to be the target of an airborne assault.[cxxxiii] On 26 April the German codewords for OPERATION FLYING DUTCHMAN were deciphered and Crete seemed the most likely next victim, but Cyprus and Syria could not be excluded. From then onwards Crete was correctly surmised as soon to be invaded, but Wavell himself remained worried about Cyprus and Syria and even Iraq . On 2 May, feasibility studies showed that the possibility could not be excluded that Syria and Iraq would be entered by German airborne forces.[cxxxiv] The strength of these was wildly overestimated, but the Intelligence estimate of the number of German warplanes likely to be available to support an invasion of Crete, was more or less accurate. There were about 700 of which over 500 were serviceable, plus nearly 500 Ju 52s and 72 gliders.

At the end of April German propaganda envisaged that a German conquest of the Middle East was about to commence. The fact that this was a cover for Barbarossa could not as yet be intelligently be surmised at the top in London. On 29 April Berlin announced the appointment of General Von Epp as Minister for Colonial affairs in Africa. Two hundred or so men comprised the German Armistice Commission in French Morocco, a suspected vanguard for the Luftwaffe and Wehrmacht. There was speculation that Spain was soon to enter the war on the side of Germany. On 22 April the DAILY MAIL headline ran 'Hitler demands passage to attack Gibraltar', though the next day it reported 'Franco bars Nazi road to Gibraltar' . At this time, a distressed Hoare in Madrid was notifying the Foreign Office that the pro-Nazi Suner, the Spanish Foreign Minister, was expecting the German capture of Suez within a month - and then Spain would make war on Britain! Press reports suggested the presence of 2,000 German servicemen in plain clothes at Spanish airfields.

Cripps reported from Moscow on 2 May, that he had learned that German diplomats there were prophesying further

German successes in the Mediterranean and Middle East. On 4 May the only widely respected German newspaper *Frankfurter Zeitung* solemnly told its readers that Mosul, close to the oilfields of Iraq, was the next German objective. The warfare in Iraq was in the balance so this too made for frightening news.

The Germans were completing the seizure of the Greek islands in the Aegean Sea including those close to the Turkish coast. This raised a further spectre that German- controlled merchant shipping would sail down the Danube into the Black Sea, and then legally under international law through the Turkish Dardanelles into the Aegean, and thence to the Mediterranean and Atlantic.

In these desperate circumstances, the atmosphere in the War Cabinet, its Defence Committee and the Chiefs of Staff was glum between 20 April and 4 May. One personal record was kept by Cadogan, who attended either with Eden or alone, representing the Foreign Office. He formed the opinion that Churchill was out of his depth as he indulged in monologues at length in the early hours of the morning to the intense irritation of ministers, civil servants and servicemen in attendance who, (unlike Churchill), had to work normal hours the next day! Churchill seemed to be at his most maverick when discoursing on strategy amidst diminishing hopes the Middle East could be held. According to Cadogan, no one seemed to have the ability to challenge Churchill, and his diary recorded his own pessimism about the outcome for the Middle East. On 16 April he had envisaged the loss of Egypt as near. A typical entry, that of 2 May, reads '*Defence Committee. All news murky. Our (still) total inadequacy in material renders us powerless everywhere. All our staff are a handful of charming amateurs pitted against the best professionals in the World*'. By 4 May 'things' were looking - '*oddly*' - '*rather better*' but then there had been three weeks of gloom. Most of those who attended these top committee meetings were expecting Egypt to be lost before long. It seemed that the highly professional German generals would not fail to take advantage of the magnificent possibilities for further easy German victories.

The night of Sunday 27 April, after Churchill had spoken on the BBC with the intention of raising public morale, saw at the Chiefs of Staffs meeting perhaps his greatest ever outburst of rage. Major-General John Noble Kennedy opined that Egypt might not be successfully defended.[cxxxv] Whilst this was a reasonable enough supposition Churchill grew incandescent at this defeatism so at odds with what he had just broadcast. He viewed with distaste the military plans to install supply dumps along the banks of the Nile, as the generals envisaged resistance to a future German offensive South of the Nile Delta. Churchill insisted that this should be effected with the minimum disclosure of information. He feared the spread of the defeatist spirit and now used all his ability to combat it. His correspondence with the Chiefs of Staff during that period made it clear that he, on the face of it, remained assertive and confident. He left it in doubt to some extent whether Singapore was more crucial than Suez (he foresaw no probability of Japan entering the war), and he emphasised the primary importance of repelling any invasion of Britain and of preserving the Atlantic lifeline.

From 20 April the main source of Churchill's depression was the likely future situation in the Mediterranean and Middle East. Churchill would have calculated that if the worst happened he might be able to rely on public support, but with distinctly less assurance on a compliant House of Commons. Most informed people at the top were now envisaging the worst would happen in the Middle East. There was no signal of an actual conspiracy in favour of replacing Churchill as Prime Minister, but there were certainly initial rumblings. Churchill probably felt he could meet opposition from Hore-

Belisha and Lloyd George. As for press criticisms, Goebbels comments in his diary that these might show real signs of opposition but on the other hand they could just be a way of "letting off steam".[cxxxvi] Churchill would not have known of this quite astute appraisal , but must have accepted that some of the press would lend weight to adverse criticism.

Inside the Government, the formidable Lord Hankey appeared as a potential ringleader.[cxxxvii] In a later government reshuffle, he was to be moved sideways from his post as Chancellor of the Duchy of Lancaster to that of Paymaster-General, presumably to show him Churchill remained boss! Lord Hankey was distinguished for having been until his retirement at the age of 66 in 1938, one of 'the great and good' as a top civil servant. A quarter of a century previously he had played a leading role in the conduct of WW1 and he later was the author of the 'War Book' which was intended to provide the administration strategy for WW2 in its first stages. Ennobled pre-war, he entered Chamberlain's War Cabinet as a Minister without Portfolio. He and Churchill disliked each other. However, due to his exceptional experience and standing, he could not be dropped from the Coalition government and he chaired an important Committee with reference to supplies.

Hankey's diary, (not all that different from Cadogan's in its sounding of alarm bells), recorded his growing concern about the situation in the Middle East and Mediterranean, and in his daily opinion, everything was deteriorating until early May 1941. His entry of 22 April refers to Churchill as *'a dictator'*, the War Cabinet as *'ciphers'*, and the Chiefs of Staff as not standing up to him. Further he records that Dudley Pound the First Sea Lord was not asserting himself and Air Chief Marshal Portal as being more or less bemused! The entry for 23 April: a shortage of shells and tanks *'a very weak point'*, and an absence of spare parts for the RAF. He was perceptive as seeing Churchill *'like a chicken in front of a cobra before*

Beaverbrook'. By 28 April he viewed meetings of the war Cabinet as *'appalling'*. Churchill's long harangues and monologues were relieved by a *'very short'* statement from Eden. No one else spoke. Boredom and fatigue prevailed. The War Cabinet members were *'yes-men'*. Churchill was *'a very tired man'*. The lateness of meetings *'wore out'* the chiefs of Staff. Hankey remembered the disaster of Norway and now there was that of Greece to add to it. He saw the meeting of the Defence Committee of 30 April as even worse. He noted that if contingency preparations for abandoning Egypt and Palestine leaked out, *'our army would be demoralised'*. Already Hankey was aware of Menzies' discontent. Sir Edward Grigg MP, a junior minister at the War Office, told Hankey that the situation was *'very anxious'* and that Churchill was *'much too complacent'*.

On 1 May Kennedy told Hankey of his belief the war would be lost if supreme control were not "put right", that Ismay Churchill's own military adviser was *'bemused'* by Churchill, that Field-Marshal Sir John Dill agreed with Kennedy, and that he may have notified Hankey of Churchill's outburst of rage of 27 April (if Hankey were not then present).

Hankey himself wanted others to act first to put pressure on Churchill to mend his ways as he saw it, and found a similar limited enthusiasm among some of his colleagues in government and MPs, (none of them Labour). Lord Simon, the Lord Chancellor wanted to pass the buck to Menzies and typically suggested delay until after the important debate fixed for 6 and 7 May. Menzies did approach Churchill to advise him to stop being so dictatorial, to no effect. Churchill told him that those around him had no ideas of their own, so he was indeed surrounded by *'yes-men'*. Another interested person was the much respected Tory grandee, the Marquess of Salisbury, who according to Hankey agreed with him, and went on to offer his view that *'Germany had a clearly thought -out strategic plan'*, for the conquest of the Middle East, whereas Britain had '*no settled initiative, though an amazing manifestation of improvised resource*'. Perhaps the ministerial son of the Marquess leaked news of this discontent so that Churchill learned of Hankey as a potential trouble-maker. Perhaps Hankey indeed wanted such a leak as a first step. Clearly so much would turn on what might happen in the Middle East, and Hankey feared the worst. Lloyd George advised him that if Cairo fell, then Churchill would lose the confidence of the House of Commons and would lose the Premiership. Of course neither Lloyd George nor Hankey were aware of the prospect of Germany invading the USSR soon. This knowledge, at first only a growing surmise, became Churchill's trump card.

Linked with Hankey's remonstrations was the anger of the Australian premier Robert Menzies present in London in April and May. He complained that there had not been proper consultation before the best Australian division had been sent to Greece only to suffer a casualty rate of one-third killed, wounded and PoWS. At times Menzies could scarcely contain his anger, which was further fuelled on 30 April by a British refusal to give him sight of vital papers on the Greek campaign. The senior civil servant accompanying Menzies felt '*shocked*'. The information concealed would presumably have shown how militarily flawed the Greek campaign was from the outset. The next day, 1 May, Menzies exploded. He told a Press Conference in London that the War Cabinet was completely ignoring him. The Press was censored regarding this indiscretion, as any publicity would have been disastrous for morale.

Menzies' outburst of anger was partly motivated by his government's fragile majority in the Australian Parliament. The powerful Australian Labour Party, in favour of Australia as an ally of Britain in WW2, was in opposition to Menzies' coalition government of the Liberal and County Parties, largely because of its glaring failure to organise the domestic war economy.

Industrial discontent came from prices rising faster than wages. The trade unions backed the Labour Party. The fall of Menzies' government was simply a matter of time. John Curtin, the leader of the Australian Labour Party, said publicly on 28 April that the British Empire was "crumbling to pieces". Fadden (the acting PM in Menzies' absence) probably too readily admitted in public that the Empire forces were fighting only a rearguard action in Greece.

A further cause of discontent for Menzies was the refusal of Churchill to take seriously enough the Japanese threat of aggression in the Pacific, southwards towards Australia. If Churchill's "paper" recognition of the threat in his communications with the Chiefs of Staff was intended to placate Menzies, no new satisfactory defence measures for Malaya and Singapore followed.

Moreover, Menzies was one focus of discontent for some MPs and part of the press in Britain, who were demanding a different sort of War Cabinet. In their opinion it should become like that under Lloyd George in WW1, when its members had been free of departmental responsibilities. In the view of some it should be an Imperial Cabinet, perhaps led by the vigorous Menzies or the South African Premier General Smuts. The discussion, partly open, continued inconclusively, except that on 1 May in a government reshuffle, Beaverbrook left the Ministry of Aircraft Production and was appointed a Minister of State with largely undefined powers.[cxxxviii] Churchill, (although doubling as PM and Minister of Defence), Beaverbrook, Attlee as Lord Privy Seal, Anderson as Lord President of the Council, and Greenwood as a Minister without Portfolio were without departmental responsibilities. Churchill refused to make any other concession or advance in this field.

During the period from 20 April through to 6 May, when at last to Churchill's private satisfaction he could feel war between

Germany and the USSR was becoming more than a possibility, Churchill showed unusually severe fits of rage and depression. 2 May seems to have represented the greatest depth of his depression. This was Colville's judgement. Churchill and Colville had on that day been visiting Plymouth to raise morale in that then much - blitzed City. They saw gruesome scenes. That same evening at Chequers, Churchill received more bad news. The courteous but negative cable from Roosevelt in reply to Churchill's plea of 29 April for some immediate American intervention, featured. Churchill also learned that a merchant ship in the OPERATION TIGER convoy had engine trouble, that a destroyer at Malta had been sunk and blocked the entrance to the Grand harbour at Valetta, and that the Iraqi 'rebel' forces were fighting vigorously. In a late-night conversation Churchill, in the presence of Colville, Ismay and Harriman, envisaged Hitler dominating all mainland Europe, Asia and Africa. The USA and Britain would then perhaps have no option but to accept a compromise peace. There was apparently a limit, (perhaps self-imposed), to a more complete and depressing elaboration by him.

Churchill on that occasion and in that select company, gave his opinion that the present crisis in the Middle East was decisive. It would not he said, (with some element of contradiction), decide whether the war would be won or lost, but on how it would be resolved. Then, after this conversation - or more likely monologue - was over, Mrs. Churchill asked Colville (familiarly calling him 'Jock') whether he thought 'we' would win WW2. He had the presence of mind to give her his no doubt "gut" answer in the affirmative. This was when expert opinion in London held that Hitler would follow the basic doctrine of strategy: where there is an advantage over the enemy, exploit it to the full.

This dread about the vulnerability of the Middle East, so prominent in the minds of ruling circles in London, was partly conveyed by some of the press to its more discerning readers. A largely inarticulate sense that things were going badly wrong was becoming widespread. Editorial comments and articles and not news reports provided the medium. Some of the public felt that the news reports were conspicuously selective and losing their appeal. These continued to mislead readers by emphasising vividly - how well the Wehrmacht and Luftwaffe were being resisted wherever. It could appear to the public at least until May, as if a line would be held indefinitely in Southern Greece . Editorial comments were much more candid and in some instances were virtually telling readers not to believe the news reports-both the *Evening Standard* and the *Daily Mail* took that line at the time!

The *Evening Standard*, owned by Beaverbrook, was edited by Frank Owen, a sometime Liberal MP with an anti-fascist reputation and who was a friend of the former General Secretary of the CPGB, Harry Pollitt, (himself an almost open critic of the official Communist policy of "imperialist war"). Its punchy editorials told some of the truth about the growing crisis in the Middle East. The *Daily Mail* clearly with a link to No. 10, dared to tell much of the truth. The Odhams Press organ of the T.U.C, the *Daily Herald*, was also outspoken. These three newspapers presumably deliberately, gave away very little inkling of a hope of the USSR becoming an ally. So their editorial warnings of Germany's imminent triumph in the Middle East were stark. Their only answer to the onslaught of the German juggernaut was lame. Tank production in Britain ought to be rapidly increased and gaining air superiority should be another priority. Britain could hope for increasing American supplies and eventually for the USA becoming an ally. Naturally there could be no suggestion of an innate inferiority of British and Empire forces in the Middle East. This would have been impossibly demoralising for all and would also be in defiance of Churchill's solemn and repeated assertions to the contrary.

The *Evening Standard* had begun April 1941 with a sense of euphoria and on the 5th had pontificated '*We need hardly fear a full-scale attack on Egypt*'. Ten days later and Frank Owen, probably with encouragement from the young Michael Foot-had second thoughts. The tone became by the 15th : '*Now the blows have fallen with pitiless fury HARD DAYS*' and Owen signed an article entitled 'WAKE UP OR PERISH'. The misleadingly cheerful propaganda which had emanated from GHQ Cairo was described as the work of '*buffoons*'. Two days later, readers were told the Germans were aiming for Mosul and after that Suez. The *Daily Mail* was as explicit in its own way. On the 14th its editorial warned of '*grim news*' to come and three days later, declared '*The loss of Alexandria our chief Mediterranean naval base, and the Suez canal would be a disaster of the first magnitude*'. To its surprise the paper found itself congratulating the *Daily Herald*. The latter had castigated the *Sunday Times* for complacently describing Germany as thrashing around like '*a harpooned whale*'(copyright The Times/Sunday Times 12th April 1941/ nisyndication.com). The *Daily Herald* had initially shared in the mood of false optimism, but by mid-April was sounding alarm bells. On 20th April The *Observer* expressed deep anxiety about the Middle East. The Editor J.L. Garvin's signed leading article had headlines 'THE CRUX OF THE WAR / A GREAT AWAKENING / GREECE AND EGYPT / BRITAIN AT BAY'. It was '*a question of life and death for the British Empire to hold Egypt and the Canal*'. Not until the last week of April did *The Times* take so strong and definitive a view.

Also relevant are press commentaries of that desperate week beginning 20 April. The *New Statesman* of 26 April, concluded '*We are deep already in a crisis greater than anything we have experienced since last June*'. On the 24th the WW1 aphorism of Lloyd George '*too feeble and too late*' was quoted by the *Daily Mail*. On the 23rd , Churchill spoke to shipyard workers at Sunderland of the need for a '*superhuman*' effort. Churchill added that it filled him with humility and with hope and prayer, that he would be worthy of the trust reposed in him. However this oratorical sentiment of his may be construed, the profundity of his then emotion at a time of deepest crisis, is apparent. It would have been entirely out of character for him to have remained passive in the face of such risk.

The Blitz and, abroad, the destruction of much of Belgrade, reinforced the general feeling that the evil of Hitlerism had to be overcome. On 2 April *The Times* had devoted its first leader to a condemnation of German treachery, and this would tend to justify in the mind of an attentive reader any step which could lead to the downfall of Nazi Germany, however unscrupulous.

Dennis Wheatley wrote later that he believed *'God intervened'* to prevent the Middle East from being conquered by the Germans. The then Queen thought the Middle East should be saved with *'any risk..... well worth taking'*. Her perceptive comment may have received too restricted an interpretation i.e. OPERATION TIGER was the right step to take.[cxxxix] Churchill himself commented on 13 April that it was *'unthinkable that we should sit idle and allow a terrible misfortune to overtake us without having taken serious risks to avert it'*. As we shall see, Churchill's armoury of diplomatic deceit was far from exhausted, however grave the military situation

CHAPTER 8

The Frog in the Cream

The reader of over sixty years later may gain the impression that Churchill took no initiative of any real value to stem the horrifying prospect of an imminent German conquest of the Middle East. It could appear that he trusted to luck, looked fruitlessly to Roosevelt to help, or succumbed to the mere hunch that Hitler would order the invasion of the USSR thus saving the Middle East for the British Empire. However this perception is implausible having regard to his ruthless personality and his great knowledge of and flair for, diplomatic and military trickery. It is not trite to mention that Churchill told the Swedish ambassador to Britain how he felt like "the frog which fell into a bowl of cream and by its exertions churned the liquid into butter on which to find a foothold so it unexpectedly did not drown". The story was repeated by the Swede to Soviet Ambassador Maisky who would not have been slow to tell others.[cxl]

In the abstract, the perceived key to overcoming the Middle East crisis of April 1941 must have been to "trick" Hitler into an invasion of the USSR. Only in this way could the Middle East be saved from an imminent German conquest. For Churchill, with his ruthless determination and guile, the crisis must have appeared insoluble in any other way. Circumstantial evidence is weighty. Direct evidence is limited, yet there is one highly significant observation in writing. It appears in the weekly bulletin of the Foreign Office entitled *Political Intelligence Summaries No. 82* of 30 April, 1941. The bulletin, each issue denoted SECRET, had a circulation of around 500. In the regular section, 'GERMANY', the author (possibly the authoritative Ivone Kirkpatrick), of the article understandably comments on the possibility of Germany invading the USSR. He considers that neither an economic nor an ideological motivation carries any weight. What he envisaged as possible, is that Hitler was possessed by a *'madman's dream'* that such an invasion would bring an easily accomplished peace between Germany and Britain, as the British governing class came to heel. Understandably there was nothing to indicate how Hitler may have been made open to persuasion by anything already done at the instance of the British Intelligence services.

The author's view that Germany would not benefit economically by invading the USSR would have been difficult to refute. As regards ideology, the author, if Kirkpatrick, could plausibly have identified many Germans as Communists manqué who would be disgusted by such an invasion. The fact that he overlooks the extreme anti-Communism and anti-Sovietism of *Mein Kampf*, may be explained by a belief that the Nazi-Soviet pact of 1939 had bonded the two totalitarian powers together in the minds of many Germans. The author of these sections also assesses much of the Roman Catholic Church in Germany as opposed to Nazism, another characteristic stance of Kirkpatrick.

Leonard Ingrams, a liaison officer with MEW, remarks on 10 May, 'We should encourage the Germans to attack Russia by misleading Hitler and hinting that large sections both in Britain and the US who preferred to see the overthrow of the German regime might be prepared to force through a compromise peace'.[cxli] Beaverbrook muses 'Hitler cannot stand opposition. Our hopes rest upon inciting him to lunatic actions. He must see the insults offered his supermen by barefoot peasants'. Beaverbook also comments on the need for British morale to be maintained and for President Roosevelt to be re-elected.[cxlii]

Some public revelation is in the News Chronicle. On 22 April during the week when the Middle East crisis is peaking, its well-informed trusted and veteran anti-fascist columnist A.J.Cummings in his regular Spotlight feature suggests that the key to victory may be Britain 'outwitting' Germany. After the invasion of the USSR, the same newspaper opines that Hitler will have been substantially motivated by his belief that Britain and the USA would be aligning with Germany against the USSR. The well-informed though arch-Stalinist editor, Palme Dutt, comments in the August 1941 Labour Monthly that perhaps Hitler fell into a trap in invading the USSR. It appears from a study of the text he was aware, at least by then, of the Foreign Office official's conjecture of a 'madman's dream'.

Before 20 April, having regard to the dispatch of that day to Cripps in Moscow, Churchill's wish that the USSR should be at war with Germany could seem only pious. Hitler could not be reckoned such a fool as to take that road to hell. He had publicly disowned a prospect of a German-Soviet war both in October 1939 and July 1940. Nonetheless it seems that what could be done by way of a stratagem was formulated.

The early April warning to Stalin from Churchill that the Wehrmacht was beginning to mass against the Western frontiers of the USSR, must have been designed to increase tension between Germany and the USSR. Churchill would have hoped that an acceleration of Soviet war preparations might spark a German war on Russia. However Stalin refused to play along, though his reacting as Churchill intended would have been in his interests. An earlier complement was the giving to Hitler a reassurance that the USSR was "easy meat" for conquest. The risk that this argument might be transparent, had to be run. Beaverbrook's *Daily Express* was chosen as the medium and claimed to be informing its readers of historical truth. On 6 March an article appeared signed by Dr. Hermann Rauschning, headlined *'Russia is Hitler's plum'*. The author, a sometime close colleague of Hitler's and an author of at least two exposes of Nazism, is nicely described as *'the man who knows'* Hitler's mind. The article suggests that a German invasion of the USSR would result in a German victory. This article must have been calculated to receive attention from German Intelligence.

The disparaging references to Soviet military strength which appeared in the British press in May and June may be the better understood in the light of this intention to trick Hitler into seeing the USSR as easily defeated. However, such were the many sincere convictions of the military experts and journalists concerned. A JIC report of nearly mid-June was remarkably silly unless it too was intended to be drawn to the attention of Hitler. This would have been easily accomplished by its being leaked to Nazi or double agents in London using the cloak of diplomatic immunity in the Japanese and Spanish embassies.

The knowledge contained in the Foreign Office dispatch to Cripps in Moscow of 20 April put the whole business of deceiving Hitler into a new and encouraging perspective. If Hitler could be persuaded that Britain and the USA would effectively side with Germany, if and when Germany invaded the USSR, here was a practical argument which Hitler could be calculated as welcome to convert his presumed dissenting generals. Previously there had been no more than a bare supposition that Hitler and his generals were at loggerheads. Churchill had merely his hunch that a German war against the USSR was intended. Now there was an opportunity for an authoritative and definitive message from Britain to achieve the seemingly impossible – to bend Hitler's will so he would order a German invasion of the USSR. This would save the Middle East, but it was obviously vital to act fast.

Some foundations already existed for the necessary and unique communication to Hitler. It was recognised that Nazi ideology included a belief that many British and American conservatives would prefer a 'decent' Nazism to Communism, if there had to be a choice between them. There could appear to be this choice in the event of a German invasion of the USSR. Consideration of an authoritative statement of British foreign policy, disregarding Churchill and Eden for this purpose, could exploit the balance between dislike of German hegemony of Europe and a loathing of Soviet penetration of Europe west of the original Western frontiers of the USSR. The war against Finland had aroused deep anti-Soviet passions in Britain and the USA. The source of this crisp evaluation was Lord Lloyd's booklet, *The British Case*, first published in December 1939 and never formally repudiated. Lord Halifax, the Foreign Secretary who served first Chamberlain and then Churchill, had written the introduction. Pre-war contacts with important pro-appeasement politicians and businessmen, including Lord Halifax, the now deceased Chamberlain, Lloyd George and the pacifist Socialist George Lansbury, had convinced some Nazis that in British politics there was a broad preference for a 'decent' Nazism if the alternative were Communism. It could seem to be of secondary importance that Hitler himself was vehemently disliked in Britain.

As viewed from London, an assessment by Hitler of a British willingness to negotiate a peace with Britain on Nazi terms had to be based partly on the Nazi illusion that the Blitz and blockade of Britain were conditioning realists in Britain to see the pointlessness of WW2.

From the outbreak of war in September 1939 and climaxing in the summer of 1940 there had been talks about peace talks between German and British diplomats and intermediaries in Sweden, Switzerland, Spain and Portugal in which Hitler had placed some hope – only for this hope to be dashed. On the British side these 'talks about talks' had arguably served the purpose of dissuading Hitler from ordering an immediate invasion of Britain. Simultaneously, to maintain British morale,

Churchill apparently sharply disowned them. In April 1941 there were talks about peace talks again. On the face of it, Germany was again threatening an invasion of Britain. Again such talks could suggest the presence of a powerful, if latent, peace movement in Britain perhaps ready and willing to take over government and negotiate an end to WW2.

The clandestine diplomacy of the last week of April should be noted. On 25 April the Duke of Hamilton declined a personal invitation from British Intelligence to volunteer to meet a German contact, - probably his German friend Albrecht Haushofer - in Lisbon. This German, a patriot but one who detested Hitler and his Nazi ways, faithfully served the German war machine as a Foreign Office official. He was a good friend of Hess, a fact obviously known by the Duke of Hamilton. Hamilton explained his reluctance to volunteer for the proposed mission due to the risk of being branded a traitor. He was himself a Wing Commander in the RAF at the time. He was being asked basically to pose as someone of importance in Britain, deemed close to the King himself as the foremost Scottish nobleman, willing to discuss peace terms with a German agent. The refusal of the Duke led to another choice of a British agent for a discussion which took place on 28 April at Geneva.

At this meeting at Geneva, Haushofer and Burckhardt were present. Burckhardt was a Swiss citizen and Vice-President of the International Red Cross. It was a second-best endeavour at giving an impression to Hitler that there was a British peace movement struggling clandestinely for ascendancy. There was certainly talk about peace negotiations. According to one informal report by Haushofer, the outcome of the talk was a prospect that a 'very important person' in the City of London would be on his way in the near future. Haushofer claimed to be satisfied, and may genuinely have believed that at last there was a chance of peace. Yet that may soon have turned to scepticism as it is on record that he firmly recognised the dominant influence of Churchill and his defiance of Hitler.

As the Geneva talk was inconclusive, it is hard to believe news of it for Hitler would have been any more than a tentative arousal of expectation. Its import has to be ranked with open news reports in the British press of around the same time.

Almost certainly the British Intelligence services tried to mislead Hitler by depicting various important people in Britain as foremost in this imaginary peace movement. These included the Duke of Hamilton. Just as Churchill recognised, as he believed, a tension between Hitler and his generals which he intended to be resolved in favour of Hitler, so he could see the advantage of suggesting a tension between himself as Prime Minister and a British peace movement. This would be a myth for Hitler's consumption, but something had to appear in the British press and in the realm of gossip, and there had to be something of a public presence to add more credibility to the pretence.

Even a few days before 20 April there was a strong indication that it would be taken at its face value by the German leadership, that Churchill was nearing the brink. On 16 April the Conservative tabloid the *Daily Sketch* (owned like the *Sunday Times* by Lord Kemsley) suggested that Parliament in Britain should be replaced by a Council of State, with its members 'dredged' from the cream of ability in the nation. A dictator would give leadership in name if not in fact. Conspicuously he remained unnamed until 18 April when Churchill was nominated. The *Daily Sketch* implied that the war was going badly for Britain. The fact that the *Daily Herald* delivered a few days later a strong attack on the *Daily Sketch* for this article gave some appearance of there being a peace movement in Britain which was gaining ground though not yet ready to become open.

The influence of *The Times,* presumed to be the organ of government or the ruling class, is clearly the most significant in this field. One climactic instance was on 28 April with a photograph of the Duke of Hamilton, showing him addressing RAF cadets who had just arrived in Britain from training in Canada. He was reported in the caption as referring to *'whatever might happen in the war'*(copyright The Times/Sunday Times 28th April 1941/nisyndication.com), arguably implying some turning point for Britain. In April and May, *The Times* gave significantly obsequious and fulsome coverage to the celebrations in fascist Portugal of a historic anniversary there. A delegation of academics from Oxford University was present. According to *The Times,* they found an almost ideal society. At a mass rally thousands of youths wore bright headscarves and sang patriotic songs. Of the more than fifty per cent illiteracy rate nothing was said. In the light of THE BRITISH CASE previously cited, there was a hint of a corporate Europe under Nazi domination as acceptable to ruling circles in Britain.

On 25 April, *The Times* commented that in relation to France *'Hitler has succeeded in respecting the case for collaboration'*! General Franco was praised as having *'a cool head'*(copyright The Times/Sunday Times/nisyndication.com). Some days later there was a lavish tribute to Strafford, a ruthless authoritarian administrator who in the 17th Century served the monarch Charles I and was later executed by sentence of Parliament. As a small but noteworthy further sign of this imagined shift towards totalitarianism, on 27 April the astrologer Naylor in the *Sunday Express* solemnly recommended a fanatical adherence to religion and patriotism with a disparagement of mere intellectual belief.

On 24 April, *The Times* published a plea in a letter from George Bernard Shaw and Prof. Gilbert Murray for aerial bombing of cities to cease. This letter could be interpreted as an indication both of the harm being done to British cities in the then ongoing blitz, and a defeatist attitude. Hopes were constantly being raised by the press in Britain of very heavy bombing of Germany in the not too distant future as a component of the road to victory.

Peace rumours circulated among top journalists who could be expected to make something of them for public consumption. At the least they could come to the ears of 'neutral' diplomats in London through the medium of the top night clubs, hotels, bars and restaurants which continued to function for the well to do.[cxliii] Charles Graves, in his diary, refers to Eric Baume and some of his staff as a source of these rumours from the first half of April onwards.[cxliv] Baume was a journalist for the political weekly *Truth*, which was virtually under Government control. A leading Conservative official held a quarter of the shares issued by its controlling Company. Anti-Semitism attracted many of its subscribers and it would have been useful for the Government to know their identity, many of them likely to be sympathetic towards Germany. The gist of these peace rumours was that Hitler would be prepared to recognise the continuation of the British Empire and perhaps British maritime supremacy provided the Nazi hegemony of the continent of Europe was recognised by Britain. Graves himself felt that Hitler could not be trusted, and this for him was a stumbling block. He conjectured vaguely that Hitler, Ribbentrop and Himmler might be replaced by acceptable Germans. Goering and some of the generals might be a good choice.

Another arguable sign of the British will to wage war being sapped was the 14 April announcement that Atlantic shipping losses would be given monthly and not as hitherto weekly. The *Daily Mail* later complained that this new deficit of information would reduce American confidence in Britain's continuing its defiance of Germany.[cxlv]

There were also anti-Communist steps taken, whose importance was easily capable of exaggeration. On 21 April the Labour Party Minister of Home Security, Herbert Morrison, well-known for his severe hostility to the CPGB, refused to meet a delegation from the former *Daily Worker* which sought the lifting of its three month old ban. On 1 May a decision took effect to ban the Communist Party daily newspaper of British occupied Iceland. Its editors were deported. If they did go to German occupied Denmark they would have found a situation where Nazi cunning had left the Communist daily paper untouched, and indeed on May Day there had been a big Communist rally openly held in Copenhagen. A handful of former full-time officials of the CPGB were about to be demobilised from the armed forces in Britain for political reasons.[cxlvi] In Australia, the Communist Party had been banned in 1939.

As a further arguable sign of a sea change, on 30 April came an announcement in the House of Lords by Viscount Cranborne that the commandants of camps for British PoWs in Germany were decent people and were not like young Nazi fanatics. Then there was the pointed governmental statement that the daughter of Lord Redesdale, Unity Mitford, reputed to have been Hitler's lover, was not intended to be interned. The Cliveden set was also publicly vindicated when a Labour MP apologised to them for his allegation of an absence of patriotism in their use of garden land.

The week beginning Sunday 20 April was to be vital for the success of the planned deception. It was highly probable that Hitler and his generals were aware that a late start for a German invasion of the USSR would be disastrous because of the Russian winter making campaigning after about mid-October extremely difficult. Napoleon's defeat of 1812 was presumed to be imprinted on any German strategist's memory. So a German war against the USSR had to be commenced in June, if not earlier. The sooner a deceptive and secret communication went to Hitler the better. Delivery on 28 April could be deemed to be safe. *The Times'* first editorial on 21 April reads *'The immediate future will be bad and full of peril. Our task is to bridge it and to reach that more distant future which holds the sure hope of victory'*(copyright The Times/Sunday Times/nisyndication.com). One must understand that this forecast and advice could have been interpreted by the Germans as a signal for Britons ready to do a deal with Hitler, however absurd this interpretation might appear for the vast majority of its readers.

CHAPTER 9

A Royal Flourish?

Flourish : a term conjurors and poker players use when they reveal or play certain cards, preselected with misleading intent.....

If Hitler were to be convinced that Britain would basically side with Germany if and when Germany invaded the USSR, then any message to him would have to be from the highest authority.

The King himself.

King George VI had in theory the constitutional power to dismiss Churchill as Prime Minister and appoint his successor. The unwritten constitution of Britain in relation to the royal prerogative had often led to disagreements about the so-called conventions of the constitution, but the topic was for legal reasoning. The point is that in April 1941,Churchill believed that he could trick Hitler into believing that Britain was ready to make peace, if necessary by means of a personal letter from the King. It was entirely reasonable to believe Hitler's wishful thinking might be strongly corroborated as a result of such a letter. The letter would in effect be a "Royal Flourish", with Churchill as the poker player behind it. Such a gesture would be born equally from Churchill's iron will to defeat Hitler and the desperate straits that Churchill's country found itself in.

The notion of Hitler's megalomania was seriously canvassed in Britain, partly in public. Outstanding were Rauschning's two books, and a work of fiction of Douglas Brown's and Christopher Serpell's first published in August 1940 under the punning title *Loss of Eden*. Due perhaps to a complaint from Anthony Eden, the title was changed in the Spring of 1941 to *If Hitler Comes*. This short futuristic novel still impresses as a story, but for us what tells is its line that a pro-appeasement government in Britain in the near future accepts peace on 'generous' Nazi terms. After not many months there is a 'peaceful' German occupation of Britain. As a result of Nazi fanaticism, democracy and the British way of life are destroyed. The royal family has already escaped to Canada, but unnamed upper-class collaborators act and resistance is crushed. The Nazis respect what they take to be the Aryan essence of British civilisation in what becomes their new brutally-ruled colony. In reality at the least, Hitler envisaged Germany and Britain becoming allies in a new German - dominated World. Kirkpatrick for one, must have known of Hitler's admiration for British rule in India .

At least two MPs contributed to Churchill's myth of a gathering peace movement in Britain, albeit unwittingly. On 22 April, Hore-Belisha was entertained at lunch at 10 Downing Street. A press photographer was outside as he arrived. It was the conspicuous presence of this guest at No. 10 which mattered. It is possible that Hore-Belisha, Jewish and deeply unpopular with many Conservatives, a victim of a hate campaign in *Truth* some fifteen months earlier, and thought to be engaging in homosexual and therefore criminal practices, was a last desperate throw by Churchill for support in face of pressure for peace talks. Whether this was the interpretation put on the event by any Nazis who would learn of it, remains unknown, but the attempt to persuade them of this nonsense would have been worthwhile.[cxlvii] Also the choice of the pacifist John MacGovern, one of the few Independent Labour Party members in the House of Commons, to speak in the Confidence debate of 6 and 7 May was possibly a ploy intended to convey the impression that many of the working class would accept Anglo-German peace talks if presented as a fait accompli.

One high point of this myth-making was Churchill's calculated abuse of Lloyd George, who had made a forceful but hardly unreasonable contribution in the same debate. Churchill in his closing speech on behalf of the government, compared Lloyd George with Marshal Petain, another hero of WW1, with the unwarranted implication that Lloyd George was already plotting behind the scenes just as Petain had done before the fall of France. Hansard reported this outburst in full. This gross defamation of character would have been duly noted by one or more 'neutral' foreign diplomats present, and indirectly communicated to Berlin. Hansard would have been available to the German embassy in Dublin a day or two later, and doubtless also in Lisbon and Madrid.

Knowledge of the psychology of Hitler and Nazism was supplemented for the few in the know by the interrogations of German PoWs. Many were keen for the most part to display their ideological and patriotic fervour, which, as they saw it, was not giving away secret information.[cxlviii] Anti-fascist German and Austrian refugees in Britain could also disclose much of value.[cxlix] Hitler's speeches were carefully studied (and indeed had been throughout the war). Ivone Kirkpatrick could reasonably have concluded that Hitler was ripe to be tricked if a 'big lie' were told.

Because of the meagre substance of the disinformation as to the existence of an influential "peace lobby" among the British political and aristocratic elite, it is abundantly clear that it would have been foolhardy for British Intelligence to have relied on this solely.[cl] It would have been logical and imperative for there to be in addition a "big lie" so as to be reasonably sure of bending Hitler's will so Hitler would be able to convince his generals of the wisdom of a German invasion of the USSR within a few weeks. The Middle East would then be saved from what was *perceived* in London as imminent German conquest.

King George VI would be Churchill's 'Royal Flourish'. The monarch was neither an intellectual nor aesthete.[cli] His becoming king nearly four and a half years earlier had been an unexpected and unwelcome development for him, and only his sense of duty and the support of his wife Queen Elizabeth (later the Queen Mother) can have made it tolerable to him. His pleasure in life came mainly from shooting grouse. That he loved his wife and two daughters was no doubt the case, but his social limitations were characterised by his stammer and shyness. His relationship with his three brothers was a mixed one. With the former King, the Duke of Windsor, he had no contact. He shared with the Duke of Gloucester a liking for physical practical jokes. The youngest of the four sons of George V, the Duke of Kent, unquestionably had a bright intellect as well as a charming manner and might have been identified by the Nazis as a genuine friend of theirs. King George VI clearly had some admiration for the Nazi revival of Germany as an advanced industrial nation with unemployment eliminated and with national pride pre-eminent, hatred of Communism, and a belief in the superiority of the white race. In fact, it cannot sensibly be doubted that whatever the strength of his admiration, his sense of duty to the British Empire fortified by his Coronation oath always remained paramount. His relationship with Churchill became firm after the first four or five months of the latter's premiership. The King had initially much preferred Chamberlain to Churchill, but perhaps the influence of the Queen latterly inclined him to view Churchill in a favourable light.

The day bombing of Buckingham Palace by a skilfully navigated German plane on 13 September 1940 was much more likely to have been intended to persuade the King and

Queen to abandon London, than to have been an assassination attempt. Six small bombs fell. One landed by coincidence some 80 yards from the King, who was shaken but not hurt by the explosion. Some damage was caused to the Palace. The King was not a coward. He had had some experience of bombardment as a naval officer at the Battle of Jutland when in his twenties. The effect of this German "sneak" bombing was probably the opposite of what Hitler wanted. The King's determination to remain in London was now strengthened and the publicity given the incident increased his and the Queen's popularity. It was unpublicised that at night they lodged at Windsor Castle. The King and Queen visited the East End and other blitzed areas and were welcomed by the dazed survivors. The King wrote to Churchill in his own handwriting a personal, modest and touching letter about the bombing of the Palace.

If Hitler had once had great hopes of the Duke of Windsor, these had evaporated by the Spring of 1941, even though the Duke's virtual defeatism was evident in the March number of the American magazine *Liberty*. It should any event be recalled that whatever sympathy the Duke of Windsor had for Nazi Germany, he was always under the control of minders whose patriotism and loyalty to the British Empire were unshakeable. Insofar as the Duke and Duchess of Windsor appeared to the Nazis to be virtual Nazi "fellow travellers", (their consistent pro-Hitler stance confirmed throughout the war by recently-released wartime FBI reports), it surely did not require a great leap of the imagination by Nazi leaders to envisage the Duke's brother as at the least, entertaining gnawing private misgivings over his Prime Minister's obduracy in prosecuting the war.

Of course, the King could not have relished being asked by Churchill to introduce himself to Hitler as a traitor. Yet there is every reason to believe that despite personal objections he would have fulfilled his patriotic duty. Much of the press during the crucial week beginning Sunday 20 April would in several ways have fortified the unusual resolution needed. The King was not a newcomer to the practice of political letter-writing. With the substantial aid of his private secretaries, he had written political letters of significance on previous occasions to heads of foreign states. In September 1938 the King had wished to write a personal and amicable letter to Hitler but was dissuaded by Lord Halifax the Foreign Secretary. He had wished to do the same a few days before the outbreak of war and again he had similarly been dissuaded. The risk of the monarch taking a line conflicting with that of the government by too eagerly seeking appeasement of Germany had to be avoided. As the war began, the King considered Hitler 'a villain' and 'a madman' and Stalin 'an ogre'.

During WW2, the King's correspondence with foreign heads of state increased. He wrote to his cousin King George II of Greece when the Italian invasion gave an opportunity for full Anglo-Greek co-operation. He tried unsuccessfully to dissuade his cousin Prince Paul the Regent of Yugoslavia, from aligning his country with Germany. He also wrote for political reasons to the Kings of Norway and Sweden and the Queen of the Netherlands. At one critical time the King wished to write to the Emperor of Japan in the racist belief that 'Orientals' would best understand a personal approach.[clii]

The King's motivation to do his duty however unpleasant, would have been fortified further by the news of the massacre of some 17,000 citizens of Belgrade by the Luftwaffe on 6 April, by the continuing blitz on British cities including the very heavy raids on London on the nights of 16 and 19 April, and by the highest ever shipping losses in the Battle of the Atlantic and in the Mediterranean. The influence of Wheatley's writings has been mentioned already. And, having met "Grey Owl" for one, the King was certainly no stranger to plausible tricksters.

The world - famous "Grey Owl" had been a hoaxer for decades. At Buckingham Palace on a December afternoon in 1937 the King, the Queen and the two young princesses were his audience. They were entranced for some two hours by the "Red Indian Chief from Canada", in reality an Englishman born in Hastings! He had hoodwinked millions by his simple and perhaps admirable "Back to Nature" philosophy. A few months later when about to be exposed as a fraud, he died. It is hard to imagine the royal family not accepting the prank with good grace. Had not "Grey Owl" behaved like the Court jesters of old? The incident may have assisted the King's predisposition to assist in a deception for patriotic purposes.

Another figure inclined to the exercise of duplicity to help his country was Dennis Wheatley (1897–1977). The role of this prolific best-selling novelist, probably inspired by the novels of John Buchan and others of that Empire-building class, has hitherto been insufficiently explored, albeit that other historians have certainly touched upon his involvement. Primarily and crucially, Wheatley saw the need to obtain advantage in war by "getting into the mind" of the enemy. Wheatley, in the summer of 1940, became an active member of Churchill's private Intelligence Committee, as presided over by Churchill's friend, Desmond Morton. In the next year or so he was to be the author of twenty papers on how the war might best be waged. Significantly King George VI was one person fascinated by these submissions. In the summer of 1941, Wheatley was given the rank of Pilot Officer.

Wheatley was a longstanding admirer of Churchill and personally had almost fascist credentials. He believed the British Empire compared with the Roman Empire for its power and civilised standards, tolerance and emphasis on justice. Though not anti-semitic, some other racist theories attracted him. His distrust of Nazism, though, was confirmed when Hitler, within six months, flagrantly broke his word as given to

Chamberlain at Munich. Wheatley favoured Mussolini until Italy entered the war, and he thoroughly endorsed Franco's regime in Spain. He wanted hundreds of Communists in Britain - *'agitators'* -imprisoned.

One of Wheatley's early novels displays sadism directed against Communism. *Black August* (1934) glamorises the hero, a British Intelligence agent, killing a Communist. At the end of this futuristic novel, 'Greyshirts' acclaim the heir to the throne (his identity unspecified) outside Selfridge's in London's West End (about to undergo renovation after it has been ransacked and looted by Communist-led mobs). In a novel of 1936, the typically upper-class hero and heroine side with the Italian invaders of Ethiopia allegedly bringing civilisation there. The next year *Red Eagle* appeared. This was an unauthorised biography of the then Soviet Minister of Defence, Marshal Voroshilov. This loyal follower of Stalin, a brave soldier in the Civil War and a *'fanatical'* Communist in his youth ought, Wheatley implies, to replace Stalin as leader of the USSR. If peace were to last, he foresees a prosperous USSR twenty years on, with nationalism replacing Communism. Years later, Wheatley disingenuously commented that he did not remember why he had written this book. Despite its odd political analysis, the book amounted to an argument likely to persuade some readers that the USSR could become a useful ally for Britain and France against a Germany threatening European security.

More significant still was *Faked Passports,* published in May 1940. Covering the period of the 'phoney war' from November 1939 to March 1940, the novel centred on the Soviet war on Finland. The personalities are standard for Wheatley: the hero as in *Black August* now accompanied by a beautiful young German woman, aristocratic and fervently anti-Nazi. The full supporting cast is also fantasised. The story line would at first sight have appeared anti-Russian with the Finns in the right, the Russians stupid, and the Nazis either sadistic brutes or aristocrats generally in a resigned state of mind. However, there are two curious and largely ignored sub-texts. The first is quite an astute political analysis of WW2 considering the phoney war was ongoing at the time of printing. The second is an emphasis on the bravery and enterprise of a few Russian soldiers, who save the hero's life at the risk of their own. Voroshilov is again praised. The reader must have been intended to conclude that despite everything, a nationalist USSR as an ally of Britain and France would be desirable.

By the time *Faked Passports* was published, Wheatley had formed the opinion that the basic Soviet motive for the expansion of the USSR West of its pre-war borders was for further protection against the risk of German aggression. The territories so acquired he nicknamed '*Voroshilov's chastity belt*'.

Following the terrifying catastrophe of the fall of France, Wheatley used his lively imagination to formulate schemes to outwit Hitler. Some of his ideas were as maverick as some of Churchill's, but even these displayed spirit. Offering Jews a National home in Madagascar was not viable. His proposal for a Jewish army would have met with much Jewish approval, if the British government had not rejected the mere suggestion. However, his idea of the building of a huge raft to be towed across the Atlantic carrying supplies was too absurd for the Admiralty to consider.

One of Wheatley's twenty papers, *This Winter*, he later claimed to be totally missing, both the original and all copies. There are grounds to suspect that it recommends that Hitler should be tricked into believing that a German invasion of the USSR would cause Britain to side with Germany. Such a ruse would come naturally to Wheatley's mind, following the plot of *Faked Passports*, where a long detailed letter from Marshal Goering is sent clandestinely to the Finnish leader Marshal Mannerheim to convince him that the Soviet colossus has feet of clay. This letter is intended to persuade the Finns to refuse the Soviet demands for a better security for Leningrad and so face war with the USSR.

In his novel *V for Vengeance,* written soon after the invasion of the USSR, Wheatley sails nearer to the wind. He relates a scenario in which the British secret service misleads Hitler into a belief that Stalin is about to order an uprising of the workers of Europe against Nazi rule; this ruse prompts Hitler to order the invasion of the USSR. Wheatley discloses by implication that this was deemed necessary to save the British Empire in the Middle East from German conquest, as he knew of this peril. He must have known something of Churchill's own views and shared them.

Little wonder if his assertion that there was a plan to bring the USSR into the war as an ally caused his employers to sack him peremptorily.

Wheatley's published papers of 1959, *Stranger than Fiction,* and his autobiography provide further proof of his confidence, well prior to June 1941, that the USSR would make a splendid ally of Britain. He sees Stalin as a thug but not an imperialist. He wants an Anglo-Soviet alliance straightaway, e.g. a Red fleet to be based in Singapore. Regarding a German invasion of the USSR which he foresees, he is confident about Soviet resistance despite likely defeats at first. The Russian winter and Communist infection of the German spirit as in 1918 are what he has in mind. Here was the mingling of realism and fantasy, typical for Wheatley. The actual tricking of Hitler would no doubt have presented an immense challenge to his ingenuity. The notion of the German war machine and Nazi fanaticism as the property of a superior militaristic (if certainly not humanistic) mentality was at that time a reluctantly-accepted factor in assessing the prospect of resistance . Wheatley for one, names a senior RAF Intelligence Officer as one of those who succumbed to this brand of pessimism.[cliii]

Wheatley was later promoted to Wing Commander but was abruptly demobilised just before Christmas 1944. His near – disclosure of top secrets in his fiction had become embarrassing to the Government. He was warned to refrain from writing about contemporary events. Unsurprisingly, he never received any recognition from Britain for his valuable services as a member of Churchill's Intelligence Committee, although he received an American award.

The actual drafting of 'the royal letter' to Hitler, of course a hypothesis, but one backed by powerful, even compelling, circumstantial evidence, would have been an exceptionally sophisticated and subtle endeavour. Kirkpatrick, a staunch Roman Catholic and monarchist, some of the King's secretaries,[cliv] Churchill, Beaverbrook , Attlee, perhaps Sinclair and the Queen, would have been in the know. Kirkpatrick and the secretaries would have been instrumental, and the King would only have had to add his personal signature and perhaps handwriting. He would have received encouragement and reassurances from Churchill.

The letter, handwritten or typed in the English language but with a German translation thoughtfully provided, could have been along the following lines after a formal address to Hitler.

'26th April 1941 . The circumstances from which I derive the inspiration to write to you almost speak for themselves. It is a tragedy of history that the two great nations of which we are the heads of state should for the last nearly twenty months have been engaged in internecine strife of an almost unendurable intensity and suffering. The lives of many millions of men of the white race are at stake, and it is with a heavy heart that I am constantly reminded by events that the present warfare *between the British Empire and Greater Germany has no apparent ending in sight other than mutual destruction of a truly terrible magnitude.*

Because of my duties and responsibilities as King, I have come to the decision that I ought to communicate some of my deepest beliefs at this unhappy juncture to yourself as Fuhrer of the most challenging adversary ever encountered by the British Empire in the hope and perhaps an expectation that combat may at an early date be terminated with negotiations leading to an honourable and enduring peace on agreed terms.

I am prepared to be frank and specific in giving an assessment of the present state of hostilities and likely developments, because I am compelled by reason to consider, despite the boldness of the proposition, that we have a mutual civilised interest in establishing the truth.

The British Empire, with whose Imperial Crown I have the honour and privilege to be entrusted by divine providence subject to a constitution which I am under oath to uphold, has moral and material sources of strength unique in world history.

Our fighting forces have demonstrated and continue to demonstrate their prowess and power. I concede that defeats have been inflicted upon them on the mainland of Europe, and recently in North Africa. Our island fortress and maritime lifelines will continue to be defended to the limit with increasing American aid. When we were at our weakest last summer, our nation held its own. Our own confidence in our own cause represents an irresistible moral force.

As a matter of reason, I acknowledge at your disposal immensely strong and competent fighting forces and a formidable vital spirit.

In brief, each of our two nations can and most probably will inflict increasing devastation upon each others' economic structures and harm upon our peoples if the war continues.

I must now reveal a profound fear. On the sidelines, Russia rearms on a colossal scale and awaits the grave weakening of Europe as a result of the prolongation of the war. I dread a prospect of an imposition of Bolshevism on war weary peoples. Already there are warning signs. Here is a fundamental threat to the survival of white civilisation. Bolshevism has been fought and largely contained since 1917, but now its looming offensive presents an unprecedented menace to which there appears to be no answer while the war persists.

The pact between Germany and Russia of August 1939 aroused our deepest consternation and suspicions for a long time, but it has become clear that it was an arrangement to satisfy the requirements of political expediency. Does its continuance now serve any real purpose? Is it not overwhelmingly clear the answer to this question is 'None'?

Let me now elaborate on what should in my view be done to solve what I believe to be our mutual problems with the achievement of peace between our two great nations a primary aim.

It is imperative that Russia should be militarily crushed without further delay. An early effect of a massive military offensive against Russia by your armed forces would be the collapse of Stalin's regime which is already in crisis according to the best of our information. An expansion of Greater Germany's power eastwards would be acceptable to us, despite our old fears, provided an end to the Bolshevist regime is guaranteed. Wholehearted support for this view comes from a majority of the most prominent and influential people in Britain.

Simultaneously with the commencement of a German war of liberation against Russia, there should be an armistice between Britain and Germany, also covering associated nations, and immediately afterwards the signing of a pact of honour and mutual respect between our two great nations to affirm the principles of a peace treaty. Supplementing definite prospects of a full partnership over a wide range, the British Empire would remain intact and Greater Germany would be recognised as established. Adjustments in particular respects would be amicably negotiated.

Negotiations in secret should commence along the above lines to be initiated at Geneva shortly. These should deal with the proposed armistice and simultaneous pact, and the drafting of a peace treaty.clv The part of our Intelligence service with whom your representatives have already been in contact, is responsible only to me and my immediate circle. Mr. Churchill has and will have no knowledge.

An alternative to the present government is in sight. The hold which the present Prime Minister has contrived to impose upon much of public opinion arose in the unique circumstances of last year and is already perceptibly weakening. It is meticulously planned that in the contingencies which I have outlined he will be dispensed with to public acclamation.

Our communications should be conducted with the utmost secrecy and confidentiality, with which, Fuhrer, I am sure you will agree, and with the assistance of my esteemed aide the most worthy Duke of Hamilton.

I have the honour at this hour of what I believe to be one of extreme peril for the future of mankind to take an initiative of great historical significance and which with God's blessing, shall succeed .'

A formal valediction would have followed and the King's signature. It would have been unnecessary and tactless openly to express any fear of the USA taking over the British Empire, although it is certainly contended that any "Royal Letter" would imply such a fear .

To arrive at Hitler's address as soon as possible the letter in several sealed envelopes with the innermost envelope indicating that it was for the exclusive sight of Hitler, could usefully have been sent by air to Lisbon in neutral Portugal. This was in the first half of 1941 a not unusual civil route. Lisbon airport was used by German civil aircraft. The transfer of the letter by a British diplomat via an intermediary to a German diplomat would have presented no difficulty. If the letter were dated 26 April and flown to Lisbon the same day, (a Saturday), it could have been in Berlin for Hitler by Monday 28 April.[clvi] 28 April was when Goebbels noticed Hitler in a *'dazzling good mood'* (the English translation) as his next day's diary records. If Hitler's elation had been due to the culmination of the Wehrmacht's victory on the mainland of the Balkans, then it would have been virtually routine for Goebbels to have been informed of this and to have noted it in his diary of 29 April.

The press in Britain reported on 26 April that the King and Queen had had their fingerprints taken at Scotland Yard the previous day, and that these had then been destroyed. It would have been a wise precaution to have had available "the royal fingerprints" if the ruse had gone badly wrong and Hitler had had 'the royal letter' published with the apparent fingerprints of the King. If that were to happen, there would of course be a total denial of the validity of such a German claim, and different fingerprints could safely be presented as proof. The avoidance of any awful embarrassment arising in relation to the royal fingerprints could explain why letters from the King and Queen to the Roosevelts, (written between five and six weeks later on 3 June), were neither acknowledged nor answered. This seeming discourtesy has hitherto not been satisfactorily explained.[clvii] If relevant, it could have been claimed the Nazis had forged the King's handwriting.

Linked with the receipt by Hitler of 'the royal letter' *The Times* among other newspapers, gave coverage to rumours of what German peace terms might be. This was the period when the German propaganda offensive against Churchill himself was at its height. Even while dismissing possible terms as *'tomfoolery'*(copyright The Times/Sunday Times 30th April 1941 /nisyndication.com), *The Times'* Tokyo correspondent gave a fairly clear account. The fullest report was on 30 April. In an Axis dominated World, the British Empire was to survive and to an unspecified extent the Nazi occupation of Europe was to be moderated. A Japanese addendum envisaged a mass emigration of Japanese settlers to Australia.

Especially during the period from Monday 21 April through to 6 May, readers of *The Times* and other newspapers could read about the devotion to duty of the King and Queen. Not only did they visit blitzed cities, they also interested themselves in a personal use of firearms and armoured vehicles and visited armament factories. An image of them as of very exceptional influence was created and for a while maintained. Princess Elizabeth, the heir to the throne, gave a radio broadcast on her fifteenth birthday (21 April). Churchill gave her flowers as a present. The celebration of St. George's Day on 23 April gave an opportunity for extolling tradition acceptable to both Nazi ideology and the monarch. *The Times* referred to St. George as *'the warrior saint'* (copyright The Times/Sunday Times 23rd April 1941 / nisyndication.com)and arguably more absurdly, the bloodthirsty crusader Richard Coeur de Lion as the embodiment of an ideal King! Here was a blatant assertion of the importance of the monarchy for Britain and the Empire. This kind of (relatively) subtle press could be reckoned to reinforce Hitler's belief that the Monarchy was soon to disown Churchill. Would it not have been seen as grand by Hitler, to have placed a treacherous egg in Churchill's nest? It is interesting and arguably significant to note that on 30 April *The Times* Leader invoked the King's broadcast on Christmas Day 1939, when he spoke of *'putting out a hand in the dark to grasp the hand of God'*. *The Times* also quoted Hitler's role model Frederick the Great's dictum *'If it is necessary to dupe, let us be rogues'*(copyright The Times/Sunday Times 26th April 1941/nisyndication.com).

How would Hitler have assessed the royal letter? In the first place it would have strengthened his megalomania. Already (Goebbels noted), a Jewish newspaper in New York had described Hitler as *' the greatest military genius of all time'*.[clviii] The letter was not needed by him to convince his generals of the case for invading the USSR, but it was useful for him to win over Ribbentrop and thus the German Foreign Office and diplomats. The civil servant von Weiszacker, the permanent head of the German Foreign Office, had submitted a powerful memorandum to Ribbentrop on 28 April, arguing against a German war on the USSR.[clix] Given the content of 'the royal letter', the gist of this memorandum would be completely refuted. As for Ribbentrop, he was won over temporarily to support Barbarossa at his 48th birthday tea party where Hitler was the guest of honour. A biographer of Ribbentrop suggests that this temporary conversion was Ribbentrop's "gift" to Hitler.[clx] Neither Hess nor Ribbentrop would have wished to challenge the leadership of Hitler, but Hitler would wisely have kept other Nazi leaders uninformed. If any of them knew, there could be a risk of Hitler's own authority being undermined. This could happen if Britain did not act as the King envisaged in his letter, or if British negotiators were to insist on dealing with an officer of state other than Hitler. The King's apparent proposed treachery would obviously best be kept entirely under wraps by the Nazi leadership until it materialised. One may compare Eden's absence of knowledge of ENIGMA in Britain in case he inadvertently or indirectly disclosed it in his personal diplomacy. Ribbentrop in his MEMOIRS, (incomplete because he was hanged following the Nuremberg trial), tells of an unspecified occasion when he obeyed Hitler's order to have "sealed lips".[clxi] Further, after the evident failure of Hess's mission, Hitler would have naturally downgraded 'the royal letter' in his mind because the incarceration of Hess proved to him that the King was weaker than anticipated.

CHAPTER 10

The Trap is Set

It is therefore contended here that at the root of the explanation for Hess's arrival, is his belief that he was responding to a direct peace offer from no less a personage than the Head of State of Great Britain, King George VI, extended just a fortnight earlier.

Pertinent to this contention is the consideration of the status and role of Hess in Nazi Germany. As Deputy-Fuhrer he enjoyed particularly close relations with Hitler himself, and this had been the case for over eighteen years. He had been practically a co-author of *Mein Kampf*, and his place in the Nazi heirarchy, although theoretically inferior to that of Goering, was recognised by the Nazi elite as of key importance and assured.

Hess was born in Egypt in 1894 and educated at a German school there. Ultra-loyal to Hitler himself and the Nazi cause and Party, personally decent (in that tainted context) and a family man, a heroic soldier, an aviator of WW1, later an air ace, a senior minister in the Reich, and an experienced politician - had a record of activity which could only command respect in Nazi circles. His capacity for deceit is evident enough now, but at the time he would have been considered astute. In the early years the Weimar Republic he may have managed, with the collusion of one or more Nazi doctors, to secure a pension for an imaginary war disability, a far from unique form of trickery.[clxii] During the six years of Nazi rule in peacetime, he had been entrusted with many roles of leadership in Party and State. These included for a while supervision over the Gestapo in relation to inner party disputes, and in relation to the mobilisation for German expansionism of some twenty million Germans or people of German descent who resided abroad. He was an experienced speech-maker on the radio and for factory workers, many of whom would once have had Social-democrat or Communist loyalties. His rhetoric skilfully introduced Hitler at the annual Nuremberg rallies, and his public voice on formal occasions became a social norm. It is clear that Hitler confided in Hess.

On 20 April 1941-Hitler's 52nd Birthday- the prayer of Hess *'Lord God preserve our Fuhrer'* was well publicised. On 1 May Hess (taking Hitler's place at short notice) spoke to a mass meeting of workers at the huge Messerschmitt aircraft factory at Augsburg, not far from his home. Dr Goebbels generally praised Hess as a good Nazi personality, though he expressed consternation at his not having much of a sense of humour[clxiii] (Hess had deplored the showing in a central Berlin cinema of a German popular slapstick comedy *'Gasman'*). This was in February. The previous March of 1940, Hess had met the American Under-Secretary of State, Sumner Welles, who was touring Europe in the vain hope of facilitating an early end to the war. Welles formed the opinion that Hess was fanatical and stupid. If he seemed stupid, it was almost certainly an outward sign of his fanaticism.[clxiv] That Hess (by Nazi standards), was not without his personal flaws, could only have added to his reputation as a model Nazi. The absence of a sense of humour and his alleged effeminacy were hardly of weight, since he was happily married with a son born in 1938. Hitler was seen as virtually superhuman, and other Nazi leaders were intermittently lauded. That Eva Braun liked Hess, is noteworthy.

That Hess believed that WW2 was a ghastly mistake so far as Britain was concerned is beyond doubt. Yet there is certainly no good reason to believe that he was other than psychologically normal. From the outset of Hess in captivity, a number of professional efforts were made to ascertain the state of his mind using contemporary psychology. The clinical assessments were not unanimous.

The Duke of Hamilton with his personal friend Albrecht Haushofer, was unquestionably assigned a historic role in April and May 1941 for a number of reasons. Born in 1905, (the same year as Haushofer), he was from birth ennobled as the Marquess of Clydesdale. He was educated at Eton and Oxford, was an amateur boxing champion in his twenties, and a Conservative MP for a Scottish seat for over eight years when he succeeded on the death of his father to the Dukedom. Further, he like Hess, was an air ace of international reputation. In 1933 he had led a flight of specially adapted RAF single-engined biplanes over the summit of Mount Everest, made famous by the film "Wings Over Everest". Before the war Hamilton commanded a Scottish auxiliary RAF bomber squadron. By 1941 he was a Wing Commander, the senior RAF officer at Turnhouse in Scotland.

International politics interested the Duke as a Conservative MP. The future of Anglo-German relations after Hitler came to power and his interest in sport, led him to attend the Berlin Olympics in August 1936. Here Hess and Hamilton met. They shared a political interest in improving relations between their countries. The personal friendship between Hamilton and Albrecht Haushofer, longstanding friend of Hess, also dates from this time. Hamilton invited Haushofer to be his guest and to lecture in London at the Royal Institute of International Affairs in 1937 on the German claim for the return of her colonies lost under the Treaty of Versailles. They corresponded at a personal level and Haushofer stayed at Hamilton's aristocratic home in the Lowlands. By the summer of 1939 Hamilton and Haushofer shared a mutual dislike of Hitler as by now they saw him as a dangerous adventurer and an aggressor on the world stage. Haushofer wrote to Hamilton in July 1939 warning him that Hitler would order a German invasion of Poland after August. Hamilton notified Halifax, the Foreign Secretary, and Chamberlain and Churchill. On 6 October 1939, an important letter appeared in *The Times* signed by Hamilton in which he suggested peace negotiations with Germany, provided a responsible right-wing government succeeded Hitler and his dictatorship, and Germany repudiated the Nazi-Soviet pact of recent date. This letter echoed Haushofer's own views.

Haushofer was the son of the distinguished founder of the pseudo-science of Geopolitics, close to, if not part, of Nazi ideology. His mother was half Jewish, and her safety, (partly provided for by the Nuremberg laws), seemed guaranteed by the deep friendship his family enjoyed. In the early 1920s, Haushofer's parents had helped Hess to survive and advance politically. Haushofer, an expert in foreign affairs, was a close adviser to Hess after the fall of France over the latter's wishes for peace and an Anglo-German reconciliation. Haushofer also wrote to Hamilton in September 1940 sending his letter to an accommodation address in neutral Portugal to be forwarded to Hamilton. The letter was forwarded to British Intelligence. When Hamilton was interviewed seven months later in the failed endeavour to persuade him to volunteer to discuss peace terms in Portugal, it was shown to him. Whether or not this letter had been read by the Duke earlier than April 1941 remains unclear.

The letter more or less pre-supposed that Britain and Germany should negotiate peace terms which would leave the British Empire intact, subject to adjustments, and that Nazi Germany should enjoy the hegemony, if qualified, over Europe which had been substantially won by Germany's victory over France. Later in September, Haushofer had warned Hess that Churchill was irretrievably antagonistic to German power, that Hess could expect no deal with a Churchill government, and that he would be in personal danger if he went to Britain. Hess himself mulled over the prospects of his own role in achieving a Nazi peace settlement with Britain. According to Nazi views of how the war was developing in Germany's favour in the second half of 1940 and the first four months of 1941, peace with Britain was no wild conjecture.[clxv] However, much of the evidence from Germans close to Hess seems tainted. Hess himself had been banned by Hitler at the beginning of the war from flying solo due to physical ill-health. This ban was for one year, and although some ill-health persisted Hess clearly felt by the Autumn of 1940 that it was lifted. He began to make tentative preparations for a solo flight to northern Britain, but with no precise date in mind. The flight would require sophisticated navigation. His plane would need fuel drop tanks. Late in 1940 and early in 1941, he may have made up to four "dummy run" flights over the North Sea. However, assertions that Hess was at that particular time attempting to fly to Britain seem totally unrealistic. Likewise, the often repeated claim that Hess felt immensely politically frustrated by May 1941. Certainly by early May 1941, Hess could be sure that the new twin-engined Messerschmitt ME.110 fighter-bomber, which he wangled from the Company's Professor Messerschmitt, was going to be ready for his flight to Scotland. By then, he was making arrangements for weather reports and for German radio beams to facilitate his northward flight over the North Sea to a point some way east of his destination.

If Hess was finally motivated by a sight of 'the royal letter' received by Hitler on 28 April, his plan to fly on the night of 10/11 May makes sense. Hess was present at Hitler's side when Hitler made his widely reported speech to the Reichstag on Sunday 4 May. It seems they had a four hour meeting, either that day or the next, which ended with Hitler amicably and jocularly rebuking Hess for stubbornness. In view of the long letter prepared by Hess to be given by his adjutant to Hitler should his mission have failed by early Sunday 11 May, Hitler's attitude makes sense. Hess knew that his mission might fail despite his own relative confidence. For that contingency he must have arranged with Hitler to declare publicly that Hess was acting on his own initiative and with probable insanity.[clxvi] No letter from Hess survives. Hearsay evidence originates from Hess's wife.

Hess again met Haushofer on or about 6 May. Haushofer maintained his insistence that negotiations with Britain with Churchill remaining as Prime Minister were bound to fail. Whether or not Hess told Haushofer of 'the royal letter' it would have provided for Hess a complete answer to this objection. If Hitler were not as satisfied as Hess over the authenticity and significance of the 'royal letter', then it would have been positive for Hitler to have let Hess go to Britain as a volunteer ostensibly on an entirely personal mission. This would hardly have been a betrayal of their personal and Nazi comradeship. Hess himself was confident his mission stood a good chance of success. He was boldly assuming a role as a peace-maker with an identifiable Nazi thrust and shrewdness comparable to those of any great figure of history or Nordic or classical myth. Even if his mission were to fail, he could hope that a German victory over the USSR that year would restore his fortunes.

If Hess also believed that it would be better for a Germany at war with the USSR no longer to have Britain as an enemy, this would have been a further incentive. The initiative for his meeting the Duke of Hamilton in Scotland would have had to have come from Hess, as if from Britain it would palpably have suggested a trap. What was required from Britain was basically only a detailed consent for Hess to come to meet the Duke at his seat, Dungavel House near Glasgow. There was an airstrip with landing lights next to the house, although it must be assumed that Hess was unaware that such a runway was actually too short for his plane to land safely· Hess anticipated that his visit would last two days . It is apparent that new drop tanks for the proposed return flight to Germany were in situ!^{clxvii}

It is necessary to emphasise that Hess never expected to have to use his parachute. Even the documentation available at the British end refers to his aiming to 'land'. Despite his record as an air ace he had never practised a parachute landing, and when it came he fumbled it, being concussed when leaving his plane and breaking his ankle on landing.

On 12 May, and in the days following, Churchill had to decide what British policy should be, both openly and clandestinely. He faced a number of problems. It would have been preferable for the Prime Minister if Hess had not survived his air journey. The biggest problem was that if Hess were negotiated with, morale for the war effort both in Britain and the USA, would collapse. The damage done in the USA both to its budding war economy and moral support for Britain could have been devastating, if there were a widespread expectation of a negotiated peace soon. On the other hand, if Hess were totally spurned, then Hitler might see this attitude as badly prejudicing Barbarossa and so order the conquest of the Middle East without delay. That would be as disastrous for Britain. So a difficult balancing act ensued.

In this tricky situation, it was necessary not to disclose anything relating to the King's involvement. So the choice of Kirkpatrick to interview Hess was wise. Fortunately Hess himself as far as we can tell on the basis of information available, was resolutely declining to betray either Hitler or the King. If he had mentioned the royal letter initially to the Duke, any harm done had been remedied in the early hours of Monday morning at his private discussion with Churchill. Churchill only had to deal with those of his colleagues who had no knowledge or suspicion of the royal letter. It was inspiring for them to learn from Churchill that Hess was *'the maggot in the (*Nazi*) apple'.* Churchill could trust Beaverbrook, Attlee and Sinclair, (if Sinclair knew), and any others "in the know", to remain entirely discreet.

Churchill authorised measures of deception in the hope of allaying Hitler's fear of any disclosure by Hess of Barbarossa, perhaps under torture. Absence of torture was no safeguard against Hitler imagining its presence. Goebbels reckoned with the possibility. On 15 May it was announced in Parliament both that the Duke and Hess were friends and that there would be a full government statement soon. Further, Hess received near praise in some of the British press. *The Times* chose to label him as an *'idealist'*(copyright The Times/Sunday Times 15th May 1941 /nisyndication.com), with only an aftermention that an idealist could be wicked. Hess was rumoured to be imprisoned in luxurious conditions, including his partaking of roast chicken dinners.·

A trump card, played as if in accordance with Churchill's wishes, was the Communist allegation that Hess had come to Britain with the belief that he would be in close contact with important and influential people keen for a British-German peace settlement, contrary to the interests of the British people and at the expense of the USSR. The Communist journalist Ivor Montagu elaborated this theme in a lively article in *World News and Views*, which appeared as late as 24 May. Montagu was of Jewish origin and the youngest son of a peer, the banker Lord Swaythling. He had co-directed *Wings Over Everest* in 1933 and assisted with making other famous British films of the 1930s. He was also a table tennis champion and initiator of international tournaments. His article was, however, careful to avoid anything libellous-possibly he believed that too much outspokenness risked internment.

A further measure of Churchill's was to draft a five thousand word statement intended for the House of Commons.

It concluded on a note of willingness for there to be negotiations with Hess. In view of subsequent events, it is hard to come to any conclusion other than that this composition was a ploy, and that its leaking to German agents was arranged. Nothing remotely approaching steps to negotiation ensued. The War Cabinet disapproved of the proposal for negotiation, no doubt to Churchill's hidden pleasure. Sinclair, who attended, ostensibly supported Churchill. Eden and Beaverbrook advised key amendments to the draft. Churchill rejected these. The proposed statement was abandoned.

Churchill, Beaverbrook, Attlee and Eden remained silent in public about Hess to a significant extent, but others in the Cabinet publicly let fly. Bevin spoke of Hess as a" murderer", Morrison of him as a "brutal thug", and Simon, the Lord Chancellor, called him a "Nazi gangster". At the same time there were denunciations of Communist methods and practices. Public opinion could arguably be satisfied that Hess was an enemy and only an enemy, but it could appear to Hitler, (so it must have been contemplated), both that there was a division at the top in Britain about whether to negotiate with Hess and that there was a shared hatred of Communism and the USSR.

Soon there came a statement from the Government that there would be no full statement to be made to the House of Commons. This was not reassuring for some MPs and some of the public, who sensed that there might be parleying with Hess. The apparent cessation of the blitz uncomfortably reinforced this suspicion. Enough MPs eventually sought a debate about Hess and one was arranged but for as late as 19 June and to be of limited duration. A previous public decision to put the crashed ME.110 on show was abruptly cancelled. This would suggest to Hitler that Hess was being taken seriously.[clxviii]

On 16 May Churchill was able to communicate to Smuts his reassuring conviction that the Wehrmacht was probably going to strike at the USSR. In the latter half of May more Enigma information strengthened this belief and unrelated war events took much of the limelight away from Hess. It did not appear that Hitler was changing his mind about Barbarossa. This was good news for Churchill but still the above "balancing act" to keep Hitler guessing, seemed a necessary preventative. The public image of Churchill's fudge was that it was desirable for that purpose. Press speculation abounded.

There remained some demand in Britain, including from some responsible for BBC propaganda for the German public, that Hess should make a broadcast. He was wrongly presumed to disagree with Hitler because Hitler wanted German friendship with the USSR! Such a broadcast was impossible of course. Interestingly, the British propagandist R. H. S. Crossman did run this line, 'the Bolshevik hare', as the Foreign Office nicknamed the project, in his broadcast to Germany of 3 June. In the USA, Roosevelt commented three days later 'I wonder what is really behind the Hess story'. He clearly realised that Churchill was concealing some of the truth, and whatever he surmised in private did nothing to rock Churchill's boat. Churchill also gave his opinion to Roosevelt of the 'ineptitude' of German Intelligence in assessing a strong peace movement in Britain. Stalin for his part was speedily informed through the agency of the mole Philby of as much as the War Cabinet was told about Hess. His deeply disturbing interpretation of the visit of Hess echoed that of the British Communists.

By early June it seemed desirable to make a further attempt to obtain more information from Hess. The advice given previously by Kirkpatrick was taken. Viscount Simon, accompanied by Kirkpatrick, was to interview Hess. Simon, the leader of the satellite National Liberal Party, had been a foremost appeaser in Baldwin's and Chamberlain's time. He had the further advantage of having met Hess six years earlier as Foreign Secretary. The three hour meeting of 9 June 1941 may be seen in hindsight as theatre. A transcript of 78 pages, perhaps not a full one, is on file at the Public Records Office.[clxix] Simon and Kirkpatrick arrived disguised as psychiatrists.

It was not the intention to deceive Hess, but to keep pressmen away. Simon was to do most of the talking with Hess, with his companion ready to act as an interpreter, although in the event Hess's English was broadly adequate. Two shorthand writers took notes out of sight of Hess. Simon wished to learn if Germany intended to invade the USSR. Again Hess disclaimed any knowledge. He again said that Soviet-German relations might deteriorate, and Germany might have to enforce demands. He had the nous to realise that if he disclosed Barbarossa, Stalin might be warned and Barbarossa would be jeopardised. Three months later, long after the invasion of the USSR began, Hess told Beaverbrook (who posed a false sympathy), that he had known about Barbarossa when he came to Britain.

Hess once more asserted that Germany was invincible and Britain would be destroyed if the war were to continue. This was not what Hitler desired but it would happen if Britain did not forthwith make peace. The generous terms which Hess claimed Hitler offered Britain were broadly what King George VI had seemingly proposed to Hitler six weeks earlier. Simon was unimpressed. He of course knew nothing of the royal letter. He challenged Hess's view of German might and British weakness. They argued heatedly over two features of the war to date; German air losses in the Battle of Britain and the damage allegedly done by RAF night raids on Germany. Here, for what it is worth, Hess had truth on his side. However, he must have known that his alarming boast of a mass building of U-boats, was a lie.

Simon with his skill as an advocate, eventually crushed Hess. If Hess as he claimed to be, was so close to Hitler, how could he sensibly claim that Hitler had not approved his mission?

Secondly, given the declaration by Hess that an Anglo-German peace would leave the British Empire more or less intact, and a German hegemony of Europe would allow innocent nations in Europe a regaining of their independence, Simon asked Hess what steps Hitler was proposing for Denmark, Norway, Luxembourg, Holland and Belgium. Given the Nazi line that these countries had been invaded by Germany "for their own protection", Hess could not cogently reply. Simon wrote to Churchill that Hess was a liar and that he did not have '*a cool cold mentality of a clever agent*'. Simon believed that Germany might be more uneasy about the war continuing than Hess pretended. Churchill's confidant and head of his private Intelligence unit Desmond Morton, purported to share Simon's opinion.[clxx]

With the exception of the Beaverbrook interview in September, the Simon interrogation was the last realistic endeavour to obtain any worthwhile information from Hess. Indeed, to the end of his life he retained his absolute loyalty to Hitler and Nazism and adhering to his Nazi code of honour, never once admitted that Hitler had approved his mission.

After the interviews in Scotland, Hess was brought to London by train on Friday 16 May and detained in the Tower of London for four days. Then he was taken to a safe house near Aldershot, where MI6 was in charge. He was kept under permanent guard in a bugged suite of rooms with a connecting staircase, with three British Intelligence agents (one possibly a Soviet mole!) as companions. That Hess knew he was bugged is almost certain. It was a Nazi practice and also a British one as he would have learned, from the information brought back to Germany before May by von Werra, a Luftwaffe fighter pilot shot down over England, who escaped, fled to the neutral USA and eventually returned to Europe. He was debriefed about British methods including the sophisticated bugging of PoWs.[clxxi]

Hess was allowed no news, which must have been for him a real deprivation. His only company was the agents. He made various unavailing requests in May and June to communicate with, if not to meet, King George VI. Hess said that in due course he would receive the thanks of the monarch for a great service to humanity. He expressed confidence in the Duke of Hamilton whom he wanted to come to see him. He anticipated a change of government. Hess believed that the King would acknowledge that he had displayed personal courage in taking the initiative to travel to Britain on his self-styled mission for peace and therefore he would be recognised as deserving an early return to Germany. He believed *'a clique'* was denying him access to the King, and that he was in the hands of a *'hostile'* secret service; all reasonable beliefs to hold, if he had been prompted to arrive from receipt of "The Royal Letter".

Hess was given a *'truth drug'* in a vain hope that he would candidly talk.[clxxii] He suspected this action and his complaint was duly distorted into an allegation of his being given poison. In a further hope of extracting truth he was told the lie that his wife and three year old son in Germany had been arrested. The forgery of a whole German newspaper containing this story was attempted but found impossible. He was told to his distress, of the sinking of the Bismarck.

The impact on Hess of his meeting with Simon must have been further deeply depressing. Six days later, on 15 June, Hess made a suicide attempt. He was able artfully to avoid the vigilance of his guards and threw himself over the banisters. The result was a broken leg and some broken ribs. The conscientious medical attention he received led to his feigning insanity, alleging that there was an intention to poison him. From 17 June he was allowed to read *The Times* daily and also *The Tatler,* the society weekly. Previously he had been allowed only innocuous reading matter, unrelated to the war or politics or the like. Reading of the German invasion of the USSR heartened him.

Probably when he intended suicide, he had erroneously concluded that Babarossa had been aborted due to his failure in Britain. His feigning insanity was consistent with the role he had agreed with Hitler should his mission fail. Hess was allowed to write home to his wife and child, but all his communications were to be heavily censored for the rest of his life.

Hess was not completely missing from the public political agenda in Britain of the first half of June. Patrick Dollan, onetime a Clydesider Labour MP, the Lord Provost of Glasgow, opined that Hess had come to Britain to procure an Anglo-German alliance against the USSR. He merely expressed what many people in Britain were now thinking. In the USA, ex-President Hoover, who had won a reputation after WW1 for organising American relief for war devastated Europe, openly welcomed the mission of Hess for a negotiated peace, as he and many Americans imagined it. Hoover's intervention was naturally unwelcome to Churchill as adding weight to the Isolationist cause.

CHAPTER 11

The Evidence for "The Royal Letter"

Those dismissive, scornful or sceptical of the above theory of there having been a "Royal Letter", should firstly wonder why the British authorities have abundantly shown ongoing concern that the whole truth of the Hess episode should not be considered fit for public knowledge. From the hours following Hess's arrival on UK soil, relevant documents have gone missing. Many that remain are as yet undisclosed.

It has been suggested that Hess had effectively supplanted the role of Ernst Bohle, a high official in the German Foreign Office, in flying to Britain, and that Hess's intervention was motivated chiefly by his egotistical desire for personal prestige as the politician who achieved peace with the Empire. Whatever the formal arrangement between the Fuhrer and his Deputy as an expression of their undoubtedly genuine friendship, it is questionable in this specific context how Hess's prestige could have increased at the time with anyone other than Hitler personally; Hess must have been conscious that wider public acclamation in Germany appropriated for himself might be viewed by The Fuhrer as a risk to his own unassailable personal standing. A plausible alternative explanation as to why it "had to be Hess" who attended, is that Hess was simply concerned that the attendance of Bohle, a mere diplomat, at peace talks prompted by The King, would be seen as an indication that the Germans were insufficiently sincere and serious about such talks-such an occasion demanded the attendance of the Deputy Fuhrer himself as envoy.

Before his departure from Germany, Hess had made enquiries about the constitutional powers of King George VI. Hitherto this circumstance has been utilised merely to show that he was "unbalanced". Yet the "holding out" to the Germans of British politicians such as Halifax and Hoare as potential peacemakers could not in itself remotely guarantee their success in overthrowing Churchill, when they would naturally have had to to corrall support "for peace" from a majority of their Conservative Party MPs. How could the British portray this obvious constitutional "problem" convincingly to the Germans who must have been to say the least, curious as to the precise procedural mechanism by which Churchill was going to be ousted? The answer lay in the power of the supreme arbiter of the British Constitution-the King- and the King's powers must logically have been perceived by the Germans as absolutely vital to the success of the proposed peace negotiations. It was the King who would have the power to install and legitimise the new British leadership, with Lord Halifax most likely at the helm. If Hess really had seen a letter purportedly from the King, such a letter would undoubtedly have motivated his enquiries over the King's powers.

It has already been suggested by others that the King's Envoy was at the least involved in the fictitious "Peace Party"; however, this must beg the question as to how much Churchill was willing to invest in the success of the operation. Surely nothing less than a completely convincing approach would suffice, with encouraging noises emanating directly from the Monarch, purporting to express his personal fears over the mutual national survival of the combatants. It is also recorded that following his capture, Hess enquired whether George VI would be willing to grant him "parole" ie. freedom to return to Germany. This does suggest that Hess was still expecting a direct approach to the Monarch to be possible.

If it is first assumed that German plans demonstrated a course of action motivated by the immense diplomatic force of a contrived "Royal Letter", there are further matters suggesting the high probability of its existence. There will have been in Britain from the outset, strong reasons for non-disclosure. The ethical dimension cannot be ignored. Nazi Germany was threatening the British Empire with extinction, so that Britain to avoid this fate, sought to persuade Germany to attack the USSR, arguably an innocent party, instead. The moral question raised is one which provides eternal fuel for ethical dispute. The 17th Century English political philosopher Harrington cited Machiavelli in relation to a nation state's desire for self-preservation '....*no consideration is to be had of what is just or unjust, of what is merciful or cruel, of what is honourable or ignominious, in case* (i.e. when) *it be to save a state or to preserve liberty...*'.Certainly Churchill's ruthlessness and guile in matters of war is a given. Preservation of the British Empire would certainly have taken firm precedence over any abstract moral debate.

Moreover, any publicity for the "trick" letter after it served its purpose, would have damaged good Anglo-Soviet relations which were vital for the defeat of Germany. At the start of the Cold war, publicity would again have damaged the moral case for Western hostility to the USSR. Another obstacle to publication would have been the impetus it would have given to nationalist movements in the British Empire, which would have gained moral ground by the revelation of the duplicity of the Crown, even if the fraud committed were deemed defensible.

It is also a given that the operation to dupe Hitler was naturally accompanied by the most stringent measures to keep it a secret. Any leakage of evidence of the "peace plan" would amount to a catastrophe for British diplomacy regardless of its true intent. The atmosphere of paranoia surrounding "those in the know" must have been palpable and prolonged. Let it be borne in mind that Churchill's subsequent concerns alighted disproportionately upon an ostensibly esoteric work of fiction "*The Life and Death of Colonel Blimp*". Shot in 1943, the now-classic film by Powell and Pressburger movingly traces the friendship between a British and a German officer across the years. Churchill vehemently and secretly conducted a campaign against the releasing of the film abroad. Why? His ostensible reason was that it poked fun at senior British officers-the "Blimp" of the title-and that this undermined morale. A more perceptive interpretation appeared in the "*Evening Standard*" on 28th June 1943; "*Public attention had mainly been focused on the picture of the British Officer drawn in the film and of his extreme conservatism. But the veto decision was not made on this point at all. It was made on a point that few people would have thought of. In the film, a young army officer wins a victory over Home Guard Colonel Blimp by fighting a "battle" some hours before the appointed zero hour. This says Whitehall, would advertise abroad that we countenance the ethics of the Japs at Pearl Harbour.*" Churchill would have every reason to seek to minimise suggestions that he acted immorally in pursuing the war. He had gained allies whom he needed to keep!

Eventually, following the end of most of the British Empire, the institution of the monarchy itself was to come under pressure. Any additional indication of the frailty (or as we might see it today, the normality) of some of the royal family, which publication of 'the Royal Letter' would give, would be anathema to the authorities.

One must of course bear in mind how few people would have known of the Royal Letter at the time. Those who did know were not only totally loyal to the King himself but also to the Crown as at the foundation of the constitution, and in addition had either taken their solemn oaths as Privy Councillors not to reveal state secrets, or at least were bound by the law of Official Secrets. Even after the disclosure of various royal scandals or near scandals, the Queen Mother's lifestyle and happiness until her death in 2002, and perhaps those of the Queen herself, might be further harmed by anything published showing the late King, the husband and father, to have been a party to deception, however morally justifiable it had been.

In the summer of 1945, Sir Anthony Blunt, as a trusted royal emissary, went on a top secret mission to a castle in Germany belonging to a German aristocrat. His main purpose was to recover documentation of a sensitive character of interest to the royal family. This much is known.[clxxiii] Blunt, who was a Soviet mole in British Intelligence, was a prestigious art historian, and would become a member of the royal household. There has never been anything publicised, (since the end of the Cold War), to show that he gave any information to Moscow about the royal family. Nor is it all that likely that he knew of 'the royal letter'. If he had come across it, disclosed it to Moscow and it had been used as propaganda, his cover would instantly have been blown. In any event it seems most probable that by the summer of 1945 his loyalty to the USSR had become qualified, and he could see no good reason to give Stalin dirt about British royalty. WW2 in Europe had been won and there was hope that despite differences, the basic unity of the big three would remain intact. For the British monarchy to be attacked by Moscow would have been counter-productive at that stage.

It is also worthwhile considering why Hess never publicly revealed the existence of 'the royal letter' about which he must have known upon its receipt by Hitler. Hess was in captivity between his arrival in Scotland on the night of 10/11 May 1941 until his death in 1987, at first in Britain and post-war in Germany. The sentence of life imprisonment imposed on him at the Nuremberg trial in his case meant life. Anything he wrote or said was censored for the outside world, including letters to and from his wife and son. Constraints were placed on all his conversations. He was isolated from all but officials until the trial at Nuremberg enabled him to have contact with lawyers.

At the trial of nearly a year's duration he was the one defendant who ostentatiously distanced himself and read a book while in the dock with his co-defendants. He retained his extreme loyalty to Hitler, whom he may have believed remained alive and he probably believed, as did most of the other defendants, that it would only be a matter of time before there was a Third World War between the West including Germany and the USSR. So he had every motive to try to escape the death penalty. His co-defendants despised him for the seeming idiocy and treachery of his journey to Britain.

The indictment against Hess was a full one though ultimately he was only convicted on two counts, Conspiracy to wage war and Crimes against Peace. The allegations of War Crimes and Crimes against Humanity were not found proved in his case. As he gave no evidence on oath he could not be cross-examined. Early in the proceedings he boasted that he had successfully feigned amnesia. His advocate advised him to plead insanity, so he dismissed his advocate. The Court deliberated and found unsurprisingly that he was fit to stand trial. The Court appointed a new advocate with whom Hess refused to co-operate. When Hess ultimately made a statement from the dock, not on oath, the Court told him in advance that he could speak for twenty minutes. He rambled on until the time limit was reached. Then he was stopped.

The fact that Hess was under immense stress must have contributed to some professional views that he was not sane. For a singular practical reason a finding of insanity could not be formally accepted by Churchill. It would have made Hess eligible for repatriation to Germany under the Geneva Convention. This had to be carefully respected by the British government because in 1941 the numbers of British PoWs far exceeded the numbers of Germans who had been captured. It was politically expedient for both Hitler and Churchill publicly to consider Hess loosely as insane. It was also helpful to Hess himself to feign insanity. His cunning, at least in May and June 1941, deserves to be emphasised. For example, he displayed a feat of navigation for his plane to reach near to his destination in Scotland, but later he was to falsify his route so as to make his undoubted prowess as an air ace seem much more distinguished.[clxxiv]

It should be understood that if Hess did mention 'the Royal Letter' to his German advocate whom he later dismissed, he would have been advised in confidence that if he mentioned it in Court, he was much increasing the chance of the death penalty. The staggering impertinence of such a claim involving the honour of the British monarch would have amounted to asking for a death sentence. He would have initially been advised that the trial was essentially a political one and that the prospect of his being found not guilty on all four counts was improbable. In the event a sentence of life imprisonment was imposed and not a death sentence.

Hess died forty-one years later aged ninety-three. Apparently he committed suicide when he knew he was shortly to be released. It was officially claimed he had hanged himself. No inquest was ever held. A detailed proposal for an inquest, suggesting a serious possibility of murder, was lodged by an experienced British police officer, and this document too, remains secret.[clxxv] There was a motive on the British side for him to die before being released, when he would no longer be censored. So he could have committed suicide as Hitler had done, perhaps given appropriate mental pressure on him. Or was he murdered? If he had been released, it would have been foreseeably impossible to stop the world's media from obtaining and publishing his own if belated uncensored account of his mission to Britain in May 1941. That has never been forthcoming.

The Hess story, both in Germany and Britain, was deliberately underplayed after June 1941, except for the British purpose of satisfying Stalin that Britain intended to remain true to the Anglo-Soviet alliance. Copious but still-incomplete documentation at the Public Record Office became available in the summer of 1992, but the royal archives remain closed indefinitely-at least for a further ten years or so.

The Duke of Kent was to perish in an air accident in August 1942 when the flying boat carrying him and others crashed into a Scottish mountain. It was on its clandestine way to neutral Sweden, where the Duke would have met their King. An unlisted passenger who died was probably a nuclear scientist,[clxxvi] and the rumour it was Hess must have been a cover. Hess by then was detained comfortably at an address in Wales. Sir Samuel Hoare may previously have met Hess in Spain between 20 and 22 April 1941. If so, Hess may have received something like encouragement from a subtle Hoare. It has been conjectured that a retired Colonel of the Guards "went too far" in some undisclosed way in relation to the mission of Hess, and remained under virtual house arrest on the royal estate at Braemar until his death in 1970.[clxxvii] Many prospective witnesses were officially deterred from disclosing evidence about the Hess visit if not for ever then for long periods of time, with few exceptions. The man known as 'C' may have had doubts about Churchill's refusal to allow negotiations with Hess, but he remained loyal.

Any unprejudiced reader will find Churchill's account in *The Grand Alliance* evasive to say the least. The arrival of Hess as an unforeseen and in a sense inevitable consequence of the suggested deception, places the episode in a far more plausible perspective. Churchill and others in the know, conveniently chose to forget anything which might damage the reputation of the King himself and the British institution of monarchy.[clxxviii]

The specific interpretation of the motivation of Hess to fly to Britain given at the outset of this chapter is not to the author's knowledge, given elsewhere. What is clear is that quite a large number of mysteries associated with Hess remain unexplained due to the unavailability of documentation. Moreover, much disinformation was spread from the outset, probably emanating from the secret services. This was to suit the interests and wishes of Churchill, and hopefully to satisfy Stalin whilst an ally. People of importance, whatever their exact views of a prospect of a negotiated peace in the spring of 1941, have never had their connections with Hess and his visit fully exposed.

CHAPTER 12

Countdown to invasion

Hitler reached the conclusion that Germany's invasion of the USSR would stand a good chance of prompting Britain and the USA broadly to align themselves with Germany. One example of how the idea spread, is to be found in the diary entry for 14 June of General Halder, the Wehrmacht's chief of staff, where he states his hope that the collapse of Russia would be followed by Britain giving in. Between 30 April and 22 June, Hitler devised more politics of barbarism as an essential feature of the invasion of the USSR. He concerned himself with the question as to how how the overwhelming build-up of the Wehrmacht and the Luftwaffe ready for 22 June might be brought about without warning Stalin, and with details of the worldwide propaganda to be disseminated by the Nazi regime on 22 June.

In Moscow, German diplomats had to continue to act as apparent friends of the USSR -something at which they excelled, perhaps due to the sincerity of most of them. However, for some time before the invasion, the diplomats' wives and children had been returning to Germany , and rather too conspicuously, any spare roubles were being splashed around in Moscow by those about to go home. The explanations for these events apparently satisfied Stalin or perhaps his compliant intimidated staff.[clxxix]

Much of the responsibility for a unique pattern of deception of the USSR and the world at large, was delegated to Goebbels.[clxxx] His first priority was the spreading of various rumours of German intentions for offensives other than against the USSR. The apparent choice of a Mediterranean strategy has limited truth - far less than Churchill initially imagined. The invasion of Crete was a one- off episode.

More emphasised by Goebbels's use of the German media, was a fictitious probability of the invasion of Britain or perhaps Ireland. It was known to Churchill that this was not planned for the foreseeable future, but he could not disclose that ENIGMA was the definitive source of this knowledge. It was deemed best for Britain to continue to be apprehensive about the risk of invasion. Beaverbrook, who must have relished the mischief, spoke fervently in public of this alleged danger as if he were taken in by Goebbels. After April he was Minister of State in the War Cabinet and closer to Churchill than ever in the conduct of the war. Some fifteen million leaflets advising the public what to do in the event of an invasion were distributed in Britain mid-May. Following the fall of Crete during May, Goebbels played with gusto, the card of an imminent invasion of Britain.

On Friday 13 June the first edition of the principal Nazi daily paper *Volkische Beobachter* contained an article suggesting that the German conquest of the island of Crete two weeks earlier was a prelude to an invasion of England. The paper was delivered as usual early in the day to the American Embassy in Berlin. Within minutes, the police were raiding kiosks and confiscating all copies. The American diplomats were intended to be impressed by the well-publicised frantic belated censorship. Goebbels appeared to be publicly disgraced for his apparent gross indiscretion. But - it was all carefully planned! Goebbels was gleeful that many members of his own staff were deceived. When he next called on Hitler, he used a back entrance and exit to maintain the pretence. A similar hoax took place a few days later, when a radio talk on plans for the invasion of England was abruptly terminated half way through.

A simultaneous rumour for popular domestic consumption - and for Stalin - was that red flags in quantity were being manufactured so as to greet Stalin, allegedly soon to come to Berlin for talks with Hitler. Public relations officers in Berlin were now spreading the fiction, which they no doubt themselves believed, of developing German-Soviet negotiations.

About this time the professional curiosity of Howard K. Smith who remained in Berlin was thoroughly aroused. Towards the end of May he had noticed that the very popular German translation of a Soviet approved best-seller, a volume of short stories by the satirist Michael Zoschenko, had disappeared from the window display of a leading Berlin bookshop. Acting on the hunch of an imminent war against the USSR, Smith asked the manager the next day what was stocked on Russia. He was shown *The Truth about the Soviet Paradise, The Betrayal of Socialism* and *My Life in the Russian Hell.* Confident he might be on the right track, Smith learned from a German PR contact that Hitler was said to be making demands on Stalin. Smith felt motivated enough to seek re-employment. He filled a vacancy in another American news agency. He met Ivan Filipoff of the Soviet News agency Tass who told him of the story circulating in Berlin that Germany was demanding a 99 year lease of the Ukraine. This could be interpreted as an opening bargaining move. They exchanged views about the apparent new looming crisis.

Smith came across further information pointing to an imminent attack on the USSR as approaching. He was in correspondence with a German soldier in the East, who wrote to say he was coming home on leave and would like to meet him. The soldier then wrote to say all leave was cancelled. Another sign was that a Hitler Youth member told him a meeting was to be held soon on changing the party line. The censor deleted all such news from his short wave broadcasts from Berlin to the USA. What finally convinced Smith an invasion of the USSR was to take place in a few days time was the occupation by the German Foreign Office of the top floor of the prestigious Adlon Hotel, for mass copying of documents behind closely guarded doors. About 3am on Sunday 22 June he, like other foreign correspondents in Berlin, was invited by telephone to attend a special press conference at 5am. Smith could guess what it was going to be about. If he recollected that on 12 June the Nazis had rescinded the ban on dancing in public, which had been a normal wartime restriction while a land campaign was being fought, he could see this as a further move to lull suspicion of war against the USSR

Over the previous seven weeks, rumours about the stability of German-Soviet relations had multiplied. The neutral capitals of Ankara and Stockholm were fertile sources. The effect on Stalin of the fiction of a gulf between Hitler and his generals was as great as it had been for Churchill on and after 20 April, but with the vast difference that Stalin believed it was the German generals who wanted an invasion of the USSR and that they were opposed by Hitler. It looks as if this theme was exploited by Hitler as part of his pattern of deception. Thus the many German reconnaissance flights deep inside Soviet territory, essential for the preparation of Barbarossa, were tolerated by Stalin until it was too late. There were only diplomatic protests. The German aerial photography proved that the Red Army was in no way ready to commence any offensive. Stalin was wondering how German generals could persuade his "pragmatic" Hitler that a preventive war would make any sense? Deliveries of raw materials by ship and train from the USSR to Germany were given further priority as part of Stalin's conspicuous policy of appeasement following 6 May.

By the end of May Hitler was increasingly confident about the prospects for Barbarossa's success. He and Goebbels discussed the choice of victory fanfares to be played on German radio. The German public remained unaware what was brewing. Even many of the top soldiers were as yet only partly informed. Many must have had some inkling as, on 30 March, Hitler had let more than two hundred elite Nazis know about Barbarossa in principle. In a mood of elation, Hitler gave a further address to a selected audience on 14 June when he gave his notorious announcement that no commissars, Communists or Jews would be PoWs. They would be shot when captured. Moreover, the warfare in the East would purposively lead to genocide of "inferior" races. Some of his audience felt shocked, but there is no firm evidence that any disobedience or non-compliance ever followed. Any claim that Hess was an enlightened man should be viewed in this context.

Barbarossa required the military participation of satellite countries, particularly Romania, Finland and Hungary. Their armies were being prepared but not to an extent where they would be able to join in the new campaign at the outset. Romania excepted, these countries' leaders were told only in broad terms about the imminent war with the USSR. In the case of Italy, reticence was justified on the grounds that it would be impossible to maintain secrecy. However, Mussolini must have deduced from his meeting with Hitler on the Brenner on 2 June, that there would be war against the USSR. Ciano in his diary entry of June reports that Mussolini told Ciano he would not be sorry *'if Germany in her conflict with Russia lost many feathers and this is possible.....'*. Rome Radio reported the Luftwaffe as leaving Sicily! By 21 June Ciano had the definite impression that the German attack on the USSR was absolutely imminent. His attitude was somewhat contradictory. He thought *'the date of the fall of Bolshevism should be counted among the most important in civilisation'*. On the other hand, he was not entirely convinced there would be a speedy German victory, a mere eight weeks campaign predicted, or indeed a German victory at all! He thought it possible the *'Soviet armies would show the world a power of resistance superior to that the bourgeois countries have shown'*, and this could have an incalculable effect on *'the proletarian masses of the world'*.

Hitler and Goebbels planned the launch of a great anti-Communist crusade. The delay was necessary so as not to obviate their claim, a mere pretext, that the reason for the invasion of the USSR was that it forestalled an attack by the USSR on Germany. This was the propaganda case being prepared at the Hotel Adlon. This crusade, (which like the military campaign itself, was disclosed to only a few people in advance), would be directed principally to obtain worldwide support for the war against the USSR from the Roman Catholic Church and its hundreds of millions of worshippers.

That Stalin was kept aware of many of the basic facts of German military capability and dispositions, in contrast to Hitler's aggressive intentions, is now well-known. Soviet agents copiously reported facts to Soviet Intelligence. It should not be thought that Stalin was other than rational, however mistaken, in disparaging these facts. It was his misjudgement of Hitler's intentions which led to terrible results for the USSR and its peoples. Yet it is fair to compare Stalin's gross failure to predict with that of Roosevelt and Churchill less than six months later in relation to Japanese intentions for war in the Far East.

The Soviets pleaded in May for reassurances from Berlin that the differences between Germany and the USSR could be dealt with peacefully. In the first half of June the absence of any reply despite the many weeks which had passed, was a source of growing anxiety to Stalin and the Politburo. The Soviet military high command appreciated the German menace more than Stalin, and did their best to notify him of its profound worries. Stalin remained adamant that messages of preparations for Barbarossa, including diplomatic warnings from Eden in London given to Maisky, were to be treated as provocations and should on principle be disregarded. In May. Marshal Zhukov had presented to Stalin a draft plan for a pre-emptive strike by the Red army, but this was totally rejected. If it had led to warfare, it would have been disastrous for the USSR. At least it was a way of showing his and his immediate colleagues' ever increasing fears. Stalin's cruel and paranoid dictatorial methods totally discouraged anyone even in the Politburo itself who might wish to express disagreement with his judgements.

On Saturday 14 June in Moscow, there was a resort to desperation. Less than a week earlier a disappointed Cripps had left for consultations in London, and his departure from Moscow could be interpreted as a helpful sign to Berlin that he despaired of any agreement between Britain and the USSR. This incident would have reflected Stalin's view that Hitler had to be constantly reassured as to how realistic the USSR was about remaining neutral and able and willing to deliver increasing supplies of vital raw materials to Germany by way of trade, even on deferred payment terms and without reciprocal imports.

A Tass news agency communiqué was surprisingly broadcast over loudspeakers in Moscow on the evening of 14 June, while many people were returning home after work. Its text had been given already to the German embassy. A summary of its contents: rumours of war and German demands on the USSR were unfounded. These were due to the malice of persons unknown. It could be implied that the recently-departed Cripps was to blame. There was no offer of any new or closer relationship between Germany and the USSR. All existing obligations by each to the other were being fulfilled. German armed forces near the USSR were so located 'one must suppose' from 'motives (having) no bearing on Soviet-German relations'. Current Soviet military moves were not preparations for war but were merely the usual annual steps for 'training reservists' and for the 'checking of railway communications'. Any suggestion of hostility to Germany was 'absurd' to say the least.

The aim of this unique diplomacy with its confusing mixture of assertions and innuendos, truth, half truth and mendacity, was to flush a conciliatory response from Berlin. Despite frantic requests in Moscow and Berlin over the next week, Ribbentrop could not be contacted and nothing more than the vaguest assurances that the matter was or would be receiving attention, was the response of German diplomats. A meeting in Moscow between Molotov and the German ambassador on the eve of the invasion was no more productive

One unforeseen consequence of the Tass communiqué was the boost it gave to the false sense of security of most Soviet people. It looked as if the continuation of peace and neutrality was guaranteed. Even as late as the day of the actual invasion which had begun by dawn, most of the press and radio in the USSR dwelt on claims of the economic and social progress of Soviet life, which seemed to confirm the attraction of this fine summer day as one for relaxation.

While civilians were misled, which was bad enough, the impact of the Tass communiqué on the armed services was much graver. Until within a few hours of the first attacks by the Luftwaffe and Wehrmacht, Red Army and air units had been very strictly ordered to ignore any signs of untoward activities and attitudes by German forces. The noisy sounds of the revving engines of German tanks, the increased presence of German patrols, the failure of German officers to return salutes, and even alarming reports from the few German deserters who crossed over into Soviet territory were to be disregarded. With a few exceptions, the nearly three million men of the Red Army (some 155 divisions) and air force who were intended to defend the Soviet frontier remained in a state of unreadiness. Training, off duty recreations and leave went on as normal. The Soviet high command badgered Stalin as far as it dared for urgent measures of defence to be implemented, but met with only a total refusal to take any step which could be interpreted as a provocation of Germany. Only the anti-aircraft defences of Moscow, the Baltic and Black Sea fleets were substantially alerted.

Towards midnight on the night of 21st June, Stalin changed his mind. The weight of evidence had become too overwhelming to disregard. However, it was too late to issue a decisive warning. Telephone messages and telegrams to headquarters were taking longer to reach all destinations than hoped for. It was a Saturday night. The result was that only some units received the order to prepare for immediate warfare. The citadel at Brest Litovsk, virtually on the frontier, was one of those few actually ready for resistance. Generally, even where action stations were taken, there was inadequate readiness for the first battle, let alone for sustained resistance and counter-attacks.

On airfields, there was no opportunity given for dispersals of warplanes which were drawn up in a series of long lines. This vulnerability was intended to guard against sabotage, which was feared if aircraft were placed in single bays adjoining perimeters. Overlooked was the appalling risk of a surprise attack by enemy bombers. These aircraft were going to be sitting ducks. On airfields to the rear there were more planes, but too many were obsolete, and few were fit for effective combat or bombing.

A patriotic loyalty together with ability and discipline naturally formed part of the self-esteem of many soldiers. The communist fervour of many, however misplaced, also sustained their morale – a fact now accepted by Western historians. However, the material, tactical skill and experience for success were at best unevenly at hand. In addition there was an underestimate of the German war machine as ideologically inferior, and a corresponding overestimate of the Soviet forces themselves. It was intrinsically difficult for Stalin in peacetime simultaneously to laud the achievements of the Soviet system and to insist on the urgency of remedying its many shortcomings. That he was aware of the necessity of the latter has been amply shown, but the practice of this was inadequately accomplished. The facile and totally futile solution to the problem of the Nazi threat was to rely on the supposed goodwill of Hitler until it was too late. That Hitler was aware of some of the dilemmas which Stalin faced, (however crazy some of his other views about the USSR were), formed part of the cunning of the military dispositions for Barbarossa. The Soviet defensive capability was simply not in place.

In Britain, Churchill remained certain that the USSR would be the next victim of German aggression. The persuading of Nazi monitors of the press that there was a real, if inchoate, peace movement in Britain which was firmly anti-Communist and against the USSR, had to be continued. There was even a British signals unit in Finland as late as June to monitor Soviet radio traffic, news of which must have been passed to German Intelligence![clxxxi] It was essential as well to keep relations with the USSR at least from deteriorating further and to maintain domestic and American morale with the hope of the USSR as a future ally in mind.

Back in London on 11 June, Cripps privately reiterated his long held view that the USSR would be invaded by Germany and would resist. His intuition impressed Churchill, and shortly after the invasion took place Cripps received the signal honour of being made a privy councillor. However, the apparent crassness of the Tass communiqué of 14 June and the difficulty of attributing any sensible meaning to it was disturbing. It seems Cripps was careful not to commit himself either way about the likely strength of Soviet resistance. The opinion attributed to him that the Wehrmacht would go through Russia "like a knife through butter", was apparently not his own but his understanding of what most foreign diplomats in Moscow believed. His legal expertise alone must have made him wary of predicting the course of the future battle, but he would have been supportive of the views of Churchill, Beaverbrook and

Eden that the USSR was probably going to be a worthwhile ally.

The government's attitude to Maisky as Soviet ambassador in London was important. There was a general affability in discussions between Eden and Maisky. So far as imports to the USSR across the Pacific were concerned which arguably might find their way to Germany, Maisky, when he complained about the British naval blockade, was sometimes given the benefit of the doubt. Maisky however could not accept that the USSR was going to be the next victim of Nazi aggression. It seemed to him that Hitler could not be so stupid. He saw the risk of an Anglo-German alliance as a result of the Hess mission, but assessed it as improbable given Churchill's predominance. Moreover, he was in touch with leftwing opinion in Britain which vaguely envisaged Britain and the USSR as allies. Labour Movement conferences showed this trend of opinion as substantial. Maisky could not easily be shaken from his complacency, which reflected that of Stalin.

As late as 12 June a representative of *The Times* and the Foreign Office, Iverach Macdonald, tried unsuccessfully to persuade Maisky that Germany was about to strike at the USSR.[clxxxii] The next day, Eden made some headway in this direction and promised to give Maisky details of the German military build-up. He further promised a British military mission to Moscow in the event of invasion; however Maisky was more seriously interested in receiving the details of the build-up and gave Eden the telephone number of the residence of the Spanish Republican exile Negrin a few miles beyond Watford, where as usual he was to stay the week-end. However, it seems that Churchill would not yet sanction what was ENIGMA information being given to Maisky. Perhaps, Churchill feared that massive Soviet preparations for defence might lead to Hitler aborting Barbarossa even at this late stage. Churchill must have changed his mind so that by the afternoon of 16th June, Cadogan (without disclosing the source) read very frightening detailed list of German units and their locations to an appalled Maisky.^{clxxxiii} Maisky notified Moscow without delay, but Stalin treated this vital information as another attempt at provoking war between the USSR and Germany. In his post-war memoirs Maisky, probably inadvertently, substituted the date 10 June for 16 June.

While a welcome for the USSR as an ally was being sketchily and furtively contemplated in Whitehall,^{clxxxiv} the official prognosis that Germany would soon defeat the USSR lay on the table. It had been prepared between 9 and 14 June by the JIC, including an amendment that a German conquest might take eight weeks and not six. It would be kind to describe this top level report as sloppy.^{clxxxv} It unquestionably reflected a traditional British upper class irrational fear and ignorance of the tenets of Communism, as well as a pessimistic assessment of the Red Army and Air Force. Notoriously omitted was any consideration of the victories won by the Red Army over the Japanese in the Far East in the summers of 1938 and 1939, new Soviet weaponry in the offing, and the significance of the industrial bases east of the Urals. Yet was this report made to be leaked so that Hitler might derive further encouragement shortly before the invasion date? In so far as it was taken at its face value, it suggested a breathing space while the USSR was being conquered, before there could be a German invasion of Britain or further offensives in the Middle East. It was expedient for Churchill, (who always had to cover the risk of any accusation of pro-Communism) to accept it. It seems that about eighty of the perhaps hundred top people who knew of this odd product of British Intelligence, shared its gloomy forecast.

An earlier decision fit for leaking to Hitler was the intention revealed at the end of May, to bomb the Baku oilfields. By mid-June the MoI under the influence of Churchill was beginning to consider how Britain should react when the USSR was invaded by Germany. In April there had been a highly secret public opinion poll which showed that over 65% of those interviewed favoured good Anglo-Soviet relations, over 20% detested this prospect, and the remainder were undecided.[clxxxvi] The Ministry supervised an internal discussion in late June and there was a conclusion that mass sympathy had to be aroused for the plight of the people of the USSR without any sharing of Communist ideology or respect for the CPGB. Churchill himself began to draft the radio speech for which he was to become famous after its delivery at 9pm, a peak listening time for the BBC, on 22 June. He toyed with the idea of speaking on the Saturday evening immediately before the invasion, but evidently considered that this golden opportunity to add to his reputation for foresight, would raise the risk that British access to ENIGMA information might be suspected by Hitler.[clxxxvii] Churchill was to rise to new heights of persuasive oratory in calling for the USSR to be treated virtually if not nominally as an ally. It is speculative that some of the moving passages of his speech referring to the plight of women and children in the vast Russian countryside would have been inspired by his wife Clementine, whose disposition was certainly more humane than that of her husband.

Meanwhile, the press as a whole continued distancing the USSR to impress Hitler according to plan. Of course many readers would have spontaneously felt disdain for Communism and the USSR consistent with Churchill's stratagem. *The Times* led the field. Even as late as 21 June with the crisis in German-Soviet relations obvious with war likely soon, the editorial line of a few days earlier persisted. THE TIMES on 16 June had advised its readers that the German threat to the USSR was probably *'bluff'* and not *'bludgeon'*. (copyright The Times/Sunday Times 16th June 1941/nisyndication.com) That Hitler was about to strike a new bargain with Stalin to the gross disadvantage of the USSR, was for many interested people in

Britain the likely outcome of the crisis. In so far as the Red Army and Air Force were commented upon, the previous line of disparagement continued. The intrinsic difficulty of a forecast, memories of past unfounded optimism and wishful thinking coupled with dislike and misunderstanding of Communism and the USSR, were bound to be major factors in any assessment of the crisis.[clxxxviii]

Churchill had on 3 May spoken on the BBC to the Polish people, nominally to the few who may have been able to hear him in occupied Poland, but in fact to the numerous exiles in Britain and elsewhere. The date was significant as Polish National day, the 150th anniversary of the Polish declaration of independence. The emphasis was overtly on the slavery of Poles under barbaric Nazi rule, but by implication the USSR was not exonerated. Roosevelt also broadcast on the occasion to the same effect. These speeches have also to be seen against the background of the Pope's ongoing calls for a just peace, notably at Christmas and Easter, which included a profound hostility to Communism and the loaded omission of the USSR from any peace settlement. Churchill did not overlook General Sikorski, the leader of Poles in exile. That Sikorski was kept partly informed of the mission of Hess and saw it as a possible opening to a negotiated peace to be at the expense of the USSR, led to his hurried return from the USA to Britain with the aim of influencing any negotiations. The governments in exile of Poland and Czechoslovakia had just signed a pact of mutual assistance and co-operation, which had also to be taken into account by Churchill.

Another person of standing whose speeches were reported in the USA, was the ostentatiously upper-class Viscount Halifax. As the British ambassador in Washington since January, his speeches were of interest to American audiences keen to listen to well presented pleas for American help for Britain. Halifax displayed his commitment to a liberal-minded Christianity, comprising beliefs values and principles conventionally asserted as representing the basis of the British and American ways of life. He was nicknamed 'the Holy Fox'. His first public speech in the USA in March was published as a White Paper in Britain. Without hectoring, he could lead his American audiences towards a conclusion that it was their commonsense duty to do all they could to support Britain in the best interests of the USA. At Kansas City in the Isolationist Midwest on the evening of 12 May, (immediately after he must have learned of the arrival of Hess in Britain), he reassured his audience that so long as the British Empire stood firm against Nazi Germany, Americans could feel safe. This contention looked at closely could be ambiguous as it was no doubt intended to be, given Churchill's plan to dupe Hitler, about which Halifax must have been told at least something. The German Foreign Office was not going to forget that Halifax had written the introduction to *The British Case*. The American media warmed to Halifax when, as an honoured spectator at a baseball game, he managed to drop his hot dog! As for the British - instigated forgery of tickets for a huge Isolationist rally in New York so as to cause double booking, that tactic risked being counter-productive. The later forgery of correspondence suggesting the imminence of a Nazi coup in Bolivia was however a great success in strengthening Roosevelt's claim that Hitler was threatening the security of the Americas.

In two principal newspapers in Britain, the Beaverbrook - owned *Sunday Express* and the TUC Sunday paper *The People,* the astrologers continued to sway much of public opinion. Their attitude towards the USSR would appear to have had little to do with astrology and a great deal to do with the requirements of British Intelligence to facilitate Churchill's tricks. The one eventuality they did not foresee was the one which was to mature, i.e. the USSR in the war and as an ally of Britain.

Perhaps the single most key sign that public opinion would favour the USSR as an ally, came from the debate in the House of Commons of Thursday 19 June, while Churchill was in the midst of preparing his decisive radio speech to be delivered on the weekend. Ostensibly, the matter raised by the independent-minded leftwing Labour MP Sydney Silverman, centred on Hess. He complained about the continued refusal of the government to make a full statement on Hess. This refusal followed an earlier promise that there would be one. Silverman's emotive speech culminated in his insistence that the government were gravely mistaken in failing to take the people of Britain into their confidence. Morale was suffering as a result. The government should trust the people.

Silverman was well-known as a supporter of the Coalition government, and also as a constructive critic. He was in that grouping which was keen to see the USSR as an ally of Britain. His strong suspicion that Germany was about to invade the USSR was not mentioned, but it must have been an underlying factor. It is equally clear that he must have suspected that there was a hidden motive behind the government's policy of silence over Hess, designed to keep Hitler guessing, as it was officially proclaimed. Probably he surmised that it was to encourage Hitler to make war on the USSR, but he could not speculate in public about that. He could do the next best thing which was vigorously to defend the essence of democracy as trust.

This message would have been recognised by perhaps a majority of MPs, particularly Labour and Liberal ones. The government certainly did. Their spokesman R.A.Butler, stonewalled in reply to Silverman. It was simply government policy not to give any more information about Hess to the public. He restated this bare justification with hardly any elaboration, but he reasonably clearly disavowed appeasement of Nazi Germany. There were only three days to go before the invasion of the USSR. No doubt his performance helped his subsequent promotion to the Ministry of Education.

Other MPs participated in the debate. J. J. Davidson, the Labour MP for a Glasgow working class seat, pertinently remarked that Communists, whom he described as 'a small group of malcontents' were able to exploit the absence of a statement on Hess by fuelling the suspicion that powerful forces in Britain wished to come to terms with Hitler to facilitate a German war against the USSR. He was able to signify, like Silverman, both his deep commitment to the war effort and his antagonism to Communism. In the atmosphere where the invasion of the USSR appeared imminent, he strongly inferred a willingness to accept the USSR as an ally. The third Labour MP to take part was Richard Stokes who sat for Ipswich. His intervention was telling; well-known as a Roman Catholic layman, a managing director of a large engineering company and with a reputation as a sometime appeaser of Nazi Germany, he took the trouble to identify himself with Silverman's motion.

Three Conservative backbenchers also spoke- two of whom making it clear that they had no respect for Hess. One had always been a fierce opponent of Chamberlain's policy of appeasement, more Churchillian than Churchill himself. He was Major Vyvyan Adams of a Leeds constituency. His onslaught on *The Times* was remarkable for its extremism. He accused it of cold-bloodedly being prepared to recommend acceptance of what was widely supposed to be the offer of Hess for peace with Britain, including an agreement that Germany should be free to attack the USSR. No MP openly disagreed with Adams. The advantage to Churchill of this attack on *The Times* must have been calculated as further "evidence" that there was a peace movement in Britain ready to spring into action on the invasion of the USSR. A Conservative backbencher who supported the government in its hush-hush policy over Hess was Henry Strauss, (once a keen follower of Chamberlain), but his enthusiasm was qualified. His reluctance to reject Hess as a prospective negotiator was ambivalent, and secondly his own son was an eloquent Labour backbench MP, an avowed admirer of Cripps.[clxxxix]

The upshot of the debate which terminated without any vote, was that it gave a green light to Churchill once more to show leadership by means of another rhetorical triumph, once the German invasion of the USSR took place. Adding strength to this growing conviction of his of popular support for an alliance with the USSR was an influential trade union journal, the *Railway Review* of 20 June. The General Secretary of the powerful National Union of Railwaymen doubted if Hitler would go so far as to order an attack on the USSR, but, with a considered assessment of Soviet military strength, expressed confidence there would be no Soviet collapse if war came.

Colville gives the best account of the evening of 21 June at Chequers, when Churchill told the company that a German attack on the USSR was about to take place. Colville wrote in his diary that Churchill said openly that he was certain the USSR would be defeated. Colville gives no hint of motive for this assertion. It was useful for Churchill to tell this white lie. It showed he was no pro-Communist, and he would have felt some anxiety that his speech the next evening might be taken as if he were. In fact this fear was groundless. Secondly, it put out a strong deceptive signal that he had not worked hard and clandestinely for a German invasion of the USSR. Churchill, unlike most of his inner circle, did believe the USSR would hold out for at least two years.[cxc] This view was certainly ruthlessly distanced from the conclusion of the JIC of little more than a week earlier! Churchill, according to Colville, thought that Hitler was counting on capitalist and right-wing interests in Britain and the USA for support. He insisted that British aid to the USSR would be a priority. John Winant, the American ambassador who was present (and who had recently consulted with Roosevelt himself), said the same would be true of the USA.

Colville was clearly feeling anxious about the imminent prospect of an Anglo-Soviet alliance, and this view represented a whole section of British opinion, mostly of the upper class. It seems he was looking for reassurance from Churchill, whose leadership by now he greatly admired. He informally told Churchill when they were alone together after dinner, that in his view Churchill was *'bowing down in the House of Rimmon'*. Churchill's response was robust. He *'had only one single purpose - the destruction of Hitler......If Hitler invaded Hell he would at least make a favourable reference to the Devil'*. Colville's diary refers to other incidents of the war unrelated to the invasion of the USSR and ends his entry for the day with a humorous mention of Eden, while earnestly talking, falling accidently backwards into the ditch bordering the garden.

Though Roosevelt, kept informed by Churchill, also prepared to declare the support of the USA for the USSR, the weeks elapsing since the arrival of Hess in Britain had seen a similar official silence about German-Soviet relations. It would be inappropriate, however, to ignore the steady movement of the USA towards formal entry into the war against Germany, although this was not to take place until a few days after Pearl Harbour, over five months later.

On 27 May Roosevelt made his much heralded authoritative speech on the place of the USA in relation to the war and the ongoing American support of Britain, short of actual belligerency. He announced a *'state of unlimited national emergency'*, a grandiose concept, but one lacking any legal definition. In the event, a little shamefacedly, it had to be admitted the next day this did not mean American planes and warships would be escorting convoys to Britain. Grand Admiral Raeder in Germany threatened war against the USA if there were such action, although such a a threat was no more at the time than a sign of displeasure. Nor was the Neutrality Act of September 1939 to be repealed, but it had already been substantially bypassed. Mussolini was outraged by the speech and Rome Radio treated it as a formal declaration of war! This Italian misjudgement was not going to distress Roosevelt, as the Duce was by now a discredited figure on the world stage. The Germans were more circumspect. They did not want to make the USA any more of an enemy, given Hitler's hopes of American complicity once Barbarossa had commenced.

An American merchant ship, the 'Robin Moor' was sunk by a U-boat in the South Atlantic on 21 May. This incident was not to Hitler's liking, but the fact that it was carrying war material to South Africa, (the cargo on deck seen from the U-boat when the stricken vessel was sinking), was of some importance. It seemed at first the crew was lost but by 10 June it was known that the crew had been rescued. In an unrelated incident, the Egyptian liner the 'Zam-Zam', with American passengers on board, was also sunk by a U-boat and some days elapsed before it was known that they too were all safe. Weeks previously, crews of German and Italian merchantmen marooned in American harbours had been plotting the sabotage of their ships. This had led to the conviction or at least internment of those involved, and seizure of the ships. Roosevelt, acting on the principle of the freedom of the seas and in protection of American interests, declared that there had been an act of piracy in relation to the 'Robin Moor'. In reprisal, German assets in the USA were frozen and German consulates ordered to be closed. Similar retaliatory measures were taken against Italy and, qualified and temporarily, against the USSR. Only a few days were to pass, as Roosevelt could now safely surmise, before Barbarossa.

American political and ideological support for Britain since the beginning of May had grown. Republican Wendell Wilkie, who had lost the election of November 1940 to Roosevelt standing for an unprecedented third term, too keenly showed his enthusiasm for the British cause by ignoring Winant, the

American ambassador in London. He was privately reprimanded.[cxci] On 20 May, the *Saturday Evening Post* switched from opposing to supporting Roosevelt. The Isolationists, however, did not cease to campaign. On 6 June, John Cudahy, the former American ambassador to Belgium, received publicity in the *New York Times* and also in *Time* for his recent interview in Berlin with Hitler himself. Here was a move aimed at a negotiated end to the war much as Hess was understood to be proposing.[cxcii] Hitler disowned any German intention to attack anywhere in the Western hemisphere. He told Cudahy such an invasion was about as fantastic as an invasion of the moon. To counter this Isolationist coup, Ickes, the Secretary of State for the Interior, 'scored' Cudahy as '*a megaphone for Hitler's shouts of obscenities*' and Robert Patterson, the American Under-Secretary of War, insisted that the USA should be prepared to fight to stop Hitler, and quickly - otherwise, Hitler would claim Canada and elsewhere, he asserted. For much of public opinion there still lingered a fear of the loss of the Middle East.

The Isolationists were far from crushed. Winant had at Churchill's request returned to Washington, and this must have been to keep Roosevelt informed about the prospect of an Anglo-Soviet alliance to mature on the occasion of Barbarossa. The return of Winant was however, publicised in the media as relating to Hess as a peace negotiator, a theme officially denied . Hoover raised the issue of food relief for German-occupied Europe, where his plea was totally rebuffed by the British government, despite Britain's stance attracting accusations of merciless intransigence.

During these weeks a constant strand of American policy was to maintain diplomatic and public pressure on Vichy France to desist from any closer alignment with Germany. The Vichy French resistance in Syria was bad enough, but the American 'carrot and stick' approach was still viable. By mid-June, it must have become known to Roosevelt, who no doubt informed Churchill, that Vichy France was further persecuting Jews ; probably taken as another sign that Barbarossa as imminent.[cxciii] The presence of the US ambassador in Vichy Admiral Leahy was useful as a source of up-to-date information.

As regards the Far East, there were differences between American and British policies towards Japan. These did not surface but the British Foreign Office feared a possible deal between the USA and Japan at the expense of British and Dutch colonial interests. This did not materialise. The American and British stands against Japan became more resolute but with a growing delusion that Japan would not dare or be ready to fight before perhaps the Spring of 1942, and that Japanese offensives could then be met. Not realised in Britain was the fact that in November 1940 the Japanese government had acquired secret documents seized by a German raider from a sinking British merchantman, indicating a (then top secret) view of the British government that the British Empire in the Far East could not be successfully defended if war in that region were commenced by Japan. The British merchantman SS Automedon sank in the Indian Ocean. It remained unknown that vital documents had not gone to the bottom but had been seized by a German boarding party and their contents later passed to Japan. Regarding the commentaries of the American military journalist Major Fielding Eliot (a regular contributor to the *News Chronicle)*, contains belated severe criticism of of his total misjudgement of Japan's armed strength not long before Pearl Harbour together with other deficiencies in his commentaries- a view shared by Cassandra of the *Daily Mirror.*

CHAPTER 13

Mission Accomplished

The invasion of the USSR by Germany on 22 June 1941 generated in Germany a new expectation that the end of the war was in sight. Victory was anticipated by Hitler and most Germans within two or three months. An example of this confidence was the bet placed with Howard K. Smith by an experienced German journalist, who staked his money on the capture of Moscow by 15 July. It became common knowledge that the German high command expected the destruction of most of the Red army West of the River Dnieper as a result of the mightiest blitzkrieg to date.

It is not the remit of this book to examine the military progress of Barbarossa thereon ; it in fact suffices to quote the extremely prescient entry in Count Ciano's diary on 18th July 1941 : *'In fact, the war is harder than the Germans had foreseen. The advance continues, but it is slow, and harassed by the very vigorous Soviet counter-attacks. Colonel Ame and General Squero ....believed that the Russians will succeed in maintaining a front even during the winter. If this is true, Germany has started a haemorrhage that will have incalculable consequences.'* For his part, General Halder still managed to hold onto and derive some comfort from the myth that most British Conservatives wanted Churchill out of office and peace with Germany.

For the majority of people in German-occupied Europe, the fact there was now a spread of the war to the East kindled a small flame of hope that Germany might eventually prove the loser, despite all appearances to the contrary. The former sharp hostility between the minority of Communists and the majority non-Communists began to be seen as capable of being bridged for the purpose of an organised resistance movement. Churchill's own resolute stand and other broadcasts from the BBC encouraged this new development, but whatever the abstract case for unity against Nazi Germany it was going to take months for positive results on the ground. There still persisted mutual suspicion and a 'wait and see' attitude. Masaryk, who as early as 25 June, was insisting on this unity, ended his moving radio address *'Foes of Hitler of all shades, unite'*. Masaryk 'admitted' that he had not expected the German attack on the USSR - *'Russia'* - *'just now'*. The probability is that he was concealing foreknowledge because he wished to give no sign of its sources.

In recently defeated Yugoslavia, remnants of the Yugoslav army which had evaded capture and were under the Serb patriot General Mihailovitch, and partisans under the inspiring leadership of a Communist and Croat, Tito, attained a degree of unity to harass German and Italian occupation forces. But the political gulf between them proved impossible to bridge; Tito's political aims struck at the root of traditional loyalty to the monarchy, the Greek Orthodox Church and the existing social system.[cxciv]

In Western Europe Nazi domination began to lose its veneer of impenetrability, as industrial sabotage - mainly Communist inspired - mounted. Imprisonments, hostage- taking and executions of patriots followed, on an increasing scale. Prior to Barbarossa, it appears that Nazi executions of resistance activists had not yet reached four figures. The growth of a Nazi reign of terror inevitably had the dual effect of deterring acts of violence against German soldiers, officials and political collaborators and sharpening the polarisation of loyalties.

However, so long as Nazi Germany appeared to be winning on the Eastern front, restraint on the part of many would-be resisters prevailed.

In Vichy France, Petain and his circle continued to use anti-semitic posturing to obtain concessions over the release of French PoWs, and as a means of reducing the German imposition of extortionate occupation costs. As French manufacturers received a boost as a result of new orders for the German war effort, Vichy was further encouraged to comply with Nazi policy in the hope of aiding a French national recovery. Legal proceedings continued for the farcical trials of politicians who were held responsible for France's entering the war unprepared.

By the time Stalin spoke to the people of the USSR on 3 July, it was already known that Britain and the USA had undertaken to be supportive of the USSR. Their official declarations to this effect were warmly welcomed, though Churchill's insistence that he remained opposed to Communism was censored. The politically-minded would have recalled that the foreign policy aims of the former Commissar of Foreign affairs Maxim Litvinov were in a way being fulfilled. At this stage of the war, the formation of an international front against Nazism across the political spectrum was a new and encouraging phenomenon.

Stalin made a broad (and for him, strangely moving) appeal for enthusiastic participation in the defence of the USSR. Not only Communists but patriots and religious believers could willingly accept what he said including his declaration of a *'scorched earth'* policy to deprive the invaders of economic gains at whatever cost. While his brief history of the twelve – day - old war was hardly accurate, it was certainly proof of determination and faith in ultimate victory. All accounts suggest the speech, typically free of flamboyance, was highly inspiring.

Five days after Barbarossa began, Cripps returned from London to Moscow to resume his ambassadorial duties. The Soviet response was now friendly, and gave him some confidence that the USSR could maintain a solid resistance. A British mission, military and civilian, was welcomed to Moscow to offer advice for the Soviet war effort. While military information about the front was disappointingly withheld - because of the huge losses and chaos - the head of the military mission, Major-General Mason MacFarlane was before long impressed by the professionalism of the Soviet high command. He put to one side his hatred of the Soviet regime. In July, British journalists began to arrive in Moscow to supplement the previously established tiny British press corps. These new arrivals included Alexander Werth, Russian born and an émigré from his teenage years, no Communist but knowledgeable and sympathetic towards the Soviet people and war effort. Charlotte Haldane also appeared in Moscow, then a fervent Communist and the wife (though separated) of the famous Communist scientist J.B.S.Haldane . Werth wrote for *Reuters* and the *Sunday Times*, Haldane for the *Daily Sketch*. Their reports to Britain about the (as yet) calm of wartime life in Moscow were valuable.[cxcv] They enjoyed some co-operation from the authorities and were able to dispel suspicions with natural friendliness. Their experience of the London blitz when Moscow was raided at night about a month after Barbarossa began, was a case in point. Cripps and the other official Britons deeply impressed Werth. He saw civilian morale in wartime Moscow as encouraging and revealing both of Soviet determination and the humanity of the Russian people.

The signing in Moscow on 12 July of an Anglo-Soviet treaty of alliance, (though it was officially described as a "common declaration of aims"), was facilitated by the British presence there, as well as by despatches from Maisky in London. The actual treaty contained only two provisions. To summarise: each party would help the other with its war effort, and neither would make a separate peace with Germany. The speeches following the signing ceremony at the British Embassy included a Soviet reference to American endorsement. Litvinov on 8 July, had broadcast in English on Moscow radio to the world at large, proclaiming democratic unity against Nazi Germany and fascism, and this too had had a positive effect. The same day, a Soviet mission arrived in Britain to purchase war equipment and raw materials.

In Britain on the morning of Sunday 22 June, the BBC gave the first news of the German invasion of the USSR. Churchill was to speak at 9pm. Immense curiosity was generated as to what he would say. During the morning Eden amicably talked with Maisky and assured him that Britain was supportive of the USSR defending itself. The previous afternoon, Cripps had invited Maisky to meet him and had warned him of the invasion about to take place. Maisky immediately warned Moscow. Churchill never showed a draft of his proposed speech to Eden. This omission may have been due to Churchill wishing to demonstrate that he was the boss!

The actual speech ,which had been finalised throughout the day, inspired millions of listeners as some of his best previous orations had done. In the interests of Britain, the USSR ('Russia' he said) was to be, by implication, an ally in the war against Germany. Economic and technical assistance would be sent to the USSR. There would be no separate peace negotiations. Churchill avowedly withdrew nothing which he had said previously against Communism, but he insisted that the great British purpose was to ensure the defeat of Nazi Germany. The emotion he displayed was persuasive. Colville's diary reports with relish friendly, though vehement, arguments at Chequers prior to the speech, when Churchill, Eden, Cripps and his wife, Winant, Cranborne and Fraser the New Zealand premier, were present. Churchill teased Cripps over his Socialist sympathies towards Communism in the USSR . Cripps must have recognised Churchill as in an adolescent mood. Cripps is reputed to have replied to ' Is Stalin popular in Russia? ' with a counter-question 'Is God popular in England? ' and merely feigned amusement.

How the coming Parliamentary debate was to be conducted was another controversial issue. Churchill was for a generous approach, but Eden and Cranborne wanted only military matters to be on the agenda. The effect on Churchill must have been to prepare him for optimal delivery of his oration.

The Sunday papers had been printed before the invasion took place, but Monday's press adequately reflected interested public opinion as largely supportive of Churchill's line. The minority of people who adhered to strong anti-Communist beliefs must have reflected that their best approach was to wait and see what might happen in this gigantic extension of the war. Britain's attitude, they could provisionally reckon, was not likely to be all that significant. The more farsighted of these were willing to uphold Churchill's attitude. It might be that the USSR would be defeated, in which case this would have been expedient. If the USSR, unlike France a year earlier, successfully resisted the blitzkrieg, this would be a contingency which would have to be met with when it arose.

On Tuesday 24 June the House of Commons debated the new situation. Churchill was present but barely participated. Eden displayed the government's enthusiasm in the opening speech. Opposition to Communism was mentioned but not unduly stressed. Virtually all MPs approved of the government's policy of support for the USSR. Attention was inevitably drawn to the speech of the sole Communist MP Willie Gallacher. He could not hide some satisfaction that the USSR had extended its frontier westward to strengthen its defences. He had been *'agreeably surprised'* by Churchill's radio speech,[cxcvi] and he must have too easily assumed Soviet invincibility. When asked by eloquent Welsh Labour MP, James Griffiths, what would now be the role of Communists towards the war effort, there was some Parliamentary knockabout. He uneasily denied that Communists had ever been concerned with '*holding up production*' and when the question was repeated, answered loftily that he needed notice to answer it. He demanded '*the Municheers and the sell-outers*' should now be excluded from the Government. The leadership of the CPGB (with Harry Pollitt once again its General Secretary), soon decided that support for Churchill's government should be unconditional, given its pronounced support for the USSR.

Gallacher was followed by a staunchly Roman Catholic Conservative MP, Commander Robert Bower, who could not resist a dig at Gallacher's evasion. Bower had always been outspoken in his hostility to Communism, but he made it clear that in politics he followed Churchill and not the Vatican. A constructive approach came from Aneurin Bevan, then a Labour backbencher and sometime rebel. He expressed concern that Churchill had not promised sufficient aid to the USSR, and he wanted a secret session for the topic to be fully aired. Discontented MPs including a few Conservatives represented a strand of opinion which Churchill could not ignore, but they kept quiet. A satisfied Maisky was present to listen to the debate. That week and following he was to be a guest of honour at many semi-public functions, more popular personally than ever.

The political problems associated with the new prospective alliance were substantial. Churchill's policy of support for the USSR had to be implemented. Mason MacFarlane, chosen to head the military mission to Moscow, was half-jokingly advised by his military colleagues that he should be prepared to rough it when the Germans captured Moscow after a few weeks. Part of his brief was to arrange the destruction of the oil wells of the Caucasus if necessary and he was told thatn if push came to shove, he might have to walk to India! Churchill had to confront this mood of defeatism with tact and guile, and pray in aid the motivation and strength of resistance to the invaders as his foremost prop. When on 8 July, a Soviet general arrived in London at the head of his country's reciprocal military mission, enough lingering anti-Soviet prejudice led to the press being instructed that there should be no photographs of handshakes shown. The *Daily Herald* showed a photograph of the Soviet entourage and their hosts walking together on a platform at Euston station. The most publicised farce was that of the refusal of the BBC to play the "Internationale" (anthem of the world Communist movement) during the morale-boosting broadcasts of the allies' national anthems on Sunday evenings. An offer of a substitute for the "Internationale" was unacceptable to the Soviet embassy. After a few weeks, the BBC ended the series with the lame excuse that time did not allow for the continuation of the programme. Much of the press could only mock at yet more silliness from the MoI, which was largely responsible for these gaffes.

The movement towards the signing of the agreement in Moscow on 12 July was greatly strengthened by the defiant speech of Stalin nine days earlier, which was favourably reported in the British press. Meanwhile, the public was kept largely in the dark on how the war in the East was going. There was a natural scepticism about official German claims. The Soviet communiqués were designed to raise morale and not to admit the terrible defeats being inflicted on the Red Army. No one could be sure where the truth lay. Churchill on 7 July wrote to Stalin a conciliatory letter which included praise of the Red army for its "magnificent resistance" Churchill had learned from ENIGMA even before the end of June that the Wehrmacht was meeting unexpected resistance from the Red army.. This tactful gesture was calculated to help to dispel any residual suspicion that Churchill might harbour a hope that the USSR and Germany should destroy each other.

In fact, after Churchill's speech of 22 June, any Soviet assessment of Britain as devious was only occasional. For his part, Churchill knew of the danger of suspicion and its role in prompting the Nazi-Soviet Pact of August 1939. Neither Stalin nor Churchill could totally eliminate their suspicion of the other, but each suppressed it. The role of Cripps in Moscow was key. As Werth put it, his idealism was more valuable than the so-called realism of others. In Cripps' own judgement, he was applying his Christian faith to politics. Much of his standpoint came from his position near the leadership of the Labour Party in the early 1930s, and from his legal representation of trade unionists and others often undertaken freely in some of the worst cases of injustice. His forthright opposition to fascism and his status as for some years the most highly paid lawyer in Britain, gave him a singularity of reputation and political importance.

Linked with the political problems presented by an alliance with the USSR, was the question of what warlike action Britain could take in support. The most obvious course was to use the RAF to hit the German economy and armed forces hard and to force the Luftwaffe to deploy more warplanes and anti-aircraft defences away from the Eastern front. Night raids on German cities became more frequent, and day- raiding on nearer targets was tried with fighter escorts where the range permitted. However night bombing by the RAF continued to be mostly ineffective until the introduction of the supremely capable Avro Lancaster in 1943 along with new technologies such as "window", to confuse enemy radar .

The most difficult question was ; what might be done by the army to open a 'Second Front'? In Mid-July, Stalin in his letter of reply to Churchill, was requesting raids and landings in occupied Europe to draw away units of the Wehrmacht from the Eastern front. Whatever Churchill himself had requested, virtually nothing happened. This was primarily down to the inertia and pessimism of the Chiefs of Staff.[cxcvii] They must have recalled all the previous British defeats on land. The RAF would have to attain and maintain air superiority and the Royal Navy would have to allocate precious warships and other vessels. No scheme proposed was regarded as feasible. However, more enterprise could arguably have been shown in relation to the thousands of miles of enemy coastline. There were high ranking officers and units, including Commandos, prepared to carry out aggressive raids. Undue caution was too ingrained for an objective assessment to be made, of the advantages and risks. Army units and ships were still kept in reserve in case Spain should enter the war against Britain on the side of Germany, and the Spanish islands in the Atlantic had to be seized.

What was most feared was a collapse of Soviet resistance and a virtual end to the Eastern front. However, the reinforcement of the Middle East was treated as the first priority. Fresh divisions were transported round the Cape, and more warplanes were delivered to Takoradi for assembly there and onward flight to Egypt. Middle East Command, now under General Auchinleck, could hope to feel secure before long, but the fear persisted that the Wehrmacht might reach the Caucasus and invade Iran and perhaps Turkey. Diplomatic arrangements with the USSR would facilitate a joint entry into pro-German Iran by the Red Army and British forces, but this was not to be until late August.[cxcviii] The threat from Japan to the Far East with its wealth of rubber, tin and oil, continued to be underestimated by Churchill. Duff Cooper, now clearly unsuited to head MoI, was sent to Singapore as political supremo. He was not a good choice and his journey took three months. The strength and proficiency of the Japanese armed forces had been the subject in April of a lecture in Singapore to senior officers by the British military attaché in Tokyo. His warnings were utterly derided by the then C-in-C, General Bond, who was present. The audience agreed with Bond.[cxcix]

The totally inadequate preparations for war seemed enough. The public too continued to be misled. Churchill himself was deceived, it seems.

A Soviet suggestion that a British expeditionary force be sent into action in the Ukraine, was rejected. Other than the presence of a few warships in the Arctic, the only fighting force to be sent, (and not until late August), consisted of two Hurricane fighter squadrons to the area of Murmansk in the North near the front line. Their prowess was acclaimed in the USSR.

Another constraint on any landing on the continent was the fear of an invasion of Britain, still feared once the enemy conquest of the USSR had taken place. In July, this eventuality was rather perfunctorily deemed postponed until September! The Home Guard continued its training. A big anti-invasion exercise was planned for late September - "Operation Bumper". The diary of the 20 year old Lance-Bombardier contains this entry for 18 July: '*From reveille we were standing to as if expecting invasion. In the afternoon the major came out & we went through an imaginary attack on parachutist(s) over by a hay stack. It went off O.K. though in my opinion a couple of men with tommy guns could have wiped us out when we charged across the open. Then we performed the gas scheme & this also seemed pretty successful....*' Wet clothes and guard duty tormented him that night.[cc]

The first 'Russian convoy' was planned to depart from Britain in August, its destination Murmansk. The Soviet delegation which had arrived in Britain on 8 July had presented a list of items needed. The Soviet economy was already deprived of some industrial areas, and worse threatened. Some contracts were negotiated for millions of pairs of boots, telephone equipment and invaluable raw materials. Tanks and planes were ordered. Even though second-rate they were better than nothing. Later military supplies such as Jeep vehicles and Mustang fighter planes from the USA were of much better quality and effectiveness. The appointment of Beaverbrook as Minister of Supply on 1 July marked another step forward for Anglo-Soviet relations. While his influence in favour of a 'Second Front' was diminished, his great drive for arranging supplies for the USSR was an asset. Churchill accepted that Lend-Lease supplies for Britain would be reduced whilst the USA met urgent Soviet needs.

Although a cloud of uncertainty inevitably hung over any prophecy of how the new conflict in the East might go, optimists were outspoken, sometimes lyrical. Dennis Wheatley reflected *'This Spring things looked about as bad as they could for us.....God intervened and 22 June would be a date that generations of our children may yet be taught to remember with thanksgiving'.* Graves reported in his diary of 23 June with unintended irony: *'Lunched at the Senior, where someone was saying that Churchill had specially requested Stalin to make all his communiqués as accurate and conservative as ours. Stalin is said to have agreed. Let's hope he sticks to It'.* George Bernard Shaw wrote to *The Times* which published his letter: *'Either Hitler is a greater fool than I took him for or he's gone completely mad. Why people seemed to think Hitler could beat Russia, I can't imagine'.*(copyright The Times/Sunday Times 23rd June 1941/nisyndication.com) Academics and military experts pointed to the destruction in the Russian winter of Napoleon's Grand Armée. Perhaps predictably, Tchaikovsky's 1812 overture became more popular than ever as a broadcast music choice .

In the darkest moments of German victories on the Eastern front, the thought of a supposedly astute Soviet military strategy sustained the morale of many. The huge Soviet military losses could only be guessed at in Britain, but the German conquest of territory and resources was evident enough. It was attractive to believe that the Red Army was retreating to draw the Wehrmacht into a colossal trap to be sprung at the onset of winter. This consideration was present in the minds of both the Soviet and German high commands. By the end of July, Hitler was seriously disappointed. The direct thrust of the Wehrmacht towards Moscow on which he had relied so much, was being held about two hundred miles west of the capital. Hitler became worried, ostensibly about the unexpected strength of the Red army's tank force. He confided that had he known of it, he would have thought twice about Barbarossa.[cci] He kept quiet about the equally unexpected determination of Britain and the USA to help the USSR.

On 23 June at Ankara, von Papen through an intermediary informed the British ambassador that Germany was ready to make peace with Britain. On 24 June Attlee said in a broadcast there would be a German peace offensive if Germany beat Russia. Von Papen must have been partly misled on 13 May 1941, either deliberately or inadvertantly, by the Turkish Foreign Minister Mr. Saracoglu. Von Papen reported to the German Foreign Office that Mr. Saracoglu had told him of his 'personal feeling that England would shortly be ready to reach an agreement' (for peace with Germany), and Mr. Saracoglu had opined further that a German invasion of Russia would fail unless Germany reached a prior understanding with 'England' and if not, Bolshevism would take over Europe. Mr. Saracoglu was pro-British,(although primarily pro-Turkish), and had presumably been influenced by the internal claim of the Foreign Office in London of 30 April about Hitler's 'madman's dream', and of course by the arrival of Hess in Britain of which the sensational news had broken late 12 May. Attlee kept an open mind as to whether Russia or Germany would win.

Hitler's only practical course as July ended, was to insist on fresh and powerful offensives elsewhere on the Eastern front. His megalomania led to his overruling many of his top generals (much to their consternation) over these proposed offensives and to his eventual assumption of supreme command. The generals began to despise him over his self-opinionated rejection of what they assessed to be the sound strategy of exploiting an existing advantage; the relative proximity to the German forces and the vulnerability of the Red Army's investment in the defence of Moscow. Stalin also, was afflicted with an overestimate of his own military aptitude which his best generals deplored. The defence of all Soviet territory was simply too much for the gravely weakened Red army. Not a hint of these internal controversies seems to have been known to Churchill.

In Britain, leftwingers in addition to Communists, pressed their case for Anglo-Soviet co-operation and increased mutual understanding, with one watchful eye on the Communist Party of Great Britain's (CPGB's) stake. The publisher Victor Gollancz quickly wrote a slim effective volume in support. While insisting that this was no time for recriminations against the USSR or Communists, he nonetheless scorned the Communist misjudgement of Nazism for the previous twenty one months. Many publications and speeches gave signs that the new alliance could work. Anti-Soviet views were being marginalised to the regret of those whose distrust of Communism and the USSR prevailed over the need for national survival.[ccii] Harry Polllitt, the new CPGB General Secretary, was wholeheartedly for harmony with Churchill as Britain's leader. Pollitt imposed his will with a diplomatic argument that traditional class struggle was now off the agenda given the new situation, and that the Coalition Government should be supported. The embarrassing challenge the CPGB presented was to inspire among many non- Communists and anti-Communists, better support for a united war effort. Admiration grew for the Red army for its infliction of (at the time), limited defeats over the Wehrmacht, as sympathy grew over the immense sacrifices of the people of the USSR. Mrs

Churchill herself was soon to lead the officially sponsored "Red Cross Aid to Russia" campaign. Uneasily co-existing with this new wave of enthusiasm, was much complacency, cynicism and war weariness ; an attitude that spoke : "Let's let the Russians do the fighting now".

The growth of these sentiments presented a dilemma for the anti-Communist Churchill, but he never was to lose sight of the paramount need for Hitler's Germany to be destroyed by the emerging Grand Alliance. Only a few Communists obtained the King's commission and became officers in the forces despite many more gaining the credentials, but police harassment of Communist street meetings soon ceased after 22 June. Public distaste for this, was evident. Communist sympathies were conspicuous in some aircraft factories. In September Churchill was (unexpectedly) cheered by the workers when visiting a Coventry factory making Whitley bombers. These outdated and utterly inferior aircraft may have been destined only for the scrapheap, such was the persistence of industrial disorganisation. Public feeling was eventually to become so strongly pro-Soviet that any open adverse criticism of the Soviet way of life was likely to be classed as pro-Nazi propaganda!

Early in 1943 came the start of the episode of the *Sword of Stalingrad*. The recapture of Stalingrad by the Red army and the final destruction of the best army of the Wehrmacht were imminent by 30 January, the tenth anniversary of the appointment of Hitler as Chancellor of the Weimar Republic and the formation of his Nazi - dominated government. A special rally was held in Berlin in celebration, though the ceremony was delayed for an hour by RAF Mosquito bombers deliberately flying above. Most British and American readers of the rally speeches would have been heartened by the whines, excuses and self-pity displayed over the failure of the German war against the USSR. Goering and Goebbels each gave a frightening warning to the German public. WW2 might be lost by Germany unless "total war" were waged. There was clearly a risk that Hitler might order the publication to the World of 'the royal letter' of twenty one months earlier with the aim of driving a wedge between Britain and the USSR. Such a risk had to be avoided at all costs.

One remedy for this potential risk lay in the reaffirmation of the British-Soviet alliance. On 26th February 1943, the public announcement that a magnificent "Sword of Honour" was going to be wrought in Britain for King George VI to present to *'commemorate the glorious defence of Stalingrad'*, its ruins finally liberated soon after 30 January. It must be noted that not until early in April, did Churchill first learn of a possible (in fact actual) Soviet massacre of thousands of Polish officers at Katyn.[cciii] The public German accusation followed in mid-April. While there was a suspicion that many Polish PoW officers had been murdered in the USSR sometime between September 1939 and the Spring of 1941, it is certainly hard to link the "Sword" with any revelation of that atrocity. What was crucial was to show the World that Britain attached tremendous importance to the war against Hitler's Germany, and the USSR was to continue to be an ally, regardless of Nazi propaganda that Britain and the USA should now openly fight the USSR and Communism.

Of course, any publication of 'the royal letter' would have led to a British denial of its authenticity. This must have been foreseen by Hitler, having in mind the news of the "royal sword". The "Sword" was presented by Churchill on behalf of the King to Stalin at the Teheran Conference of the Autumn of 1943. Churchill jocularly mentions in his CLOSING THE RING, that it was dropped by Voroshilov after it had been kissed by Stalin.

The news of the German invasion of the USSR found most Americans in a confused state of mind. Even if there were sympathy for the victims of this new aggression, most commentators believed the blitzkrieg would again triumph, and soon. On the other hand, Churchill's speech of 22 June did register an impact. It gave a cue to Roosevelt to announce on 24 June that the USA would assist the USSR in the war, because Hitler's Germany was the common enemy. The USSR was to be free to purchase American goods, including weapons, industrial equipment and raw materials, but Lend-Lease would not be extended. Soviet financial assets in the USA would be immediately unfrozen. In fact they were seen as adequate for all foreseeable purchases. This adherence of Roosevelt to normal profitable business practice was indicative and deliberate.

The bulk of public opinion and Congress supported Roosevelt's initiative. The argument deployed by the future Vice-President - and subsequently President - Senator Truman, summarises the conflict of opinion over the new attitude to be taken towards the USSR. He declared that if *'Germany were winning the USA should help Russia, and if the latter were winning then the USA should help Germany'*. Such weasel words were expedient for routing the opposition to Roosevelt. It was glaring that the first limb of Truman's cynical proposition was applicable. The second limb was to become a total anachronism by the time it became applicable. Of course, the Isolationists were not going to be silenced, and they foresaw with relish the end of Communism. However, their main supporters on the Left, the American Communist Party, had immediately joined ranks behind Roosevelt. Their change of allegiance came literally within an hour or two. Sherwood tells the story of how Communists were picketing a pro-Britain rally on the Saturday evening and by the time the rally was over and the news of the invasion had arrived, the pickets had disappeared.[cciv] The incidence of strikes in war industry began perceptibly to diminish.

The famous airman and political reactionary, Charles Lindbergh, remained outspoken and publicly declared at an

'America First' rally at San Francisco ' *I would a hundred times rather see my country ally herself with England or even with Germany with all her faults than with the cruelty, the godlessness and barbarism that exists in Soviet Russia'.* William Bullitt, the first American ambassador to the USSR, was even more ferocious: ' *Stalin and Hitler are like twins out of hell....we ought to rejoice that Satan and Lucifer are fighting each other'.* The Roman Catholic bishops found themselves in a dilemma, but the distinctly conservative American Legion at their national Conference on 2 July pointed the way forward for many. They called for increased aid to Britain, the defence of the freedom of the seas and opposition to Communism, Fascism and Nazism. Here was a formula which could be interpreted as supportive of American sales of weapons to the USSR. The bitter anti-Communists could console themselves with an inner belief in a German victory in the East soon. The Vatican broadly supported the new Nazi 'crusade' against Communism and remained notoriously inert over the genocidal application of anti-semitism.[ccv]

In contrast, there was a special role for the American ambassador to Moscow of 1936 to 1938. He was the irrepressible Joseph E. Davies, a wealthy capitalist and important in the Democratic Party, who viewed sympathetically the rapid modernisation of the Soviet economy. From the outset of the invasion, he did his best to persuade the administration in Washington to build new friendly relations with the USSR. He was confident that probably the Red army would offer successful resistance. His efforts helped the equally alert Vice-President, Harry Hopkins, to travel in July on behalf of Roosevelt first to London, and then to Moscow.

The amicable relationship which developed between Stalin and Hopkins facilitated the flow of American and British supplies to the USSR, and for the planned Moscow Conference to organise this. The conference was to be attended by Beaverbrook from Britain and Harriman from the USA. When the Soviet Purchasing mission arrived in Washington towards the end of July, Davies learned with enthusiasm of superior models of Soviet tanks and planes capable of being mass produced in the USSR out of reach of the Luftwaffe, and forcefully advocated massive aid for the USSR from the USA. This aid was to materialise in the course of the war. It is no exaggeration to state the view that with this action, firm foundations for Allied victory in World War 2, had been laid.

CHAPTER 14

Reflections

It cannot be emphasised too highly that the immediate events of April and May 1941 leading to Hess's surprise arrival, remain shrouded in mystery. *Just what is deemed so sensitive that it cannot be disclosed sixty years later,* even now (and especially after the collapse of the USSR)? A "neutral" royal's participation in international deception in wartime may be viewed as one such deeply sensitive issue, for no politician would dare to expose such a scheme and in doing so, implicitly acknowledge either that the credibility of such a diplomatic "weapon" has been lost forever, or (worse still!), try to attempt to justify such an amoral action by a civilised power retrospectively to the rest of the world, including confirmation to Russia that Britain's self-preserving machinations may have indirectly caused the deaths of some 20 million Soviet civilians? Either option would entail a high risk of career suicide. If Churchill felt unable to broach the above, it appears unlikely *in extremis* that any of the modern crop of bland careerist-administrators comprising the Government of the United Kingdom would put their heads above the parapet until positively compelled to. In addition to the above, which modern politician would remotely wish to contemplate the domestic impact of past royal participation in such a deceptive scheme, upon the ideological justifications advanced for the continuation of the Monarchy itself?

Concerning the art of deception in warfare, it is not as if deception and obfuscation has declined in modern diplomacy-quite the opposite, and one need not look far for recent major examples of military action and alliances motivated by dubious (to use a neutral word) intelligence.

The release of the Royal Archives may yet supply the answer and if the theory expounded in this book proves correct as to the specific motivation for Hess's flight, the sensational but wholly appropriate adage "You Read It Here First!" will apply.

CHRONOLOGY

Some key dates of WW2 March to July 1941

March 11	Lend-Lease becomes law in the USA
	In Yugoslavia, Belgrade Coup overthrows pro-German government
	In East Africa, imminence of collapse of Italian Empire
	Victory of RN at Battle of Cape Matapan
April 3	In Libya, Germans capture Benghazi
April 6	Germany invades Greece and Yugoslavia
	In Libya, Germans besiege Tobruk
	Germans capture Belgrade
April 15	Evacuation of Empire forces from Greece becomes inevitable
April 17	Yugoslav army surrenders
April 18	In Iraq, Indian army units arrive at Basra to reinforce British occupation
April 22	Greek armies in Epirus and Macedonia surrender
	Germans capture Athens
April 30	Evacuation of Empire forces from Greece virtually completed
	In Berlin, Hitler fixes 22 June as date of German invasion of USSR
May 2	In Iraq, British base at Habbaniyah besieged

May 6	In USSR, Stalin replaces Molotov as Prime Minister
May 10,11	The heaviest German air raid on London (virtually the end of the Blitz)
	Rudolf Hess the German Deputy-Fuhrer lands by parachute in Scotland
	Failure of British offensive in Western Desert
	Italian C-in-C in East Africa surrenders
	German airborne troops invade Crete
	German battleship Bismarck sinks the pride of the RN HMS Hood
May 27	RN sinks Bismarck
	President Roosevelt makes major pro-British speech
May 31	End of the hostile regime in Iraq
June 1	Evacuation of Empire forces from Crete virtually completed
	In Britain, clothes rationing begins
June 8	British and allied forces enter Syria and are opposed by Vichy French forces
	Further British offensive in Western Desert fails (Operation Battleaxe)
June 22	Germany invades USSR
	Churchill in a sensational speech declares Britain will support USSR
	President Roosevelt declares the USA will support USSR
July 12,13	In Moscow, Anglo-Soviet agreement signed with American approval

Selected Book List

A

Paul Addison The Road to 1945 British Politics and the Second World War London 1975

Louis Allen Singapore 1941–1942 London 1993 edn

Martin Allen The Hitler/Hess Deception London 2003

Leo Amery The Diaries of... ed John Barnes & David Nicholson London 1988

Anon The Battle of the Atlantic London 1946

Anon The Campaign in Greece and Crete London 1942

Anon History of the CPSU(B) (transl) Moscow 1938

Anon The Nazi Kultur in Poland London 1944

Anon Science in War London 1940

Jim Arnison Hilda's War Preston 1996

B

Constance Babington Smith Evidence in Camera London 1957

Michael Balfour Propaganda in War 1939–1945 London 1979

Vernon Bartlett And Now Tomorrow London 1960

Max Beaverbrook Politicians and the Press London 1925

Ed. Richard Campbell Begg and Peter H Liddle For five shillings a day, Experiencing war 1939–45 London 2000

Tuvir Ben-Moshe Churchill/Strategy and History London 1992

Joan Beaumont Comrades in Arms London 1980

Cajus Becker (transl Frank Ziegler) The Luftwaffe War Diaries London 1966

Geoffrey Best Churchill A Study in Greatness

George Bilainkin Diary of a Diplomatic Correspondent London 1941

London 1941London 1944
Michael Bloch Ribbentrop London 1992
Willi A Boelcke The Secret Conferences of Dr Goebbels
   October 1939-March 1943 (transl
   Ewald Osers) London 1967
Robert Boothby I Fight To Live London 1947
Michael J F Bowyer 2 Group RAF A Complete History
   1936–1945 London 1974
Alexander Boyd The Soviet Air Force since 1918 1977
Sarah Bradford King George VI London 1989
Noreen Branson History of the Communist Party of Great
   Britain 1927–1941 London 1985
History of the Communist Party of Great Britain 1941–1951
   London 1997
Bertolt Brecht (transl HR Hays) Compact Poets London 1972
Douglas Brown & Christopher Serpell If Hitler Comes London
   1941 edn
Abraham Brumberg Neighbors London 2001
Arthur Bryant Turn of the Tide/The Alanbrooke Diaries
   London 1957
Alan Bullock Hitler A Study in Tyranny London 1952
T D Burridge British Labour and Hitler's Wars London 1976
Michael Burleigh The Third Reich London 2000
Kendal Burt & James Leasor The One That Got Away London
   1958 edn
Ewan Butler Mason-Mac (a biography) London 1972
J R M Butler Grand Strategy vol II London 1957

C
Sir Alexander Cadogan (ed David Dilks) Diaries London 1971
Angus Calder The People's War London 1969
David Calton Anthony Eden – a biography London 1981,
   Churchill and the Soviet Union
Manchester 2000
David Carroll Dad's Army The Home Guard Stroud 2002
Robert Cecil Hitler's Decision to Invade Russia London 1975

Sir Henry Channon, (ed Robert Rhodes James) Chips, The Diaries of...London 1967

John Charmley Churchill The End of Glory London 1993

Anne Chisholm & Michael Davie Beaverbrook A Life London 1992

Arthur Christiansen Headlines All my Life London 1961

Winston S Churchill The Gathering Storm London 1948
  Their Finest Hour London 1950
  The Grand Alliance (TGA) London 1950
  The Hinge of Fate London 1951
  Closing the Ring London 1952
  Triumph and Tragedy London 1954
  History of the English Speaking Peoples Vol 1 London 1956

Ciano (ed Malcolm Muggeridge, transl) The Ciano Diaries 1939–1943 Great Britain 1947

Alan Clark Barbarossa London 1995 edn

Peter Clarke The Cripps Version The Life of Sir Stafford Cripps London 2002

W P & Zelda K Coates A History Of Anglo-Soviet Relations London 1944

G D H Cole A History Of The Labour Party From 1914 London 1948

Richard Collier The Years Of Attrition 1940–1941 London 1995 edn

John Connell Wavell Scholar and Soldier (to June 1941) London 1964

John Colville The Fringes Of Power Vol I London 1985

R W Cooper The Nuremberg Trial London 1947

John Cornwell Hitler's Pope London 2000

John Costello Ten Days That Saved The West London 1991

John de Courcy Behind the Battle London 1942

Milton Crane The Roosevelt Era New York 1947

Martin Van Creveld Hitler's Strategy 1940–41 The Balkan Clue Cambridge 1973

D

Hugh Dalton (ed Ben Pimlott) The Second World War Diary Of.... London 1986

Jospeh E Davies Mission To Moscow London 1942

David Day Menzies And Churchill At War Oxford 1993

I C B Dear (general ed) The Oxford Companion to the Second World War Oxford 1995

Len Deighton Blood, Tears and Folly London 1995 edn

Sefton Delmer Black Boomerang London 1962

Robin Denniston Churchill's Secret War Oxford 1997

Roy Douglas New Alliances 1940–1941 London 1982

James Douglas-Hamilton Motive For A Mission London 1985 edn

Tom Driberg Ruling Pasions London 1977

R Palme Dutt India Today Bombay 1949

E

Bill Eburn Be My Guest - The Autobiography of An Ex-Japanese PoW London 1985

Sybil & David Eccles By Safe Hand – Letters of…1939–1942 London 1985

Anthony Eden The Reckoning (The Eden Memoirs) London 1965

Ruth Dudley Edwards Victor Gollancz (a biography) London 1987

I Ehrenburg Eve of the War 1933–1941(transl Tatiana Shebunina in collab'n with Yvonne Knapp) London 1963

Paul Einzig In The Centre Of Things London 1960

John Ellis The Sharp End London 1990, Brute Force London 1990

John Erickson The Road To Stalingrad London 1975

Facts on File Yearbook vol 1 1941 ed. Bernard Pearson

F

Michael Foot and others (sub-nom "Cato") Guilty Men London 1940

Debts of Honour London 1980
M R D Foot Resistance European Resistance to Nazism 1940–1945 London 1976
SOE The Special Operations Executive 1940–1946 London 1984
The Forrerstal Diaries ed. Walter Mills London 1952
Anne Frank The Diaries of (transl B M Mooyaout) London 1954
Julius Fucik Report from the Gallows (transl & ed Stephen Jolly London 1957
Gusta Fucikova Julius Fucik Prague 1955

G

G Gafencu Prelude to the Russian Campaign (transl E Fletcher-Allen) London 1945
William Gallacher The Rolling of the Thunder London 1947
David Garnett The Secret History of PWE London 2002
Martin Gilbert Finest Hour 1939–1941 London 1983
Second World War London 1989
Churchill A Life London 1991
In Search of Churchill London 1994
Goebbels Diaries 1939–1941 (transl Fred Taylor) London 1982
Victor Gollancz The Betrayal of the Left London 1941
Russia and Ourselves London 1941
Gabriel Gorodetsky Stafford Cripps' Mission to Moscow 1940–1942 London 1984
Grand Delusion, Stalin and the German invasion of Russia London 1999
Charles Graves Off the Record (a diary) London 1942
Jack Green & Alessandro Massinagni The Naval War in the Mediterranean 1940–1943
London 1998
J M A Gwyer Grand Strategy vol III pt 1 London 1964

H

Paul Hagen Will Germany Crack? London 1943

Charlotte Haldane Russian Newsreel London 1943, Truth will Out London 1949

Franz Halder The Halder War Diaries 1939–1942 ed Charles Burduck & Adolf Jacobsen London 1988 edn

Donald Hamilton-Hill SOE Assignment London 1975 edn

Averell Harriman & ElieAbel Cairo HQ/ Special Envoy to Churchill & Stalin 1941–1946 London 1976

John Harris & M J Trow Hess The British Conspiracy London 1999

Roy Harrod Lindemann The Prof (biography of Lord Cherwell) London 1959

Oliver Harvey The War Diaries of…..1941–1945 ed John Harvey London 1978

Max Hastings Bomber Command London 1979

Konrad Heiden Der Fuehrer (transl Ralph Mannheim & Norbert Guterman) London 1944

Margaret Heinemann Britain's Coal London 1944

R E Herzstein The War that Hitler Won - Nazi Propaganda London 1979

Trumbull Higgins Hitler and Russia 1937–1943 London 1966

Robin Higham Diary of a Disaster British Aid to Greece Kentucky 1986

F H Hinsley British Intelligence in the Second World War Its influence on strategy and Operations Vols 1 2 3 4 6 (5@) London 1979–1990

HMSO Persuading the People London 1995

Harold Hobson The First Three Years of the War (a diary) London 1943

Vere Hodgson Few Eggs and No Oranges (a diary) London 1976

Michael Howard (5@) Strategic Deception London 1990

Emrys Hughes Winston Churchill in War and Peace Glasgow 1950

Douglas Hyde I Believed London 1951

I

David Irving Hitler's War London 1991
Lord Ismay The Memoirs of London 1960
Anthony James Informing the People London 1996
Robert Rhodes James Anthony Eden London 1986
Mark Johnson Fighting the Enemy Australian Soldiers
  Cambridge 2000
R V Jones Most Secret War London 1978
Judex Anderson's Prisoners London 1940
Carl Jung Essays on Contemporary Events (transl Elizabeth
  Welsh,
Barbara Hannah, Mary Briner) London 1947

K

John Noble Kennedy The Business of War London 1957
Ian Kershaw Hitler Nemesis 1936–1945 London 2000
Louis C.Kilzer Churchill's Deception Simon and Schuster 1994
Warren F Kimball Churchill and Roosevelt The Complete
  Correspondence Vol 1
Princeton 1984
Cecil King With Malice towards None (a diary) ed William
  Armstrong London 1970
S W Kirby The War against Japan vol 1 The Fall of Singapore
  London 1957
Singapore: The Chain of Disaster London 1971
Ivone Kirkpatrick The Inner Circle London 1959
Victor Klemperer The Diaries of... (abridged & transl Martin
  Chalmers) London 1999 edn
Frida Knight The French Resistance 1940–1944 London 1975
MacGregor Knox Hitler's Italian Allies Cambridge 2000

L

Richard Lamb Churchill as War Leader London 1991
D A Lande Occupied Europe and its Defiance of Hitler
  Wisconsin 2000
R Langhorne (ed) Diplomacy and Intelligence in the Second
  World War Cambridge 1985

Harold Laski Where do We Go from Here? London 1940
Joseph P Lash Roosevelt and Churchill 1939–1941 London 1977
Sheila Lawlor Churchill and the Politics of War Cambridge 1994
Barry Leach German Strategy against Russia Oxford 1973
James Leasor Rudolf Hess The Uninvited Envoy London 1962
Jennie Lee Our Ally Russia The Truth London 1941
Raymond Lee The London Journal of.....1940/ ed. J Leutze London
B H Liddell Hart The Other Side of the Hill London 1948
Lord Lloyd The British Case London 1939
Stefan Lorant I Was Hitler's Prisoner (a diary)(transl James Cleugh) London 1935

M

Malcolm MacEwen The Greening of a Red London 1991
Fitzroy Maclean Eastern Approaches London 1949
Ivan Maisky Memoirs of a Soviet Ambassador The War 1939–1943 (trans Andrew Rothstein) London 1967
Thomas Mann This War (transl Eric Sutton) London 1940
Olivia Manning Friends and Heroes London 1965
Jan Masaryk Speaking to my Country London 1944
Mass Observation People in Production London 1942
Arno J Mayer Why did the Heavens not Darken? The Final Solution in History London 1990
John McLain (otherwise John Harris) The British Conspiracy 1994
Ian McLaine Ministry of Morale London 1979
Major A M Meerloo Total War and the Human Mind London 1944
W Franklin Mellor Casualties and Medical Statistics London 1971
Derek Mercer (ed) Chronicle of Second World War London 1990

Allan Merson Communist Resistance in Nazi Germany London 1985

Henry Metelmann Through Hell for Hitler Staplehurst 2001

Martin Middlebrook & Chris Everitt The Bomber Command War Diaries 1939–1945 London 1985

Clara Milburn Mrs Milburn's Diaries ed. Peter Donnelly London 1979

Alan S Milward The German Economy at War London 1965

Economy and Society 1939–1945 London 1977

Ewen Montagu Beyond Top Secret U London 1977

Ivor Montagu The Traitor Class London 1940

Lord Moran Winston Churchill: The Struggle for Survival 1940–1965 London 1966

Ian Morrison Malayan Postscript London 1942

H V Morton Atlantic Meeting London 1943

R Motz Belgium Unvanquished London 1942

Tor Myklebost They Came as Friends (transl Trygvo M Ager) London 1943

N

Robert Neillands The Bomber War, The Desert Rats London 1991

Peter Neumann Other Men's Graves (transl Constantine Fitzgibbon) London 1958

Harol Nicolson Marginal Comment London 1939

Diaries and Letters 1939–1945 ed Nigel Nicolson London 1967

Francis Noel-Baker Greece the Whole Story London 1946

O

Odhams Press The Second Year of War in Pictures London 1941

The British People at War London 1943

Ian Ousby Occupation The Ordeal of France 1940–1944 London 1999

Richard Overy War and Economy in the Third Reich Oxford
1994
Russia's War London 1998
Oxford Companion to the Second World War (see I C B Dear)

P
Peter Padfield Hess The Fuhrer's Disciple London 2001 edn
Mollie Panter-Downes London War Notes London 1972
Bernard Pares Russia London 1941
Roger Parkinson Blood, Tears.Toil and Sweat London 1973
Vladimir Peniakoff Popski's Private Army London 1950
Barrie Pitt The Crucible of War Western Desert 1941 London
1980
Churchill and the Generals Newton Abbot 1981
Major-General I S O Playfair The Mediterranean and Middle
East vol II London 1956
Clive Ponting Armageddon The Second World War London
1995
B N Ponomaryov & Others History of the Communist Party
of the Soviet Union
(transl & ed Andrew Rothstein) Moscow 1960
M M Postan British War Production London 1952
M.Powell and E.Pressburger The Life and Death of Colonel
Blimp Ed. Ian Christie
Faber and Faber 1994
J B Priestley Postscripts London 1940, British Women go to
War London 1945
Lynn Pricknett & Clive Prince & Stephen Prior & Robert
Brydon Double Standards The
Rudolf Hess Cover-up Great Britain 2001
D N Pritt from Right to Left (autobiographical) London 1965

R
Nicholas Rankin Churchill's Wizards Faber and Faber 2008
Hermann Rauschning Hitler Speaks Great Britain 1939
Germany's Revolution of Destruction (transl E W Dickes)
London 1939

Hitler's Aims in War and Peace (transl as above) London 1940

The Beast from the Abyss (transl as above) London 1941

Make and Break with the Nazis (transl as above) London 1941

Makers of Destruction (transl as above) London 1942

Henry Reed Naming of Parts (poem)

John Rees ed The Case of Rudolf Hess London 1947

Laurence Rees World War Two Behind Closed Doors BBC Books 2008

Denis Richards RAF 1939–1945 vol 1 London 1970

Ernie Roberts Strike Back London 1994

Stephen Roskill The War at Sea Vol 1 London 1954

Hankey Man of Secrets Vol III London 1974

Lord Russell The Scourge of the Swastika London 1954

S

Albert Seaton The Russo-German War London 1971

Walter Schellenberg The Schellenberg Memoirs (transl & ed Louis Hagen) London 1956

Anna Seghers The Seventh Cross (transl James A Galston) London 1943

Robert E Sherwood The White House Papers of Harry Hopkins vol 1 London 1948

(Otherwise Roosevelt and Hopkins)

William L Shirer Berlin Diary London 1941

The Rise and Fall of the Third Reich London 1959

Konstantin Simonov Victims and Heroes (transl R Ainsztein) London 1963

Derrick Sington & Arthur Weidenfeld The Goebbels Experiment London 1942

Howard K Smith Last Train from Berlin London 1942

Christopher Somerville Our War London 1998

Albert Speer Inside the Third Reich (transl Richard & Clare Winsten) London 1970

David Stafford ed Flight from Reality Rudolf Hess and His Mission to Scotland

Great Britain 2002
Joseph Stalin Correspondence with Churchill, Attlee, Rossevelt
and Truman London 1957
Edward Stettinius Lend-Lease London 1944
William Stevenson Man Called Intrepid The Secret War
London 1976
Patricia Strauss Cripps - Advocate and Rebel London 1943
Yuri Suhl ed They Fought Back London 1968

T

A J P Taylor Beaverbrook New York 1972
John Terraine The Right of the Line London 1985
Frank Thompson There is a Spirit in Europe (ed T J T & E P
Thompson) London 1947
R W Thompson Churchill and Morton London 1976
R M Titmuss Problems of Social Polic London 1950
H A Trevor-Roper (ed) Hitler's War Directives 1939–1945
London 1964
Ernest Trory Imperialist War Brighton 1977

W

Geoffrey T Waddington Ribbentrop and the Soviet Union
1937–1941
Walter Warlimont Inside Hitler's HQ (transl R H Barry)
London 1964
Evelyn Waugh Officers and Gentlemen London 1965 edn
Charles Webster & Noble Frankland The Strategic Air
offensive against Germany 1939–1945
London 1961
Alexander Werth Moscow '41 (a diary) London 1942, Russia
at War 1941–1945
London 1964
Barton Whaley Codeword Barbarossa Cambridge(Mass) 1973
Denis Wheatley Black August London 1934
Red Eagle London 1937
Faked Passports London 1940

V for Vengeance London 1942
Stranger than Fiction London 1959
The Deception Planners 'My Secret War' ed Anthony Lejeune
London 1980
Autobiography Vol 3 Drink and Ink London 1981
Richard Woodman Arctic Convoys London 1994
Llewellyn Woodward British Foreign Policy in the Second
World War vol 1 London 1970
vol 2 London 1971
Jacob Wern-Muller Norway revolts against the Nazis London
1941

Y

Marion Yass This is Your War London 1983
Yegeny Yevtushenko A Precocious Autobiography (transl
Andrew R MacAndrew)
London 1965 edn
The Press: Daily and Sunday newspapers and Weeklies as in the
text and Notes. Also The Economist and Tribune. Monthlies
as in the text and Notes.
Hansard , Facts on File, and Keesings Archives.

Permissions And Acknowledgements

Where extracts appear unaccredited, the editor avers that reasonable efforts have been made by the author and editor to contact the copyright holders.

Specific thanks are due to the following :-

Use of the front cover illustration "Valez (SIC) vous jouer avec moi Mr. Hitler?" by Marinus Kjeldgaard, by kind permission of Mr. Gunner Byskov

Extracts from The Daily Mail by kind permission of The Daily Mail

Extracts from The Times by kind permission of News International PLC

Extract from "Few Eggs and No Oranges" by Vere Hodgson, by kind permission of Persephone Books

Extract from "Tempestuous Journey" by Frank Owen published by Hutchinson. Reprinted by kind permission of the Random House Group Ltd.

Extracts from "The Goebbels Diaries" by kind permission of Penguin Group (UK)

Extract from "The Diary of Sir Alexander Cadogan " by David Dilks published by Faber and Faber, by kind permission of David Higham Assoc.

References

[i] The SUNDAY TELEGRAPH 21 February 1999 p 54.

[ii] PRO WO/99/3288A.

[iii] Sight of the microfilm FO 1093/1 pp18/9 suggests a typewriter in London to the order of Churchill.

[iv] Padfield pp 368–370.

[v] The Duke spoke on the phone to Colville (his diary 11 12 13 14 May). Colville recollects his memory at the time of a novel by Peter Fleming THE FLYING VISIT of which he had dreamed. The novel tells a story of Hitler landing in England by parachute and very soon easily winning first prize in a village fancy dress competition – finally he is returned to Germany by parachute.

[vi] Letter of 1 July Donald Somervell (Attorney–general) to the Treasury Solicitor. PRO Hess microfilm FO 1093/ reels 6 to 12.

[vii] THE TIMES law report 19 February 1942.

[viii] Collier (1941) p 3.

[ix] e.g.Balfour and McLaine.

[x] PRO inf 1/292 (HIWR).

[xi] e.g. Graves 6 May.

[xii] DAILY MAIL 30 April.

[xiii] e.g. THE TIMES 2April: a letter from the Director of Public Relations at the Ministry of Home Security and many official notices.

[xiv] e.g. Middlebrook and Everitt. Boothby pp 227–229 was one of the very many millions who were taken in by exaggerated claims of success by the RAF. Churchill admits his own doubts about the efficacy of RAF raids on

Germany as from late 1940 (see para 5 of Ch XVI of THE HINGE OF FATE).

xv   PRO INF 1 894 & 149B (April 1941).

xvi   Driberg pp161/2.

xvii   THE TIMES 15 March.

xviii   e.g. Stettinius pp 90 - 91.

xix   Masaryk, broadcasts of 5 & 12 March.

xx   Goebbels 18 March.

xxi   Zweininger-Bargielowska are informative.

xxii   Titmuss is authoritative regarding wartime social problems.

xxiii   His speeches in HC on 3 April and 7 May.

xxiv   e.g. correspondence in THE TIMES and the DAILY TELEGRAPH regarding horse-racing. The DAILY MIRROR complained vociferously of such waste.

xxv   e.g. Heinemann and debate in HC on 28 May.

xxvi   e.g.Shinwell in HC on 7 May and at the Whitsun Labour Party Conference.

xxvii   Sinclair in HC on 11 March ; Beaverbrook in HL on 23 April.

xxviii   MP for Hythe in HC on 9 July.

xxix   Cole p 392 Price controls, selective though these were, also featured.

xxx   HC debate 27 March.

xxxi   Judex and Arnison.

xxxii   Day pp 115/6.

xxxiii   e.g. Branson, Hyde and Hinsley vol 4 pp79–85.

xxxiv   DAILY EXPRESS 10 January 1941.

xxxv   John Mason, a shop steward of Mexborough was released after about a year (Hinsley cited as above) and arguably T.E.Nicholas detained later for a few weeks.

xxxvi   e.g on Churchill's flaws R.W.Thompson and Lamb.

xxxvii   SUNDAY TIMES 16 March 1941: the banned Communist composer Alan Bush praised Ralph Vaughan Williams: 'what action could be nobler'.

xxxviii   e.g Einzig pp 217/8 and Lamb Ch 6.

xxxix   Shirer's BERLIN DIARY regarding Hitler's speech of 4 September 1940.

xl   e.g. Moran.

xli   Bunting. General Smuts was promoted to Field-Marshall on 24 May 1941.

xlii   Question Time in HC on 9 April 1941.

xliii   Letter in Owen p.751.

xliv   These diaries include those of Graves, Colville, the Lance-Bombardier Vere Hodgson and Mrs Milburn.

xlv   His diary. Also Graves 27 March. Press reports contemplated an RN base at Kotor and an RAF base at Mostar.

xlvi   Francis Noel-Baker.

xlvii   Graves 28 March and 1 April. The booklet was succeeded by a more sumptuous and illustrated one which also sold exceedingly well.

xlviii   Day, Higham and Lawlor .

xlix   Dalton p177 and Hamilton-Hill p 82. Hinsley vol 1 pp 369–370 . Boelcke mentions bribery as referred to by Goebbels on 6 April.

l   WNV 3 May 1941.

li   In the NEWS OF THE WORLD, Hore-Belisha, in his regular article of 2 March headlined 'Let us try a master-stroke in Moscow', hopes the USSR will help to save Turkey from German aggression.

lii   TGA refers to Yugoslav preparations to meet a German attack as inadequate.

liii   Goebbels 9 April.

liv   According to Dennis Wheatley in his autobiography, Desmond Morton told him that Churchill had told Morton 'How wrong I was to allow Anthony (i.e Eden) to persuade me into agreeing such a disastrous operation.' The DAILY MAIL of 17 and 24 April contained strong and adverse criticisms of Eden as Foreign Secretary. However, in the House of Commons debate of 6th and 7th May, Vernion Bartlett MP spoke in defence of Eden.

lv   Mme Tabouis in SUNDAY GRAPHIC 20 April and Vernon Bartlett in HC on 7 May.

lvi   HWIR for April and May and Frank Owen in the MANCHESTER GUARDIAN 9 June where he opined 'British communiques...the despair and laughter of the World'.

lvii   I rely on Gilbert's SECOND WORLD WAR figure of German dead.

lviii   Graves 9 April.

lix   e.g. Middlebrook and Everitt.

lx   HWIR for April and DAILY MAIL 18 April.

lxi   Articles by Cecil Brown.

lxii   I accept Macgregor Knox as authoritative.

lxiii   e.g. Sherwood Ch xii and Stevenson and Lash.

lxiv   Harold Nicolson's diary 9 April.

lxv   Colville 27 & 28 April. Vere Hodgson 29 April.

lxvi   In an article by Emrys Jones MP (National Liberal).

lxvii   DAILY HERALD 3 May.

lxviii   e.g.Delmer.

lxix   There will have been confidential mandatory directives to the press. See infra. And as for broadcasting when W. J. Brown well-known BBC political commentator spoke early May 1941 about the war, absence of his mention of the USSR was conspicuous. See THE LISTENER May 8 1941.

lxx   These manoeuvres gave rise to a much publicised embarrassing incident. When marching GIs wolfwhistled some women among golfer, who included General Lear, the infuriated General ordered these unfortunate soldiers on a long-distance march in full kit under blazing sunshine; they inevitably fainted.

lxxi   Sherwood p 281.

lxxii   Cadogan 30 April and e.g. Colville 2 May.

lxxiii   e.g. Colville 11 May.

lxxiv   This incident 8/9 March. DAILY HERALD 21 March

lxxv   According to German leaflets dropped over Britain in early June. Roskill THE WAR AT SEA Ch XX1.

lxxvi Ch xii Sherwood.

lxxvii LUFTWAFFE WAR DIARIES Ch 9 pt 1.

lxxviii Goebbels 10 April.

lxxix Churchill admitted this adverse feature in his HC speech of 7 May.

lxxx In the HC debate of 7 May .

lxxxi TGA p 215.

lxxxii The press in Britain obviously as directed claimed Cyprus was strongly defended. Hinsley vol 5 Ch 2 for references to dummy guns and tanks etc in situ in Cyprus.

lxxxiii Churchill's opinion TGA p 268.

lxxxiv TGA p 269.

lxxxv e.g. Hinsley vol 1 Ch 13 p 423.

lxxxvi Hinsley vol 2 p 81. A JIC estimate 2 June.

lxxxvii Hinsley vol 1 ch 13 ; The Operations in Greece, Iraq, Crete and Syria' and Roskill THE WAR AT SEA Ch XX.

lxxxviii Goebbels 1 May.

lxxxix Goebbels 18 March and 18 &19 April.

xc Sweden, Switzerland, Spain, Portugal and Turkey.

xci Goebbels 22 March.

xcii Masaryk in his broadcast of 16 July 1941 mentioned Banse, who in his bellicose RAUM UND VOLK IN WELTKRIEG of the 1930s relished the prospect of the downfall of the British Empire.

xciii Goebbels 1 & 22 May.

xciv For vivid descriptions of youthful enthusiasm for Hitler e.g. Henry Metelmann, Lorant & Neumann.

xcv HISTORY TODAY vol 52(12) December 2002 David Welch on Hitler's Historic Films.

xcvi E.g Shirer's BERLIN DIARY 21 September & 25 November 1940, and Cornwell.

xcvii e.g. Merson.

xcviii e.g. NEWS CHRONICLE 24 April and PRO HO 213/ p 144

xcix	THE RISE OF THE FRENCH COMMUNIST PARTY by Edward Mortimer, London, 1984, pp 304 & 305.
c	Goebbels 18 March.
ci	Goebbels 17 April.
cii	Goebbels 24 & 28 April and 3 May.
ciii	E.g. Hinsley vol 1 p 464.
civ	Gorodetsky.
cv	For some of the text of this letter of 21 June 1941 and commentary GRAND STRATEGY vol 3 pp 86/7 and Shirer THE RISE AND FALL OF THE THIRD REICH pp 849–851.
cvi	World News and Views for complimentary reports.
cvii	PRO FO371/21489.
cviii	PRO FO371/29480.
cix	Ponting estimates 170,000 from the three Baltic states.
cx	NEWS CHRONICLE 2 April.
cxi	De Courcy reports PRAVDA 19 April – p 206.
cxii	Cadogan 31 May and Hinsley vol 1 Ch 14 p429 et seq.
cxiii	Churchill's speech on 20 August 1940, Bevin's on 12 October 1940.
cxiv	Sherwood p 259
cxv	PRO AIR 40/ 2232 28 March and Hinsley vol 1 p 451.
cxvi	Hinsley vol 1 Ch XV.
cxvii	Woodward vol 1 p 613.
cxviii	Woodward vol 1 p 612 et seq PRO FO/ 371/ 29479 78 p17.
cxix	Eburn pp 27/8 for Major Hooper's post-war admission.120 An adage of Admiral of the Fleet Jackie Fisher (1841–1919).
cxx	An adage of Admiral of the Fleet Jackie Fisher (1841–1919).
cxxi	Colville 19 October 1940.
cxxii	Bullock p 638. Forrestal p 205 (10 September 1946). Kennedy pp 102–126.
cxxiii	The first telegram Kimball p 176 c-83x and the second Kimball pp181/2 c-84x. Also see TGA pp208/9.
cxxiv	Sherwood Ch XIII.

cxxv   An assessment 2 June Hinsley vol 2 p 81 presumably post-dating actual knowledge by weeks.

cxxvi   GREENMANTLE a 'Boy's own' type of story centres on an imminent 'holy war' by Islamics against the British Empire. The plot is foiled by the four heroes , British secret service agents including one American, the denouement in an oriental setting. First published October 1916 and running to very many editions.

cxxvii   Hitler's War Directive No. 30. TGA p 234.

cxxviii   Halder 6 May 1941.

cxxix   Appendix 7 of Playfair THE MEDITERRANEAN AND MIDDLE EAST vol II lists aircraft arriving in the Middle East including Malta, by all routes January-October 1941.

cxxx   e.g. Roskill THE WAR AT SEA vol 1 Ch XX p 422 et seq.

cxxxi   Ch 3 p.

cxxxii   TGA p 217. Roskill THE WAR AT SEA vol 1 Ch XX pp 434–436 .

cxxxiii   Hinsley vol 1 p 416.

cxxxiv   Hinsley vol 1 Appendix 14.

cxxxv   Kennedy pp 102–126.

cxxxvi   Goebbels 17 April.

cxxxvii   HANKEY MAN OF SECRETS vol III Ch 13 pp 467–496.

cxxxviii   Edgar Granville MP in HC debate on 7 May.

cxxxix   FINEST HOUR (Gilbert) p 1086 (1983 edn). Ch 55 ref Greece and Crete: 'hard times, but the end will repay'. This would appear to have been an assessment after Churchill could be reasonably sure Germany was about to invade the USSR

cxl   Maisky p144

cxli   HESS THE BRITISH CONSPIRACY p 124.

cxlii   MAN CALLED INTREPID no source given.

cxliii   Hinsley vol 4 Ch 6

cxliv   e.g .Graves 16 & 20 April 1941.

cxlv   10 May.

cxlvi   Trory p 177.

cxlvii Hore-Belisha remained a Privy Councillor. Probably Churchill confided in him only superficially.

cxlviii Burt and Leasor.

cxlix Delmer.

cl Clausewitz regarding Intelligence information in warfare: a great part contradictory, a still greater part false and by far the greatest part of a doubtful character. CLAUSEWITZ ON WAR ed Anatol Rapaport transl JJ Graham London 1968 edn p 162).Hinsley vol 4 on double agents in Britain sending misleading reports to Germany about top people in Britain wanting peace to be negotiated.

cli Bradford reports this as the opinion of the French ambassador M.Massigli after the King's death in 1952. However, Winant and Hopkins admired the King for his interest in and understanding of WW2. The Duke of Kent is commented on in DOUBLE STANDARDS.

clii Bradford on the King as a correspondent. On 14 April 1941 he wrote to Halifax in Washington warning of 'a great deal more strain this summer'.

cliii Autobiography pt 3 p 695 et seq.

cliv Whittaker's Almanac lists the King's secretaries.

clv Padfield pp 368–370 credibly suggests, though his source insists on remaining anonymous, that in London in great secrecy and with much circumspection a draft peace treaty prepared in Germany, and in the German language, was being scrutinised. It would be a fair inference (my own) that this draft peace treaty was sent to Britain through whatever medium because it was understood by Hitler it would be welcomed here by whoever received it. It would have been seen as a sign of German weakness if it had not been requested either expressly or by implication from the highest authority – i.e. obviously not Churchill himself as he was persona non grata but from the monarch as the British head of state.

clvi e.g. Quentin Reynolds in SUNDAY GRAPHIC 23 March 1941 about his flight to Lisbon.

clvii Bradford does suggest that Roosevelt could not wisely simultaneously communicate with Churchill as PM and the King as head of state.

clviii   Goebbels 13 April.

clix   TGA pp324/5.

clx   Bloch p332.

clxi   THE RIBBENTROP MEMOIRS p 152.

clxii   Lorant, 27th April 1943, gives an indication of this possibility.

clxiii   Goebbels 15th and 16th October 1940, 26th November 1940, 20th February 1941 and 12th March 1941.

clxiv   Sherwood p294.

clxv   eg Much in Goebbels and LAST TRAIN TO BERLIN Ch 11 Myth's Progress.

clxvi   The late Frank Roberts , the Foreign Office expert on the topic of Hess, held the opinion at least ultimately that Hess knew about Barbarossa and so presumably, was duly authorised by Hitler to fly to Britain. Costello p 450.

clxvii   DOUBLE STANDARDS Ch 8.

clxviii   The cancellation presumably intended to suggest to Hitler that Hess was being taken seriously.

clxix   PRO FO/1093/1 microfilm pp70–147.

clxx   Desmond Morton ultimately destroyed his relevant papers (R.W.Thompson).

clxxi   e.g. Burt and Leasor.

clxxii   DOUBLE STANDARDS Ch 10.

clxxiii   See ANTHONY BLUNT HIS LIVES by Miranda Carter, London 2001, p311 et seq for Blunt's sojourns in Germany post-war.

clxxiv   e.g. DOUBLE STANDARDS Ch 5.

clxxv   Richard Norton-Taylor in THE GUARDIAN 29 January 1997. The senior police office Howard Jones submitted his report to the Crown Prosecution Service. See also Padfield.

clxxvi   This is my own interpretation. E.g. Hinsley vol 2 Ch 17 pp 125/6: a decision could have been taken on 14 August 1942 urgently to contact Niels Bohr in Copenhagen via Sweden. DOUBLE STANDARDS does not refer to this possibility at all. Bohr (1885–1962) escaped to Sweden in September 1943 and was then flown to Britain.

clxxvii   A possible explanation: Had he sometime murdered the German who had been present with Hess at the Simon interview of 9 June?

clxxviii   Kirkpatrick in Ch 8 of 'THE INNER CIRCLE' treats the whole episode of Hess as a comedy! As do Sybil and David Eccles in BY SAFE HANDS. Sybil writes to David 18 May 1941 'L'affaire Hess was a lark, wasn't it? ".

clxxix   Regarding reports of the USSR at war and during the last few weeks of peace : Gorodetsky, Erickson and Werth.

clxxx   Goebbels and Howard K. Smith for details of the German deception measures.

clxxxi   As mentioned by Eunan O'Halpin at a Conference at the PRO June 2001. At the time there remained in Finland some 400 former British volunteers for Finland's defence in the winter war 1939/1940 and also RN seamen whose warship had been lost off Narvik in April 1940.

clxxxii   Macdonald's report to the Foreign Office is at the PRO.

clxxxiii   Regarding the Eden-Maisky discussions see Note above, and also Woodward vol 1.

clxxxiv   Memo of 17 June Harold Nicolson MP, the junior Minister at MoI. See also Mclaine p 195 in the Chapter 'Stealing the Thunder of the Left'.

clxxxv   Hinsley vol 1 Ch 14 and GRAND STRATEGY vol 2 p 593.

clxxxvi   MoI HIWR report 18–25 June 1941.

clxxxvii   TGA p 329.

clxxxviii Cadogan 31 May et seq, Colville 7 12 & 16 June, Harold Nicolson 18 June, Graves 24 May & 17 18 & 21 June.

clxxxix   George Strauss MP for a Lambeth (London) seat since 1934. He had been expelled from the Labour Party with Cripps in 1939 but had later been readmitted.

cxc   Gilbert CHURCHILL A LIFE p 701 and Woodward vol 1 p 615.

cxci   e.g Lash Ch 17.

cxcii   Lash as cited above.

cxciii   FACTS ON FILE 13 June: 12,000 Jews interned in Vichy France.

cxciv   e.g. Lamb Ch 19 pp 250/1.

cxcv   e.g. Werth's MOSCOW '41, Haldane's RUSSIAN NEWSREEL and Ch XI of her TRUTH WILL OUT.

cxcvi   Branson (1927–1941 vol) p 331.

cxcvii   e.g. Gwyer Ch iv part (iv) p 94.

cxcviii   Woodward vol 2 p 24 A reference to Afghanistan vol 2 pp 57–58.

cxcix   SINGAPORE THE CHAIN OF DISASTER p 74.

cc   SINGAPORE THE CHAIN OF DISASTER p 74.

cci   e.g. Collier p 142.

ccii   De Courcy's BEHIND THE BATTLE of 1942 must have been intended to appeal to those who accepted the USSR as an ally as a thoroughly deplorable necessity.

cciii   THE HINGE OF FATE Ch XLI.

cciv   Sherwood p 303.

ccv   eg Collier p132 and Cornwell Ch 14.